POPULAR SPIRITUALITIES

In our contemporary post-modern world, popular forms of spirituality are increasingly engaging with notions of re-enchantment – of self and community. Not only are narratives of re-enchantment appearing in popular culture at the personal and spiritual level, but also they are often accompanied by a pragmatic approach that calls for political activism and the desire to change the world to incorporate these new ideas.

Drawing on case studies of particular groups, including pagans, witches, radical faeries, post-modern tourists, and queer and goddess groups, contributors from Australia, the UK and North America discuss various forms of spirituality and how they contribute to self-knowledge, identity, and community life. The book documents an emerging engagement between new quasi-religious groups and political action, eco-paganism, post-colonial youth culture and alternative health movements to explore how social change emerges.

Popular Spiritualities

The Politics of Contemporary Enchantment

Edited by
LYNNE HUME
and
KATHLEEN McPHILLIPS

ASHGATE

Published by
Ashgate Publishing Limited
Gower House
Croft Road
Aldershot
Hants GU11 3HR
England

Ashgate Publishing Company
Suite 420
101 Cherry Street
Burlington
VT 05401-4405
USA

Ashgate website: http://www.ashgate.com

British Library Cataloguing in Publication Data
Popular spiritualities : the politics of contemporary enchantment
    1. Popular culture – Religious aspects 2. Cults 3. Spiritual life 4. Rites and ceremonies
    5. Mysteries, Religious
    I. Hume, Lynne II. McPhillips, Kathleen
    306.6

Library of Congress Cataloging-in-Publication Data
Hume, Lynne.
  Popular spiritualities : the politics of contemporary enchantment / Lynne Hume, Kathleen McPhillips.
      p. cm.
  Includes bibliographical references and index.
  ISBN 0-7546-3999-1 (hardcover : alk. paper)
  1. Cults. 2. Spirituality. 3. Religion and politics. 4. Popular culture—Religious aspects.
I. McPhillips, Kathleen. II. Title.

  BP603.H85 2006
  201'.7—dc22

2005021896

ISBN 0 7546 3999 1

Printed and bound in Great Britain by Antony Rowe Ltd, Chippenham, Wiltshire.

Contents

Part 2　　Queer Enchantment and Religious Borderlands

Part 3　　Disrupting the Rational: Enchantment as Political Response

List of Plates

Contributors

Michael Carden is an honorary research advisor and sessional lecturer in biblical studies and comparative religion at the University of Queensland. He has published a number of essays on the Bible, sexuality and religion, including contributions to the anthologies *Queer Commentary and the Hebrew Bible* (2001) and *Redirected Travel: Alternative Texts, Readings and Spaces in Biblical Studies* (2003). Michael is also a contributor to the internationally collaborative queer Bible commentary project, *The Bible in Translesbigay Perspective* (forthcoming 2006). His book, *Sodomy: A History of a Christian Biblical Myth*, was published by Equinox Publications in 2004. He is currently researching the Jewish provenance of Virgin Motherhood ideas and other Marian motifs.

Tanice G. Foltz is an Associate Professor of Sociology and an Adjunct Associate Professor of Women's Studies at Indiana University Northwest in Gary, Indiana. In her book *Kahuna Healer: Learning to see with Ki* (Garland Publishing, NY, 1994) she explored an alternative healing group in Southern California. Her research on feminist Witchcraft and the Goddess movement also led her to explore drumming as a healing modality and the phenomenon of 'drum circle facilitation' as community service. Tanice has published two articles in the area and she is working on a book that examines drumming circles and communities, gender issues related to drumming, drumming in spiritual and religious practices and healing, and drumming as a political action as well as a global movement.

Margaret Gibson gained her PhD in Sociology at the University of New South Wales, Australia. She is currently a lecturer in the School of Humanities, Queensland University of Technology, Australia. Margaret has published widely on topics such as menstruation product advertisements; polygraph machines as technologies of truth; death scenes in film; mourning and material culture. She is currently working on a book project titled *Objects of the Dead*.

Wendy Griffin is a professor of Women's Studies at California State University in Long Beach. Among the first to publish academic research on contemporary Goddess Spirituality, she is the author of numerous articles and chapters on the topic. She is the editor of the anthology *Daughters of the Goddess: Studies of Healing, Identity and Empowerment* (2000), and a co-editor of a series in Pagan Studies, published by AltaMira. She serves as the co-chair of the Consultation on

Pagan Studies for the American Academy of Religion and is currently working on a book that examines contemporary Goddess rituals in and outside of 'traditional' religions, in places as varied as a women's prison in California, a shrine tended by nuns in Ireland, and a middle class home in Puerto Rico.

Graham Harvey is Lecturer in Religious Studies at the Open University, UK. Broadly speaking, his research has engaged with the creation and performance of identities among indigenous peoples, Pagans and Jews. His most recent research and publications have considered indigenous diasporas and the new animism. In addition to various edited books about indigenous religions, his main publications include *Listening People, Speaking Earth: Contemporary Paganism* (1997), *Animism: Respecting the Living World* (2005).

Bob Hodge is Foundation Professor of Humanities in the Centre for Cultural Research at the University of Western Sydney, Australia. He has published *Social Semiotics,* 1988, with Gunther Kress, *Dark Side of the Dream* 1991, with Vijay Mishra, and *El hipertexto multicultural en México posmoderno* 2004, with Gabriela Coronado. He is currently working on a book length study on Atlantis and the Goddess.

Lynne Hume is an anthropologist and Associate Professor in Studies in Religion at the University of Queensland, Brisbane, Australia. She has researched and published widely on Australian indigenous culture, contemporary Paganism, and new religious movements, and is currently working on a book on altered states of consciousness. Her publications include: *Witchcraft and Paganism in Australia* (Melbourne University Press, 1997), *Ancestral Power: The Dreaming, Consciousness, and Aboriginal Australians* (Melbourne University Press, 2002), and, with Jane Mulcock, an edited collection of papers on fieldwork, *Anthropologists in the Field: Cases in Participant Observation* (Columbia University Press, 2004).

Andy Letcher is a freelance teacher, writer and researcher based in Oxford (UK). He was awarded his PhD in Religious Studies at King Alfred's College in 2001, for which he studied performance in contemporary Druidry and Eco-Paganism. Since then he has taught Contemporary Spiritualities at Bath Spa University, and held postdoctoral research positions at Sheffield Hallam University, with the *Sacred Sites Project*, and the Open University. He is currently interested in psychedelic spirituality, and is writing his first book, *Shroom: The Cultural History of the Magic Mushroom*, to be published by Faber and Faber in 2006.

Kathleen McPhillips is a Senior Lecturer in Humanities at the University of Western Sydney. She has written extensively in the area of the sociology of religion with particular attention to the role and experience of women. She is co-editor of

Australian Religion Studies Review and is currently writing a feminist hagiography of Australia's only saint Mary MacKillop.

Adam Possamai is a Senior Lecturer in Sociology at the University of Western Sydney. He is also President of the Australian Association for the Study of Religions, Vice-President of the Executive Board of RC22 (Research Committee on the Sociology of Religion) from the International Sociological Association, and co-editor of the *Australian Religion Studies Review.* He is the author of *Religion and Popular Culture: A Hyper-Real Testament* (P.I.E.-Peter Lang, 2005) and *In Search of New Age Spiritualities* (Ashgate, 2005).

Bill Rodgers has been in the deep, dark academic past, an anthropologist of religion with a keen interest in queer neopaganism. His qualifications include a BA (Hons in Ethnobotany), and a MA (Studies in Religion). He has published articles on queer neopaganism in the journal *Social Alternatives,* and contributed an entry on Radical Faeries in the *Encyclopedia of Lesbian and Gay Histories and Cultures Volume 2 (Garland Publishing: NY).* He currently enjoys teaching children how to use computers in a small, rural primary school, while living a satisfying self-sufficient lifestyle on 40 acres with his cow, dogs, chickens and a garden full of faeries.

Patricia Rose is an independent writer, researcher and facilitator. Recent work includes studies of women's spirituality, medieval romance texts, contemporary women's writings, and spiritual feminist myth and ritual. She has published in the Sydney *Women-Church Journal* and *Texas Studies in Literature and Language.* Patricia is currently exploring the emerging nature and role of the Goddess in/of Australia, and is preparing a book of applied Goddess thealogy.

Graham St John is a Postdoctoral Research Fellow in the Centre for Critical and Cultural Studies at the University of Queensland. As a cultural anthropologist with an interdisciplinary research interest in contemporary youth cultures, techno culture, countercultures, ritual and performance, he has published widely in the fields of anthropology, cultural studies, Australian studies and studies in religion. He recently edited *Rave Culture and Religion* (New York: Routledge, 2004); is author of *Technomad: Global Pathways of Post-Rave Counterculture* (Berghahn, forthcoming); and editor of *Victor Turner and Contemporary Cultural Performance* (Berghahn, forthcoming).

Steven J. Sutcliffe is Lecturer in Religion and Society in the School of Divinity at the University of Edinburgh. He has published widely on New Age religion, including *Beyond New Age: Exploring Alternative Spirituality* (co-editor: Edinburgh University Press, 2000), *Children of the New Age: A History of Spiritual Practices* (Routledge, 2003) and *Studying 'New Age': Reconfiguring the Field* (guest editor, *Culture and Religion* Vol. 4 No. 1, 2003). He is editor of *Religion: Empirical Studies* (Ashgate 2004) and is currently editing *What is Religious Studies? A Reader in Disciplinary Formation* for the series 'Critical Categories in the Study of Religion' (Equinox, 2006).

Des Tramacchi is currently completing a PhD in the department of Studies in Religion at the University of Queensland. His thesis, *Visions and Vapours*, concerns the entheogenic use of DMT in Australia. His research interests include the psychedelic and entheogenic movements, neo-shamanism, trance, and consciousness studies. He has published several papers in these areas.

Acknowledgements

The editors would like to express their thanks to all the contributors for their hard work and their patience throughout the editing process. We hope that this volume will not only demonstrate their prowess in the field of popular spiritualities but also the unique approaches and writing styles of each of them. Thanks to Tim Haydon for editorial advice and assistance. We would also like to acknowledge the financial support in the form of a Publications Grant given by the University of Western Sydney, Australia in 2003. And at Ashgate Publishing, many thanks to Sarah Lloyd for her support and advice.

Introduction

Lynne Hume and Kathleen McPhillips

This book explores the evidence for the emergence of a re-enchanted world in the modern West. Fifteen essays explore the myriad ways in which post-traditional religion is becoming more vital and personally significant to people and communities. It has become increasingly clear that traditional religions, particularly in West, have lost their spiritual efficacy and are largely reliant on either aging populations or fundamentalist agendas. Outside of tradition, rather than religion diminishing, we are witnessing the emergence of new forms of spiritual and religious practices that are entwined with the political, the social and the popular.

The project of modernity is largely credited with the process of the de-legitimating of religion as an important social institution: enchantment was gradually abandoned in favour of rationality, the pre-eminent sibling of modernity (see David Tacey, 2000; Morris Berman, 1981). This led to what Max Weber (1993) described as the 'dis-enchantment of the world' because it was in religion that meaning was generated and without religion, the creation of both social and individual meaning became a problem. This certainly may have been the case in the nineteenth and twentieth centuries as secularism became dominant but in the last fifty years at least there has been an increase in spiritual inventiveness (Fenn, 2001), which in this book we are referring to as re-enchantment. Enchantment might take various forms, but can be defined as the sensation when one experiences events or circumstances that produce a sense of the mysterious, the weird and the uncanny (Schneider, 1993). While disenchantment distances the realm of magic and imagination from the world of the secular and mundane (Lee and Ackerman, 2002), re-enchantment brings back the imagination and the possibility of magic into our everyday lives. As Lee and Ackerman (2002) suggest, a secularized environment may provide the impetus for innovative groups that address the search for religious meaning. This is an interesting phenomenon and begs the question of the nature or status of religiosity as a phenomenon of knowledge. Is religion, as Durkheim suggested (1976), a fundamental necessity to social life; an inherent element of humanity?

A re-enchanted world appears to be not just about what is popularly known as New Age practices. Re-enchantment is clearly operating in established as well as new religious movements (Partridge, 2004) as various authors demonstrate here. It appears that this post-modern enchantment makes little distinction between religion and magic, utilizing both in the imaginative drive. Here we can see that magic is much more than just simplistic expressions of imaginative change. Post-modern magic is much more sophisticated and engages with understandings of personal and social responsibility. This is particularly clear in the modern Goddess movements which have re-defined magic. The well known witch Starhawk discusses the use of magic in one's personal life as a guide to responsible change, as well as in forums of political change to raise energy and motivate new directions (1988). Magic can easily sit side by side anthropomorphic expressions of divinity, such as the Goddess and is integrated into modern expressions of individualism and consumerism. This of course begs serious questions about the forms of religiosity that post-modern culture gives rise to and while this has been addressed by scholars such as David Lyon (2000) and Elisabeth Arweck (2004), this book is unique in that it provides a focus on case studies of enchantment in action.

The Spiritual Drive

The book proposes that the drive and desire for religiosity and experiences of the sacred are far from lost in contemporary western societies. However, the nature of religiosity – or its more popular form, spirituality – itself an ambiguous term which allows for flexibility in its definition (Frohlich 2001) – is undergoing significant material and symbolic transformations. The term 'spirituality' is derived from the Latin, *spiritus*, and the Greek, *pneuma*, which both refer to the 'breath of life' (Schneiders 2003, p.5). Like the breath, which rises out of the body, spirituality stems from an inner quest that reflects a 'deep, inner hunger for meaning and connectedness' (Murchu 2000, p.192). This 'inner hunger' at grass roots level seems to be unsatiated in our times, where high technology, scientific advancement and an insistence on rationality has left many lives devoid of meaning. The essays in this collection demonstrate that people are searching for community, meaning and something sacred or supernatural, and that the new spiritualities are eclectic, imaginative, and experiential. As well, while some aspects of the new spiritualities are celebratory and uplifting to the individual, there are many dark aspects to enchantment, where people delve into the shadow sides of themselves; indeed, unlike New Agers, who tend to emphasize a light and happy (and highly commercial) attitude to life, some of the new spiritualities embrace the dark, sometimes macabre and frightening depths of the inner self, seeing them as essential to the process of individuation. The eclectic nature of popular spiritualities can also lead to the borrowing/appropriation and commodification of another culture's material and spiritual properties.

Each of the authors in this book explores the spiritual aspects of popular culture, recognizing that there is a deep engagement with re-enchanting self, culture and community. Lack of faith in traditional mainstream religions has resulted in de-institutionalization and distrust of dogma and doctrine, yet it has not resulted in a secularized world that is devoid of spirituality. The exploration of inner personal experiences is demonstrated in the rise of interest in Buddhism in the West, in the rediscovery of the esoteric, and in the revival of Romanticism. The latter, suggest Lee and Ackerman (2002, p.40) is not incompatible with post-modern culture because it does not negate the importance of emotions and feelings.

The post-modern demonstrates a profound move towards new understandings of self and spirituality, spirituality and the environment, and self-reflexive spirituality that often leads to social change and political activism (Lucas and Robbins, 2004). The authors in this collection demonstrate, through case studies and theoretical reflection that the spiritual quest comes in some very surprising and innovative forms. The elusive nature of contemporary spiritualities requires an interdisciplinary lens. Authors have drawn on cultural studies, anthropology, sociology, religious studies, as well as fantasy literature to focus on the emergence and identification of popular spiritualities that clearly transgress traditional definitions of religion. Many are on the borderlands of religion and popular imagination.

Indeed, what becomes clear is that post-modern religion encourages a disintegration of old dichotomies such as fact and fiction, real and imaginary; perimeters are fluid and flexible. Some of the chapters highlight the move away from traditional religious dogma that has long characterized mainstream religious frameworks that focus on a particular text as a basis for belief, or a synthesis of some traditional ideas with a new slant that result in a hybrid cocktail of beliefs and practices. At the same time the collection reveals the perennial need of individuals for community and identity (even within their own searched-for communities of like-minded people), which is still an important aspect of being human. Historical accuracy is often dismissed or re-worked in the search for something that is felt should be present for all of us, but is now missing. Legends become history, and fiction reality, dissolving the real and the imaginary. Identity is continually negotiated, often mythologized, and sometimes re-invented (see chapters by Hume, Carden, and Rodgers), and fidelity to community is negotiable (chapter by Gibson).

Multiple choices about one's place in the cosmos leads to a spiritual bricolage (Frohlich, 2001) and inventiveness. What were once considered fixed religious frameworks, based on inerrant texts, become experimental forms based on individual preferences; boundaries are open, permeable, and unpredictable (chapters by Tramacchi, and Sutcliffe). The sacred is being unearthed in some unlikely spaces and places. Where once people looked to religious scriptures for guidance, many are finding inspiration from other kinds of texts such as myths (chapters by Rose and Hodge), comic books (chapter by Possamai), fantasy literature (chapters by Hume and Harvey), and from the natural environment (chapters by St John and Letcher). The spiritual quest is also taking individuals on voyages of discovery to distant places (chapters by Hodge and Foltz) and religious leadership is negotiated and re-invented (chapter by Griffin).

All the authors in this book approach the question of re-enchantment as a phenomenon to be described and understood. It is clear that enchantment has as many shadowy aspects as it does celebratory tropes. Authors question how emergent spiritualities contribute to self knowledge, subject formation and identity, community life, and most importantly, how social change can emerge from such processes. Religion is often considered to be a stringent force of conservatism and traditionalism in western societies. This collection takes the opposite view and suggests that the forces of re-enchantment and desire for spirituality are deeply associated with contemporary forms of social change.

While our collection is neither exhaustive, nor even representative of the different spiritualities that abound in the West today, it nevertheless articulates the diversity and breadth of post-modern alternative forms of spirituality and points to some important trends. Lynne Hume describes the Western vampire sub-culture, pointing out the ways people legitimize their beliefs (Berger, 1969), rationalize the irrational, and negotiate their own identities. The line between real and imagined becomes blurred as individuals align themselves with fictional blood-drinking vampires. Hume also shows how alignment with others that are similar in their differences can create a sense of family and *communitas* (Turner, 1969) in unexpected places.

Patricia Rose shows how the quest for meaning takes the form of enacting medieval myths and romantic literature through women's rituals. A medieval mythic pattern forms the framework for contemporary women's identity and spirituality. She demonstrates this by identifying the key motifs in the fourteenth-century tale of Sir Gawain and the Green Knight, how these motifs inform and inspire contemporary women's rituals, and the effect one of these rituals had for her personally.

Bob Hodge also takes a self-reflexive approach, as he recounts his journey of self-discovery via his own post-modern pilgrimage to Mediterranean sites in search of Atlantis and the Goddess. Many tourists, he writes, want to escape their mundane worlds to seek places which are personally spiritually meaningful. He explores the connections between tourism, post-modernity and spirituality, using his surprisingly revealing personal journey as a case study.

Graham Harvey focuses on fantasy fiction, in particular Terry Pratchett's *Discworld* series and Robert Holdstock's *Mythago Wood*. He suggests that ideas contained in these works of fiction offer alternative worldviews that are highly relevant for contemporary British Heathens. Magic, imagination and humour are celebrated, as is the very real possibility of encountering other beings, such as dwarves, trolls and pixies. Heathens extend their community of humans to a 'wider-than-human community' that encompasses faeries and elven folk, badgers, trees and many other beings. His personal experience enhances the notion that strange things can occur in an enchanted world where magic happens.

Adam Possamai utilizes Baudrillard's notion of the hyper-real to discuss modern society as a social world constructed out of models or 'simulacra' which have no foundation in any reality, except their own. Hyper-reality is structured via signs and symbols in such a way that it becomes difficult to distinguish the real from the unreal. Possamai assesses the contribution of popular culture to the development of post-modern enchantment tropes, using super-hero comics, such as Superman, as examples. He poses the question; do the processes of re-enchantment have socio-cultural repercussions? Citing Wedgewood, Possamai suggests that individuals have two conflicting impulses – one to resemble one's fellows, the other to be different from them, a paradox which is mirrored in the two-in-one figures of Clark Kent and Superman.

Margaret Gibson describes a broad range of modern communication technologies that enable the creation of sacred and transcendent events of community. To exemplify her argument she discusses the death, grief and memorialization of two particular events: post-September 11 rituals of mourning, and Princess Diana's death and funeral. As media events, writes Gibson, they illustrate 'the power of death in creating community, however fleeting, across divisions of time, space, language and nationality'. She points out that virtual media technologies are a core aspect of spiritual access and religious community in contemporary societies.

Michael Carden discusses his own involvement in the evolution of a queer community at a university in Australia, and how a particular event designed to confirm identity and sustain solidarity among the students developed a quasi-religious character. The importance of putting on a 'good show' and laughing at one's incongruous position can create a curious admixture of reverence and ridicule. Camp, writes Carden, is 'a creatively transformative strategy for sustaining identity positively in the face of social proscriptions'.

Des Tramacchi discusses spirits that can be encountered using entheogens (psychedelics). In his account, communication can occur between humans and disembodied entities in hyperspace, thus breaking down the perceptional barrier of real and unreal, human and spirit. He recounts his own experiences and those of others. Impressions of 'formless vibration, strange plant-like forms, alien machines, intelligent entities, and otherworldly music and language' often form part of the experiences of 'psychonauts' ('trippers') during entheogenic 'encounters'.

Wendy Griffin conducted interviews with women in the U.S. who are priestesses of Goddess spirituality. She first explores the process of becoming a priestess who is legitimately recognized by members of her community, and then discusses how these women magically enchant their world through ritual performance. Priestesses, she writes, take participants to 'a liminal place where magic is possible' and perceive their role to be 'facilitators of enchantment' for others.

As a participant observer, Bill Rodgers travelled to the U.S. to conduct fieldwork with people who call themselves Radical Faeries. After his sojourn with a community he found that their sense of identity as gay people is hard to pin down as they are 'continually reinventing themselves'. The communities nevertheless provide a uniting forum for some queer people; one of the principal uniting figures is the Drag Queen who 'bridges gender' and, like shamans, are 'walkers between the worlds'. The Drag Queen 'suggest[s] communion with the otherworldly, fantastic, spiritual realms' and 'mediate[s] between the physical and political worlds'. Faerie Circles are spiritual places where queer people can act up and act out, and provide an opportunity for queers to demonstrate their anarchism to heterosexual norms and pigeon-holing through 'ritual form[s] of unification and fellowship'.

Other types of communities that are developing around the world, writes Tanice Foltz, are communities of drummers, who are involved in the process of re-enchantment, 'whether they know it or not'. Foltz contends that the contemporary drumming phenomenon can be viewed as a tool for spiritual re-enchantment because it levels out differences and brings people together in abandoned play. Importantly, drumming can alter consciousness to the extent that the drummers become part of a single entity in 'a unique creative experience'. Drumming is therefore, she contends, a form of spirituality, healing the self and creating community. Further, 'drumming for peace' takes leisure drumming into the arena of action for social change as drummers promote international peace worldwide.

Kathleen McPhillips demonstrates David Lyon's (2000) notion of 'cultural crossovers' to show how the Virgin Mary has been 'released into new realms of enchantment' in the post-modern world by looking at three contemporary sites of Marian devotion in Australian culture. Polyvalent signs move between images and community making traditional pilgrimage and miracle sites accessible to a much wider audience. As well, a site that 'may appear traditional and religious' has the potential to develop quickly into 'a post-modern, post-Christian source of enchantment' and tourist-style spiritual pilgrimage. Contemporary Marian apparitions, writes McPhillips, 'could be understood as part of a broader phenomenon of technologies of enchantment' as religious actors construct their identities from the variety of offerings of religious groups, 'bypassing the regulatory forces of the Church'.

The implications of New Age epistemology, argues Steve Sutcliffe, are political as well as soteriological, unpredictable and 'cut all ways'. Instinct and feeling can punctuate everyday conversations in appropriate encounters and settings, writes Sutcliffe, and 'disrupt the dominant epistemological order of instrumental rationality'. He closely examines three practices: guidance, meditation and healing and the political alignment of those practices as part of a wider argument to view the New Age as 'popular' rather than 'alternative' religion.

Andy Letcher's chapter outlines the spiritual component of activist mass Eco-Pagan protest activities against the felling of old forest for new road construction in Britain. As Letcher points out, Nature is not only given primacy over economic rationalism, but is regarded as 'sacred, enchanted, and crying out for protection'. While not all ecological protestors are Pagans, Eco-Pagan narratives of enchantment suffuse the movement as a whole and give impetus to the political tactics of resistance. The forest becomes enchanted, peopled with other beings like those of Tolkien's *Lord of the Rings* or Enid Blyton's *Enchanted Forest*. Trees are other-than-human persons, with their own personalities. Cultural norms are transgressed, categories of time and space are transformed, and political protestors rail against a corrupt modernity. Protest camps, writes Letcher, become liminal sites of *communitas* (Turner), heterotopic (Foucault), carnivalesque (Bakhtin) or temporary autonomous zones (Bey).

Graham St. John also considers ecological consciousness and activism, but in another part of the world. St. John focuses on the protection of Goolengook Forest (Victoria, Australia) from the encroachment of modernity's 'environmental despoilation'. In addition to relaying how people are consciously acting to protect the forest, he connects these factors with the efforts at reconciliation with Australia's indigenous inhabitants. There is, he says, 'a post-colonial spirituality manifested in nationalist discourse'. He suggests that the 'feral character at the heart of eco-strategies' is a 'meta-narrative of enchantment'.

Clearly, there is dissolution of some hitherto almost sacrosanct boundaries. Some of the authors have demonstrated the merging of the real and the imaginary, human and nature, human and non-human beings, and the breakdown of distinct gender boundaries. There is frequently a sense of play which sometimes provides a ludic overlay to some very serious issues, including contesting our own place in the world, or protesting the human destruction of that world. As well, the experiential and experimental are given primacy over text-based faiths.

Post-modern spiritualities are elusive, sometimes bizarre and seemingly limitless in their creativity. There is also a political edge to many of these new spiritualities, which changes not just how individuals privately regard their religious beliefs, but how those beliefs can transform society and bring about social change. The search for spirituality in the West is evolving, evocative and innovative; it can also uncover some very important, sometimes disturbing, contemporary trends that change and challenge social norms and the way we view the world and our own place in it.

References

Arweck, E. (2004), *New Religious Movements in the West: Constructions and Controversies*, Routledge, New York, NY.

Berger, P. L. (1969), *The Sacred Canopy*, Anchor Books, New York.

Berman, M. (1981), *The Re-enchantment of the World*, Cornell University Press, Ithaca.

Durkheim, E. (1976), *The Elementary Forms of the Religious Life*, George Allen & Unwin, London.

Fenn, R. K. (2001), 'Editorial Commentary: Religion and the Secular; the Sacred and the Profane: The Scope of the Argument', in Richard Fenn (ed.) *The Blackwell Companion to Sociology of Religion*, Blackwell, Oxford.

Frohlich, M. (2001), 'Spiritual discipline, discipline of spirituality: revisiting questions of definitions and methods', *Spiritus*, vol. 1, pp.65–78.

Lee, R. L. M. and Ackerman, S. E. (2002), *The Challenge of Religion after Modernity*, Ashgate, Aldershot.

Lucas, P. C. and Robbins, T. (eds), 2004, *New Religious Movements in the 21st Century: Legal, Political and Social Challenges in Global Perspective*, Routledge, New York.

Lyon, D. (2000), *Jesus in Disneyland: Religion in Post-modern Times*, Polity Press, Cambridge.

Murchu, D. O. (2000), *Religion in exile: a spiritual vision for the homeward bound*, Gateway, Malaysia.

Partridge, C. (2004), 'Alternative Spiritualities, New Religions, and the Re-enchantment of the West', in James R. Lewis (ed.) *The Oxford Handbook of New Religious Movements*, Oxford University Press, New York.

Schneider, M. (1993), *Culture and Enchantment*, University of Chicago Press, Chicago.

Schneiders, S. M. (2003), 'Religion vs. spirituality: a contemporary conundrum', *Spiritus*, vol. 3, no.2, p.163.

Starhawk (1988), *Dreaming the Dark: Magic, Sex and Politics*, Beacon Press, Boston.

Tacey, D. (2000), *Re-Enchantment: the New Australian Spirituality*, Harper Collins, Sydney.

Turner, V. (1969), *The Ritual Process: Structure and Anti-structure*, Aldine, Chicago.

Weber, M. (1993). *The Sociology of Religion*, Beacon Press, Boston.

PART 1

Re-enchantment Tropes in Popular Culture

Chapter 1

Liminal Beings and the Undead: Vampires in the 21st Century

Lynne Hume

When I was a young child my mother read me fairy stories. Tucked up in my cosy bed, my imagination was filled with gnomes wheeling barrows full of gold, fairies with gossamer wings, elves with pointed shoes, and princesses with flowing golden hair. Later, when I was older, my parents took me with them to the movies on a Saturday night, and when I came home I would stare in the mirror and imagine I was the glamorous star of the movie I had just seen. It did not matter that the face reflected back at me was that of an eight-year-old girl; to me, that face had been transformed, and for a short time I could believe that I was indeed a woman of great beauty. My imaginary world was one I could move into at will – a good distance from the mundane suburbs of a big city.

The playful imagination has been explained as the capacity to extend the imagination and to place oneself in an 'illusionistic world of the mythical and the metaphorical' (Pruyser, cited in Bainbridge, 1997, p.9). Theorists such as Singer (1995) tell us that the make-believe play of children has a dimension that can be termed the realm of the possible, which lets them entertain the possibility of alternative actions and life situations. In much current, popular spirituality, there is an element of make-believe that allows such a possibility to be entertained by adults. Indeed they may arrive at a new belief system that seems to answer epistemological questions and provide a new self-identity and a new type of community. What I am interested in is the process of legitimation[1] (Berger, 1969, pp.29–34) that can occur among individuals and groups of people who become ensconced in a *fantasy* world and use it to re-enchant their *everyday* world. At first their imagination may be sparked by fictional characters and plots or by role-playing games, then they may move to dressing up and acting out their fantasies in the company of others. If they go a step further, by taking role-playing seriously, a new lifestyle or even a new belief system might present itself as a possibility. I will be using as a case study of this process the world of contemporary 'vampires'. I ask: why are people in the twenty-first century calling themselves vampires? Do they believe that they are indeed 'real' vampires, and if so, how do they arrive at this self-identification? And how do they rationalize their sense of self to others?

Contemporary Vampire Culture

The vampires of Bram Stoker's (1897) *Dracula* might not recognize their modern counterparts. The nineteenth century vampires of European folklore were undead corpses who dwelt in graves or crypts by day, roamed about at night, and returned to their sleeping places before sunrise. During their night vigils they would search for unwilling victims from whom to drink the living blood they needed to survive. Sunlight was anathema to them, mirrors did not reflect their image, and they could be kept at bay by crucifixes and garlic.

The present-day vampire subculture grew out of the Gothic movement of the 1970s, a youth culture that celebrated death, the dark side of existence, the macabre, the occult, blood, and vampires.[2] These 'Goths' were largely the product of a combination of rock music, movies, fiction (eighteenth and nineteenth century Gothic literature and horror literature), and role-playing games. Later, when the Internet enabled ideas to spread rapidly and widely, vampires came to form only a small part of Gothic interest, and present-day vampires are not necessarily Gothic. The focus on vampires developed more fully in the 1980s and 1990s, due in no small part to the increasing interest in fantasy literature and role-playing games and to the widespread use of the Internet.

Many of today's vampires model themselves on the erotic and glamorous vampire figures of novelist Anne Rice rather than on the Bram Stoker figure of old. Sarah (www.darksites.com/souls/vampires/vampdonor/essays/roses.html) admits that she had absolutely no interest in vampires whatsoever until she read Anne Rice books when she was nineteen. Rice's books, which include *Interview with the Vampire* (1977), *The Vampire Lestat: the second book in the Chronicles of the Vampire* (1985) and *The Queen of the Damned: the third book in the Vampire Chronicles* (1990), are acknowledged by many as important in promoting a different image of the vampire:

> These days, partially due to contemporary authors such as Anne Rice, vampires have shed much of their superstitious air and come to embody the darker desires of humanity's ideal. The vampire has become a sensual creature of passion and beauty, immortally young, powerful, and free of inhibition... (www.darkwaver.com/subculture/blood-drink.php)

As a genre, fantasy literature is powerful and evocative. The works of J. K. Rowling, J. R. R. Tolkein, Ursula Le Guin, C. S. Lewis, Anne Rice, Bram Stoker, Terry Pratchett and Marion Bradley, to name only a few, describe enchanted realms where we can transcend our mundane selves and share in the adventures of mythical heroes and fantastic creatures. Myth, suggests Andrew Schopp (1997, p.232), 'constitutes a mirror that reflects shifting cultural desires and fears'. The vampire myth provides readers with the possibility of subverting the social order (by challenging socially-imposed barriers) and of experiencing 'both sublimated and conscious desires' (Schopp, 1997, p.232). 'A fantastic narrative reality', writes

Eric Rabkin (1976), 'speaks the truth of the human heart'. It leads the reader into a 'keener self-understanding', says Timmerman (www.religion-online.org/cgibin/relsearchd.d11/showarticle!item_id+1809, p.3). Indeed, the crucial significance of fantasy literature is often an interior spiritual one of self-realization. Fantasy literature as a genre has the capacity to move a reader powerfully and it often affects his or her personal beliefs, ways of viewing life, hopes, dreams and faith. Authors of fantasy, adds Timmerman, are often 'visionaries of the spiritual nature of man'. David Keyworth's (2002) findings on the vampire subculture seem to confirm that vampire fantasy literature has had a powerful effect on many of today's youth, who have made it the basis of their belief system.

Around 1990, role-playing games such as *Ravenloft* and *Dungeons and Dragons* spurred interest in acting out fictional characters and events. In 1992, the White Wolf Company introduced a role-playing game called *Vampire: The Masquerade* (V:TM), which requires players to act out a variety of vampire roles (Keyworth, 2002, p.304). Role-playing games, in general, involve the creative acting-out of fantasy and imaginary situations. Players often identify strongly with their characters (http://members.ozemail.com.au/~tarim/rpg/workshp0.htm), exploring what it would be like to be a different personality and to push beyond limitations of a moral or physical nature. Role-playing is cathartic: violence is permitted, yet only symbolically, so no-one gets hurt; enemies can be killed, yet there are no (actual) reprisals. Anything is possible. Some role-players say that in a virtual world subconscious fears can be brought to the surface and faced, and dreams can become animated. (http://members.ozemail.com.au/~tarim/rpg/workshp0.htm).

In *Vampire: The Masquerade*, players adopt a favourite persona (sometimes based on the vampire novels of Anne Rice), each with its own affiliations and attributes, and act out their characters in the company of others. *The Masquerade* characters and plots are a significant model for many contemporary vampires and the impetus for numerous vampire websites from 1992 onwards. Many of the vampire groups model their lifestyles on this role-playing game, although some are loath to admit this and explicitly state that they are not game players. When asked how she felt about role-playing versus real vampirism, Sangi (of the Sanguinarius) replied: 'I think that V:TM does have some very good ideas on vampiric culture … some of the materials they have created could be useful as "inspiration" and ideas for developing and shaping the vamp community into an actual culture for ourselves and our future generations'. But although Sangi neither advocates nor discourages role-playing, she notes that: 'Anybody who happens to be a real vampire who DOES play the vampire RPG games is summarily blacklisted by others'. A role-player, continues Sangi, 'has come to stand to mean a poser or fake' (*Vampire Church*, March 2004, p.4).

Who is a 'Real' Vampire?

Vampire groups are diverse and their beliefs about concepts such as blood, dress, and lifestyle vary considerably.[3] The vampire subculture consists of vampire game role-players, people who believe they really are vampires, willing blood-donors, and occult-based and mystically-oriented groups (Keyworth, 2002, p.356). There are magazines (for example, *Bloodstone, Bite Me, Bloodlines*) that focus specifically on items of interest to vampires, and there are commercial providers of customized fanged teeth and Gothic-style clothes. Numerous websites offer information on vampires, and chat-rooms are available for anyone interested in delving further into the topic. According to Stephen Kaplan of the Vampire Research Center, New York, there are four types of vampires: 'true vampires' who drink blood every day and see themselves as having a different genetic and metabolic make-up to 'normal' people; 'blood-fetishists' who use blood as a fetish for sadomasochistic sex; 'psychic vampires' who feed upon the psychic energy of others (and do not necessarily drink blood); and 'vampire-like people', pretenders who like to dress Gothic style, sleep in coffins, and copy fictional vampires (Kaplan, 1984, pp.147–153). The latter often participate in role-playing games and on occasions may consume blood.

Identity and Blood

Blood was essential for the continued existence of the nineteenth century vampire, and the consumption of blood appears also to be at the heart of contemporary vampirism. Some of the other nineteenth century vampire 'criteria' have, however, been modified by contemporary fans. One said that many of today's 'vampires' 'love the taste of garlic', 'have had holy water on their skin' and 'used mirrors' – all without ill effect – and that:

> Many of us are highly sensitive to the sun and burn rather easily, but we don't burst into flames or any such nonsense. … What IS true is that vampires require ingestion of blood on a somewhat regular basis to function properly physically, mentally, emotionally, and spiritually. Forget trying to repel us by showing us crosses; many of us wear and/or own them. If you are looking for our sleeping place, don't expect a coffin; though some people do have them just for effect, the majority of us prefer a nice cosy bed with a little room to move around, just like anyone else (www.geocities.com/vampirereality/QandA.html).

There is much dispute about what the consumption of blood actually means. Some have convinced themselves that they crave and need blood in order to survive, some insist that only human blood should be consumed, others substitute human blood with animal blood or blood squeezed from meat bought at a supermarket; yet others say that symbolic blood-substitutes, such as red cordial, are entirely adequate.

To the question, 'How do I know if I'm a vampire?' the response inevitably turns to the issue of blood consumption. It is a question often asked of vampire website owners. The answer, according to one website, is straightforward:

Do you feel a need to ingest blood?

Do you suffer physically, mentally, and psychically when you have not ingested blood recently?

Does your ingestion of blood result in improved physical, mental, and psychic function?

If you answered 'yes' to all of these, chances are better than not that you are a vampire. (www.geocities/com/vampirereality/AmIaVampire.html)

Another person's response to the question 'do vampires really drink blood?' is:

Yes they do. There are some who call themselves psi-vamps who do not drink blood, but real vampires not only drink blood, but NEED to do so in order to maintain 'normal' function. They do not do it just as a sexual stimulus, but actually need it to not feel crummy and/or sick (www.geocities.com/vampirereality.QandA.html)

Some even talk about 'bloodrage' or 'bloodlust' as an overwhelming desire that 'pervades their consciousness' but say they 'work very hard at controlling [their] needs so that [they] never become a danger to others' (www.geocities.com/vampirereality/QandA.html).

When Sangi, who runs a group called the Sanguinarius Vampires, first came into contact with other people who claimed they were vampires, she discovered self-descriptions that 'ranged anywhere from those with a blood fetish to those who claimed to be several hundred years old'. As well, 'there were those among them who seemed to be something close to what I was'. For Sangi, who calls herself a 'blood vampire' or 'sanguinarian', the issue of human blood is very important:

Hell, it's got to be right from the vein. I've got to suck it out myself. I'm beginning to think, however, that there is something more than just blood that I need[4]... If I tried to feed psychically, I can't. I do not consider myself a psi-vamp or a psychic vampire. Just a vampire. I am a blood vampire or sanguinarian. There is nothing else quite like feeding on blood... fresh blood would be the only thing to satisfy. (*Vampire Church*, 2004)

While Sangi thinks that meat from the store is 'dead', other vampires insist that human blood is not necessary; indeed, they refer to the drinking of human blood as cannibalism. One of the rules explicitly stated on The Temple of the Vampire website is, 'No drinking physical blood' (http://www.vampiretemple. com/law.html). It is generally acknowledged that some try drinking blood just out of curiosity and experimentation, and others for the erotic experience:

Sex is a way to share yourself with your partner. For some people, blood drinking can also be a part of this sharing experience. Often it is viewed as a more deeply bonding and erotic way to experience the essence of another person. (www.darkwaver.com/subculture/blood-drink.php)

A strong sexual element pervades most of the website chat-rooms and vampire narratives. 'Feeding' on one's sexual partner seems to be a highly erotic exercise for many. Sarah explains:

> I used to feed primarily during sexual contact. I was like a succubus. I'd go on the prowl for lovers, nearly always getting what I wanted and have to turn down ten times as many suitors as I accepted …I would get high off their passion and sensation, leaving them drained and exhausted while I bounced off the walls. (ibid)

Blackened hair, white skin, black clothing and sometimes false fanged-teeth, yellow contact lenses and long false nails, transform people's outward appearance into something resembling what they believe is their true character. Like the arguments concerning blood, there are diverse opinions about how to present oneself in public, and dress differs according to individual preference. People may change their names (for example, to Gwennifer, Lucifyra, Dante, Vyxyn, Sabretooth, Lilith, Grim Reaper, Sphynxcat, Dark Rose) as well as their lifestyles. As for wearing fangs, one vampire fan said that when she walks into a hotel with her fangs in and smiles at someone, there is 'a look of shock, of disbelief', people tend to back away:

> They see me in black, they see the fangs, they see the contact lenses. They say you can't fight the system or buck the system, well yeah you can, but in your own way. (cited in Williamson, 2001, p.150)

Vampire fans, suggests Williamson, establish 'a proto-political act of subverting mainstream society' through their non-conformity and the 'construction and affirmation of self' (p.150). Dress is a part of this construction.

Identity and Community

Guiley (1991) refers to the generation of youth that grew up in the 1970s and 1980s as Generation X. The collective traits of this generation of young people include confusion, loneliness, a sense of hopelessness, and the need to be somebody. The following statements are typical of modern vampire narratives:

> By the time I hit puberty I was having a miserable time of it. The onset of puberty gave me a nervous breakdown and terrible depression. I pulled myself out of it only to discover a loneliness so intense that I could not breach it even when I was among close friends. (http://www.darksites.com/souls/vampires/vampgonor/essays/roses.html)

Many (GenXers) see themselves in Rice's characters because they feel a similar malaise, an uneasy despair that persistently seeks release. (Mark, cited in Ramsland, 1998, p.244)

Dresser (1989) thinks that today's vampires are yearning for a loving relationship. Guinn (1996) suggests that the common pattern in the biography of contemporary vampires includes a disturbed upbringing of abuse, neglect, alienation and abandonment. Some vehemently disagree with this blanket reference to Generation X'ers – 'We're not all disenfranchised Gen-Xers' (*Vampire Church*, March 2004, page 5) – but admit that there was something missing in their lives that gave them the impetus to search for others who might be like themselves. The editor of *Vampire Church* (March 2004) conducted an interview with Sangi, of the Sanginarius Vampires. Asked how she started Sanguinarius, Sangi replied:

It started out originally as a personal home page which had some information on real vampires, some FAQs and some tips for others like me who stumbled across it. Also had a list of the links to other pages which I felt were about real vampires or at least trying to give accurate information. Back then, everybody was isolated and didn't know about the others or their pages. I figured they were just as lonely for like company as I was, so I scoured the net incessantly, searching out new vamp pages … I also started to offer resources like message boards so that those who came to my site would have some place to congregate and communicate openly and freely about themselves … (*Vampire Church*, March 2004, p.1)

The mixture of alienation, yearning for community, and wanting to find a way of expressing oneself is perhaps what Giddens means when he refers to the problem of the maintenance of self-identity in a world where most traditional systems of meaning and social order have dissolved. The 'reflexive self', writes Giddens (1992), 'is searching for something to hold on to in a fragmented, rootless world,' and this involves a more or less continuous interrogation of past, present and future. Individuals are now engaged in a heightened reflexivity about life and its meanings, about their own identities, and, in finding some way of expressing themselves in all this. In *Modernity and Self-identity*, Giddens (1991) writes about the unprecedented individualization of the body and postulates that self-identity has become deliberative. Currently there is a focus on the body as the visible site for political statements about the self and the self's position in the world.

Instead of making more attempts to fit in to society at large, many vampire fans exaggerate their difference. The liminal figure of the vampire, neither truly living nor truly dead, suspended between life and death, human-like but not human, provides a niche for young people who feel they are on the fringe of society:

At school I found it difficult to make friends and wear trendy clothes. I didn't fit in so you're looking for something else to be instead … I don't know, perhaps that's why you identify with vampires because you feel a bit of a misfit. (A vampire fan interviewed by Williamson, 2001, p.141)

This comment seems to confirm what Williamson (2001, pp.141–157) suggests, that the attraction of vampirism is that it addresses both the pain of being an outsider and the strength of non-conformity. Vampirism seems to indicate a desire for an alternative way of being in the world, and the construction of an alternative identity enables individuals to re-enchant their feelings of difference.

In the liminal phase of rites of passage, which Victor Turner (elaborating on Arnold Van Gennep) discusses, liminal personae are neither living nor dead, as well as both living and dead; they express the ambiguity of the seclusion period of a rite of passage; they are 'betwixt and between' (Turner, 1969, p.95). Although Turner is referring to ritual, his liminal personae could equally apply to youth attracted to the vampire scene. The vampire hovers 'betwixt and between' the world of humans and non-humans. Similarly, contemporary vampires feel that they are social 'misfits'. Once they have found a group of others with similar feelings of liminality and outsiderness, a sense of community can develop.

This brings to mind Turner's concept of *communitas*, which refers to liminality, marginality, inferiority, comradeship and equality among the liminal personae and is defined in opposition to structure (Turner, 1969, p.95). A generic bond is created between the liminal beings because of their marginal position vis-à-vis the rest of society. *Communitas* can be experienced on the margins of mainstream society, and ideologies can be developed to valorize this *communitas*. This, I think, aptly describes the vampire sub-culture which Keyworth (2002, p.355) describes as a 'multi-faceted, socio-religious movement with its own distinct collective community and network of participants who share a similar belief system and customary lifestyle that reflect their concept of the vampire'. *Communitas* becomes extremely significant, in fact, and many of the vampire websites emphasize the importance of a community of like-minded others that is different to mainstream society:

The community is very important to me. This is something bigger than me, or a marriage or a relationship. (*Vampire Church*, March 2004)

> The need for community is great and No Troubled or seeking Vampire will be turned away. This is a community for all Sanguinarians ... As a community we can meet and come together and keep our own community alive. (House Night Breed, http://www.angelfire.com/art2/ulgrave/frontpage.html)

> If consequences become dire, reach out to us here, and we will guide you the very best we can. This is not merely an organization, but a family ... (*Vampire Church*, March, 2004)

In Turner's notion of *communitas* there is invariably the development of a sense of intimacy in the process of liminality. A collective sentiment may be expressed when individuals are released from conformity to general norms. This sense of liminality and *communitas* is evident in the following passage from the Temple of the Vampire website:

Those who have thus found the Temple willingly try to honor the intentions of their found Family. If a member were to resist these four simple requirements[5] this would be clear evidence that they were human after all and be removed from membership. The Temple is for Vampires alone and would only be a source of frustration to any human.

From Fantasy to Reality

Stoller (1985, pp.1–6) suggests that popular culture is now characterized by a new kind of symbolic arena – 'protected domains' – that make it possible for people to act out their fantasies, embodying their fears and desires in ways that are not possible in everyday life.[6] The settings, situations and actions out of which they are created, are life-like representations: fiction masquerading as authenticity. Watching movies and television and reading books may engage the individual passively, but what many people want today is an engagement with fantasy that is active. They want to experience the fantasy for themselves. Symbolic arenas are life-like fictions that can move the actor from the realm of play to a lifestyle that immerses his or her total being. Some symbolic arenas allow participants to experience the illusion of transcendence, not only from time and space but from the roles they play in society. They become part of stories that are larger and more interesting than those in everyday life. They can face and overcome simulated angers and problems, and they can enter into a more exciting simulated lifestyle, playing out desires in fantastic realms that are far removed from the ordinary world.

When acting out fiction in the company of others, a group sense of reality can develop, and continued group interaction can help consolidate that sense of reality. The leap from acting up and acting out in role-playing games, to actually living a vampire lifestyle and identifying as the liminal figure of the vampire, seems to be arrived at over time and is only relevant to some vampires. Sarah admits:

> Somewhere around age 20 or so I think I finally decided that I was some sort of succubus or vampire. I had a couple of lovers who noticed it in me, and it sounded right. (*Vampire Church*, March, 2004)

When she was 21, Sarah met another young woman who claimed to be a vampire. They became friends and during sexual encounters with the young woman and her boyfriend (which included biting and draining blood from each other) Sarah began to consider the possibility that she too was a vampire:

> I started thinking a lot more about blood, and I got really interested in vampires because I wanted to find myself. (*Vampire Church*, March, 2004)

Her vampire 'tendencies' increased 'dramatically' and she started wanting blood regularly during sexual encounters (http://www.darksites.com/souls/vampires/vampdonor/essays/roses.html).

Tanya Luhrmann's notion of interpretive drift is pertinent here. When researching witchcraft in England, Luhrmann noted that there was 'an unacknowledged shift' in the way people interpreted events as they became more and more involved in practising witchcraft. People slowly came to think and act differently as they increasingly immersed themselves in the practice of magic and in participation in group rituals. There was a shift in the types of assertions they made about the world, accompanied by a strong defence of their new practices. People 'drifted' away from their 'previous moorings' toward a new type of believing and belonging (Luhrmann, 1989, pp.312–5). This phenomenon also seems to occur among self-professed vampires. When the same role is continued over time and in a community of like-minded others, the line between the real and the imagined sometimes becomes blurred and the fantasy becomes a major part of identity: a line has been crossed between play and reality, moving beyond Stoller's 'protected domains'. Indeed, self-professed vampires look back to earlier times in their lives and re-cast their life narratives in accordance with how they see themselves in the present:

> Many of us vampires grew up so alone, social outcasts because we couldn't relate to the world of 'mortals'. Many of us had to hide what we were because society just doesn't understand. (www.geocities.com/Area51/Labyrinth/2497/)

The idea that one is a vampire from birth crops up in different personal accounts on websites. 'Vampires' start to believe that they truly are more than human – different from the 'herd of humanity':

> We are true Vampires, members of the Vampire religion. Vampirism is not easily understood and is reserved only to those who are born to the Blood, those who feel the draw of the Night, those who find they are different from the herd of humanity and glory in that difference. (www.vampiretemple.com/tov.html)

> Unlike the world of fiction, vampires do not make other vampires. Either you are one, or you are not, much like one cannot be made into another race than that of their birth. (www.geocities.com/vampirereality/QandA.html)

Another website, *The Dark Aesthetic: Living the Vampire Lifestyle*, points out that being a vampire is an 'alternative lifestyle' for people who are 'something other than a mere mortal' (www.geocities.com/Area51/Labyrinth/2497/). This includes having certain powers such as heightened senses, heightened charisma, and magical abilities.

While researchers explain the attraction of the vampire as being due to the need for a loving relationship (Dresser, 1989) or to a disturbed childhood of abuse, neglect and abandonment (Guinn, 1996), vampires like those quoted reverse the cause and effect model, saying that any psychological and/or social problems they encountered were a direct result of their difference. Indeed, their genetic predispositions *caused* them to be different (other-than-human):

I guess I was the weird kid that was in every school. I couldn't relate to the other children, so my early childhood was filled with pain and loneliness (plus my homelife sucked real bad). I felt deep down inside that I was a Vampire. I understood what I was, but I didn't know why I was the way I was. (Quoted in Thorne, 1998, p.194)

Conclusion

In many of the sub-cultures and spiritual groups that exist today, people seem to want to do more than merely read about enchantment, they want to actively engage with their fantasies, extend their imagination, and live enchanted lives. When people discuss their feelings and experiences with others who have participated in similar events, shifts in individuals' perceptions can occur – about self, world and their own place in that world. This seems to be a reflexive process that serves to explain and justify the participants' own actions and social milieu, or, to use Peter Berger's terms, legitimation takes place. All forms of legitimation maintain socially-defined reality (Berger, 1969, p.32). To summarize Berger's idea, the essential purpose of legitimation can be described as 'reality-maintenance', both on the objective and the subjective levels (1969, p.32). Role-playing is engaged in by all of us most of the time – we act the role of our profession, we act the role expected of us when we play sports, and so on – it is always dependent upon the recognition of others. That is, we identify ourselves with a role only insofar as others identify us with it. In the case of the 'vampires': within vampire discourse, being a 'real' vampire is not only within the realms of possibility, it is a stated fact that only depends upon certain criteria being met. Self-identification as a vampire becomes correspondingly deeper and more stable the more one is engaged in vampire discourse within the vampire collectivity.

As we have seen, some vampires convince themselves that they 'need' blood to survive. What begins as a playful pastime sometimes has a way of erupting into more serious pursuits: socially prohibited actions, experimentation with social alternatives, and flouting cultural norms. For some vampire groups an ethical component emerges that conforms to mainstream normative ideology.[7] The moral component that underlies stated rules could be attributed to the fact that when small emerging groups grow larger and more organized, they tend to seek to legitimize themselves to the outside world and may conform in some ways with society at large (Stark 1996). Or, it might be that their own sense of morals has not radically veered away from a Judeo-Christian (for example) upbringing. More research would have to be done to fully ascertain the reasons. For other vampire groups, however, vampirism provides an arena where they can contest mainstream ideas of identity, flout social norms, and find a space for themselves, their differences and their sense of otherness. A thread running through most of their narrative accounts is loneliness, the desire for family and community, the need for positive recognition of their feelings of difference, and the yearning for a spirituality that addresses their needs. The role of the vampire, says 'Clint' is:

... a demand for connection with the body and spirit. It's anathema to polite society, power books, sterile office cubicles, safety nets. It's a terrifying display of the truth of the need for feeling. The vampire is about the search for something genuine in an era when almost anything can be faked.[8] (Clint, cited in Ramsland, 1998, p.238)

According to David Miller (1970), play and fantasy serves to free humans from fossilized thinking, opening up new ways of looking at life. We might be living in a fragmented, rootless world, as Giddens suggests, but through fantasy and the acting out of imagination the search for meaning continues, as it always has, and the freedom to explore can result in some highly imaginative outcomes that disrupt, challenge and sometimes disturb the *status quo*. The vampires' expressions of identity and community might be a path not all of us would wish to tread, but for some it provides a creative niche from which to explore issues of identity, belonging, and community.

Notes

1   Legitimation, according to Berger, is socially objectivated 'knowledge' that serves to explain and justify the social order, that is, what passes for knowledge in a given collectivity.
2   For more on the emergence and development of the Gothic milieu, see Massimo (2000).
3   Perusing the Internet, diversity is apparent. Although researchers discuss the vampire subculture as an entity, there are many disagreements among various groups on issues such as the necessity to drink real blood, how 'real' vampires behave, types of rituals, group organization, and purported lineages. There is no overarching centre or religious head, rather, groups exist independently, are segmented, and polycentric, which means there is no specific religious body to make decisions about doctrine. The Internet allows easy dispersal of information and communication between individuals and groups but this does not mean that they all agree. It merely provides a forum for polemics.
4   Many allude to the fact that drinking human blood enhances their life energy.
5   The four requirements are: Abide by the Law, No drinking physical blood, Do not represent the Temple without our explicit written permission, Do not betray the Temple Mission.
6   Stoller, R. J. (1985). "A culture Based on Fantasy and Acting out", pp.1–6. www.transparencynow.com/actout.htm
7   For example, the Temple of the Vampire requires that their members be 'sensible' and abide by the law: not committing any criminal offense that would send them to jail, not drinking human blood, and 'not belonging to racist, neonazi or similarly antisocial fringe groups' (http://www.vampiretemple.com/).
8   'Clint', quoted in Katherine Ramsland. 1998. *Piercing the Darkness: Undercover with Vampire in America Today*. New York: Harper Prism, p.238.

References

Bainbridge, W. (1997), *The Sociology of Religious Movements*, Routledge, New York.

Berger, P. L. (1969), *The Sacred Canopy*, Anchor Books, New York.

Dresser, N. (1989), *American Vampires: Fans, Victims and Practitioners*, Norton, New York.

Droogers, A. (1999), 'The Third Bank of the River: Play, Methodological Ludism and the Definition of Religion', in J. G. Platvoet, and A. L. Molendijk (eds), *The Pragmatics of Defining Religion: Contexts, Concepts and Contests*, Brill, Leiden, pp.285–312.

Giddens, A. (1991), *Modernity and Self-identity: Self and Society in the Late Modern Age*, Polity Press, Cambridge.

Giddens, A. (1992), *The Transformation of Intimacy: sexuality, love, and eroticism in modern societies*, Polity Press, Cambridge.

Guiley, R. (1991), *Vampires Among Us*, Pocket Books, New York.

Guinn, J. with A. Grieser, (1996), *Something in the Blood: the underground world of today's Vampires*, Summit Publishing Group, Arlington, Texas.

Introvigne, M. (2000), 'The Gothic Milieu: Black Metal, Satanism, and Vampires', CESNUR www.kelebekler.com/cesnur/eng.htm.

Kaplan, S. (1984), *Vampires Are*, ETC Publications, Palm Springs.

Keyworth, D. (2002), 'The Socio-Religious Beliefs and Nature of the Contemporary Vampire Subculture', *Journal of Contemporary Religion*, vol. 17, no. 3, pp.355–370.

Luhrmann, T. (1989), *Persuasions of the Witch's Craft*, Blackwell, Oxford.

Miller, D. (1970), *Gods and Games*. World Publishing Co., New York.

Rabkin, E. (1976), *The Fantastic in Literature*, Princeton University Press, Princeton.

Ramsland, K. (1998), *Piercing the Darkness: Underground with Vampires in America Today*, Harper Prism, New York.

Rice, A. (1977), *Interview with the Vampire*, Futura, London.

___(1985), *The Vampire Lestat*, Futura, London.

___(1990), *The Queen of the Damned*, Futura, London.

Schopp, A. (1997), 'Cruising the alternatives: Homoeroticism and the contemporary vampire', *Journal of Popular Culture*, Spring, vol. 30, no. 4, pp.231–243.

Singer, J. L. (1995), 'Imaginative Play in Childhood: Precursor of Subjunctive Thought, Daydreaming, and Adult Pretending Games', in A. D. Pellegrini (ed.), *The Future of Play Theory*, State University of New York Press, Albany, N.Y., pp.187–219.

Stark, R. (1996), 'Why Religious Movements Succeed or Fail', *Journal of Contemporary Religion*, vol. 11, no. 2, pp.133–146.

Stoller, R. J. (1985), 'A Culture Based on Fantasy and Acting out', www. transparencynow.com.actout.htm, pp.1–6.

Thorne, T. (1998), *Children of the Night: of Vampires and Vampirism*, Victor Gollancz, London.

Timmerman, J. H. (2004), 'Fantasy Literature's Evocative Power', www.religion-online/ org/cgi-bin/relsearchd.d11/showarticle?item_id=1809, pp.1–7.m. Reprinted from *Christian Century*, May 17, 1978, pp.533–537.

Turner, V. (1969), *The Ritual Process: Structure and Anti-structure*, Aldine, Chicago.

Vampire Church, http://www.network54.com.Forum/15069.

Williamson, M. (2001), 'Vampires and Goths: Fandom, Gender and Cult Dress', in William Keenan (ed.), *Dressed to Impress*, Oxford: Berg, pp.141–157.

Chapter 2

The Quest for Identity: Spiritual Feminist Ritual as an Enactment of Medieval Romance

Patricia Rose

Over fifty years ago John Speirs wrote that 'medieval romances are at the end of a process of evolution from myth or ritual to romance' (1982, p.65). Today I would argue that the rituals of spiritual feminism are a development, as well as an enactment, of the enduring romances of the Middle Ages. I suggest that medieval romances are texts of enchantment; and that, through the rituals of spiritual feminism, which echo the structure and the themes of medieval romance, women can claim – or reclaim – a sense of enchantment for their own lives. In this chapter I will explore these propositions by analysing first the mythic structural framework common to medieval romance and spiritual feminist ritual and then the key motifs through which romance and ritual convey their message. To illustrate the argument, I will draw on the tale of *Sir Gawain and the Green Knight* as representative of the romance genre of medieval England, and on the celebration of the full moon as an example of spiritual feminist ritual.[1] As well as providing an analysis of the structural framework and romance motifs common to both, I venture a personal reflection upon my own participation in a full moon ritual, to discuss the way in which these romance characteristics are enacted in it and to demonstrate how the ritual's actions, words and symbols created an enchanted space for all participants to deepen their personal and spiritual self-understanding.

Underpinning this analysis and providing a context for the study, is an awareness that aspects of medieval life have received wide-ranging spiritual, artistic and commercial interest in recent years. In western society medieval myths and motifs are emerging in novels such as those of Marion Zimmer Bradley, Mary Stewart and Rosalind Miles,[2] in films like *Excalibur*, *Sword of the Valiant*, *Beowulf* and *A Knight's Tale*,[3] and in music, art, fairs, and fashion trends.[4] Luce Irigaray observed that 'in this age of sophisticated technical apparatus we still frequently turn to the Middle Ages in search of our images and secrets', and she wondered, 'Is this because we still need a little time to dream?' (1993, p.58). One might equally well ask: Is this because the Middle Ages provide a source of magic, mystery and enchantment that satisfies the contemporary desire for new – or renewed – models of spirituality? Certainly the current interest in all things medieval seems to support these propositions: the romanticization evident in recent cinematic portrayals of the European Middle Ages,[5] the belief that the medieval world view was more holistic than modern-day ideologies, and the conviction that a living pagan tradition existed in medieval times (Starhawk, 1989, pp.19–22; Sjöö and Mor, 1987, pp.298–329).[6]

With this resurgence of interest in the (actual or idealized) Middle Ages has come renewed interest in medieval writings and, in particular, in the romances – those magical tales of love, adventure, and the quest for personal and spiritual meaning, beloved by both upper and lower classes in medieval times.[7] Today these romances are being rewritten in modern language for the popular (mostly female) market,[8] and feminist literary scholarship is contributing fresh insights into their origin, meaning and contemporary value (Markale, 1986; Orenstein, 1990; Matthews, 1992; Grey, 1993). Medieval romances, particularly Arthurian romances, are included on recommended reading lists for pagans today.[9] Most significantly, for this essay, medieval romances may be contributing to both the mythic structural framework and the content of the rituals of contemporary spiritual feminism.[10]

While diverse opinions abound as to the meaning, origin and matter of medieval romances, there is general agreement that romances are, by their very nature, religious texts, with significant pagan mythic overtones.[11] In a Christian context, W. H. Lewis noted that 'any amount of theology can … be smuggled into people's minds under cover of romance without their knowing it' (1966, p.167). G. K. Chesterton referred to this type of work as 'alternative theology' (Sammons, 1988, p.1). Northrop Frye dubbed medieval romance 'secular scripture' (1976, pp.136–7), and W. R. J. Barron noted that romance reflects 'the perennial tension between ideal and reality' (1987, p.9). The relationship between romance and theology is a complex and fascinating one, as is the relationship between myth, ritual and romance which has engaged generations of scholars. According to one school of thought the romances are the remnant of long-forgotten pagan rituals, which were themselves the physical expression of much older myths.[12] Another approach sees medieval romance as a reflection of pagan myth and ritual extant at the time the tales were compiled.[13] Despite the seeming incompatibility of these two opinions, what they have in common is far more significant than their differences: that is, an acknowledgement of the close link between myth, ritual and romance. This, then, is romance, the complex literary genre that is helping to inform and shape spiritual feminist ritual practice today.

Bronwyn Davies (1997) suggested that myths and fairytales – and, by extension, medieval romances, which share many of their features – have been very damaging for women, inscribing oppressive roles and symbols. Indubitably, some of the subject positions occupied by women in medieval romances are stereotypically female, and less than ideal from a feminist perspective. Scholars have demonstrated that myths can be, and have been, suppressed or reshaped in support of dominant ideologies.[14] Nevertheless, as Caitlin Matthews notes, although women often occupy primarily supportive and nurturing positions in medieval romances, encouraging and empowering the male protagonists, more commonly they bring 'healing, insight, challenge and difficulty as well as empowerment' and they bear 'distinct traces of the Goddess in her many aspects' (1992, pp.xxvi–ix).[15] This may be part of the appeal of medieval romance for spiritual feminists, who read these texts as sources of the Goddess-centred 'alternative theology' which they are reclaiming and celebrating in ritual. It could also be a weakness of spiritual feminism, where nostalgia or sentiment shapes the way the tales are read and any content or subject positions potentially demeaning to women are ignored, denied or simply not acknowledged.

While mythic themes, motifs and symbols can, wittingly or unwittingly, be distorted and misinterpreted in support of a dominant ideology, the basic mythic structural pattern cannot, as Joseph Campbell argued, be so easily denied or destroyed but survives in the human unconscious, erupting in story, song and ritual action. This mythic structural pattern tells of seeking, finding and following one's own truth.[16] It is the pattern of the quest for meaning of any human being, male or female, the pattern that shapes romance literature. Thus it is possible that, even in texts that originate in patriarchal cultures and perpetuate an androcentric ideology, the underlying mythic structure may convey an alternative hope and vision for women. In contemporary times this mythic pattern is providing a framework for ritually retelling, 're-membering' (Daly and Caputi, 1987, pp.92–3) and reliving the mythic tale of women's courage to find their own identity, name their own goals, and follow their own dreams. This is the mythic pattern that is central to medieval romance, and celebrated in spiritual feminist ritual.

Within the mythic structural framework of medieval romance are two motifs that have also become central to spiritual feminist ritual:[17] magic, and female power or agency. In medieval romances magic is a tool for achieving goals and altering reality, and it is frequently wielded by women: in *Sir Launfal* the enchanted gloves given to Launfal by his mother, in *Sir Perceval of Galles* the magic ring Perceval's mother arranges for him, in *Thomas of Erceldoune* the intricate magical adventures directed by the fairy queen, and in *Sir Gawain and the Green Knight* the magical adventures of Gawain coordinated by Morgan le Fay (Rose 2001, pp.74, 225).[18] In spiritual feminist ritual, magic is the power of the will to effect change, a tool to empower women and improve society. As Melissa Raphael writes: 'the transformative power of the Goddess cannot be detached from that of a woman's own wise, resistant female self … woman as a magical activist' (2000, p.155).

Not every romance tale, nor every spiritual feminist ritual, includes all elements of the mythic structural pattern or focuses on the two key motifs. However, there are significant parallels between the medieval and the contemporary modes of expressing and exploring the human quest for personal and spiritual identity. This essay will outline the structure of *Sir Gawain and the Green Knight* and identify the text's key motifs. It will then explore the presence and function of these characteristics of medieval romance in a contemporary spiritual feminist full moon ritual. Through a combination of analysis and personal reflection, my aim is to make evident the fascinating parallels between the adventures of Gawain, as choreographed by 'Morgan the Goddess' in the enchanted world of *Sir Gawain and the Green Knight*, and the spiritual feminist ritual journey to an enchanted space.

The Romance of *Sir Gawain and the Green Knight*

Sir Gawain and the Green Knight is a fourteenth-century Arthurian romance from north-west England, an anonymous, elegant, alliterative poem. It is the story of Gawain's journey of personal and spiritual growth, initiated and directed by a three-fold female figure variously described as a beautiful lady, an aged crone and a goddess. A midwinter festival poem, it begins at the Arthurian court where the king and queen, with their knights and followers, are celebrating Christmas Day. Suddenly, an enormous green knight appears, riding a green horse and carrying a green holly branch. He issues this challenge: one of the knights may behead him on the condition that if he survives, he will in turn behead that knight in a year's time. Gawain volunteers, and cuts off the knight's head. Miraculously, the Green Knight picks up his severed head and goes to leave, but not before reminding Gawain of his promise; and they agree to meet at the Green Knight's chapel on New Year's Day twelve months hence.

A year passes and Gawain rides out to face his own beheading test. He journeys through the winter landscape until at last, almost magically, a castle appears in the frozen woods. Here he is offered hospitality for the few days before New Year. The lord of the castle, Bertilak de Hautdesert, is the Green Knight in disguise, and the outcome of the beheading test will depend on how Gawain conducts himself at the castle. The castle is home to Bertilak, to an unnamed lady who is his wife, and to a very old woman, also nameless. To enliven the waiting time, the two knights agree that each evening they will exchange the fruits of their daily labours. While the lord and his men spend their days hunting, Gawain is pursued by the lady of the castle, who seeks to test his commitment to the knightly virtues of courtesy and chastity. Gawain succumbs to temptation and accepts kisses from the lady, which he then gives to Bertilak in accordance with their agreement. Gawain also accepts the lady's magic girdle, which will protect him from death when he meets the Green Knight for the beheading challenge; this he does not surrender to Bertilak.

On New Year's Day, Gawain rides out to the mysterious green chapel where the Green Knight awaits him. Gawain submits his neck to the giant's axe, yet receives only a small cut. He also receives a very long lecture for failing to keep his bargain to give the Green Knight all that he earned, namely the magic girdle. The poem ends with the dual revelations that Bertilak and the Green Knight are one and the same, and that the aged crone and the beautiful young lady are both incarnations of Morgan the Goddess, who was the instigator and driving force behind all Gawain's adventures. Gawain returns to court a much wiser man, and is greeted with gladness and celebration.

Romance Characteristics of *Sir Gawain and the Green Knight*

Like other medieval romances, *Sir Gawain and the Green Knight* comprises a number of key motifs in a common mythic structural framework, all of which are to do with the growth and development of the protagonist. Typically these tales commence with a gathering of a broad community (in *Sir Gawain and the Green Knight*, this is the royal court). Within this broad community there is a smaller, select group (the knights). From this group emerges the protagonist (Gawain) who identifies, or accepts, a task to be undertaken (the beheading challenge). The significance of this task is always, symbolically, the quest for self-knowledge. The quest begins, often with the protagonist entering a magical or mysterious natural setting (the castle in the frozen forest) in search of the goal. There is an encounter with a mentor or wise one (the Lady and/or Bertilak), who offers advice and guidance and often a talisman as a reminder of the past and a promise for the future (the exchange of gifts, the Lady's girdle). This talisman may also provide strength or protection (the magic girdle). The protagonist continues on the journey through the magical land, growing in maturity and wisdom, until the allotted task is completed (the encounter with the Green Knight at the woodland chapel), and finally returns to the community (the Arthurian court) to be welcomed with joyful celebrations and feasting.

The two key romance motifs – magic and female power or agency – are crucial to the tale of *Sir Gawain and the Green Knight*. Not only does the Green Knight magically restore his decapitated head, the castle appears mysteriously in the desolate winter landscape, the castle residents exhibit multiple and magical identities, and the Lady offers Gawain her magical girdle. The entire action is choreographed by Morgan, described as 'the Goddess', but also known to readers of other romance stories as an enchantress and a witch. *Sir Gawain and the Green Knight* takes the reader on a journey into an enchanted world, to encounter mysterious characters and magical adventures that offer opportunities for growth, and for escape from the mundane, pragmatic realities of daily life.

Romance Characteristics of Spiritual Feminist Ritual

Spiritual feminist rituals vary greatly, but most include the following structural elements, which mirror the elements of the mythic structural framework of medieval romance: welcome, discussion of the ritual's purpose, purification and/or blessing, casting the circle, the Charge of the Goddess, drawing down the moon, meditation or visualization, magical work, raising energy, sharing ritual food and/or drink, and opening the circle.[19] The order may vary according to group preference or convention.

The welcome and the discussion of the ritual's purpose reinforce the values of the gathered women. The blessing and casting of the circle represent the women's separation from the wider community and their movement into an enchanted space. The blessing and the Charge of the Goddess represent the imposition of a task on each woman, that of finding the Goddess, as well as the symbolic sending out of each woman with the reminders that '[t]hou art Goddess' and 'that which you seek' will be found only 'within yourself'. Drawing down the moon could be construed as each woman's acceptance of her commission. In the visualization, the quest is undertaken. The magical work and raising of energy assert the power of sacred womanhood, the strength of will of this committed group and their growth in courage and confidence. The activities of sharing the goblet, opening the circle and feasting reinforce the bonds of this special community and symbolize their return from the enclosed ritual space to the wider community.

The meditation, or visualization, also follows the mythic structural pattern of medieval romance. It is, in effect, a mini romance set within the larger romance of the ritual itself. In it the women usually undertake a journey to their 'centre' – however this is imagined – to seek out their deepest desires, identify their strengths and clarify their needs. For each woman it is an intensely personal journey, undertaken within the communal journey of the ritual. During the visualization the women are led deeper into an enchanted psychic space where spiritual insights become possible and where opportunities for personal and spiritual growth abound. Each woman is the protagonist in her own spiritual quest, which ultimately leads her to a deeper knowledge of herself, her place in this small group of like-minded women, and her role in and responsibility to the wider community of women committed to remembering ways of being strong, sacred, female.

The spiritual feminist ritual journey of self-discovery emulates the quest for identity central to medieval romances. Like romance tales, these rituals invoke and generate magic and female power as resources for the journey. In the next section I describe my own spiritual journey in a full moon ritual and explain the ways in which the ritual's mythic structural pattern provided a framework for personal challenge, reflection and growth. Like Gawain, I too entered an enchanted landscape that was both challenging and empowering.

Romance Enacted – Personal Reflections

Participating in spiritual feminist ritual always energizes me. No matter how tired and stressed I am before a ritual, I always leave feeling nourished and nurtured, as if I have tapped into a sustaining source of energy. Full moon rituals, in particular, evoke this response; and this one was no exception. The quiet suburban park where we met for the ritual, with its central space encircled by tall gum trees, was private and very beautiful in the moonlight. As Mari welcomed us and spoke of the purpose of the ritual, I knew that once again it would provide me with a space for reflection, a time for taking stock of my life.

After the blessing, we stood to cast the circle, ending with the assurance that 'We are between the worlds, beyond the bounds of time, where night and day, birth and death, joy and sorrow meet as one.' As always, these words thrilled me, because they conveyed an aura of mystery, of entry into a place beyond the everyday, an enchanted world, a safe space, where anything was possible.

The closing words of the Charge of the Goddess – 'if that which you seek you find not within yourself, you will never find it without' – were both familiar and awesome. They challenged me to seek full, authentic, mature womanhood and oneness with the Goddess. I felt almost overwhelmed by the thought of the task ahead. Fortunately for my quest, the act of drawing down the moon reminded me that I was not without access to sources of power and energy, and it gave me the courage to accept the charge laid upon me by the Goddess.

As I entered into the meditation I felt a sense of excitement and anticipation, as if I was poised at the threshold of a quest. I trusted that this journey, like so many other ritual journeys, would give me entry into a world of empowerment, understanding and affirmation, where I could deepen my commitment to the Goddess and to the responsibilities that entailed. I was not to be disappointed. I followed Mari's gentle words as she led me away from the group, out of the ritual space, deep into a rainforest:

> As you look at one of the huge tree trunks you become aware of a presence. There is a woman sitting on the roots of the tree. Look closely at her. What does she look like? She greets you by name. She tells you her name. She asks you gently, 'What do you want?' She asks another question: 'What gifts do you already have that will help you achieve what you want?' She asks, 'What do you need?' She takes your hand and places a gift on your palm. It is a small round pale pebble from the pool. She closes your fingers around it. It is warm from her body heat. When you look up the woman is gone.

I was a little frightened by the darkness of the forest, the dankness of the earth, the possibility of spiders – and worse! – lurking beneath the leaf litter; yet when I became conscious of the woman my fears faded. She seemed like the forest, young and vibrant as well as old and wizened. Her voice resonated with the forest's ancient sounds. As she spoke my name, I experienced a sense of being known intimately, accepted, as if the boundaries between us had dissolved and I had merged into her.

As we spoke I felt my burden of responsibility lift, to be replaced by a quiet confidence that, with her help, all would be well. I felt, rather than heard, my answers to her questions. I knew that what I wanted was to know her. I understood that my heart, my body and my unconscious already knew her. I recognized that I needed courage and confidence, to live the truth of this knowledge. I saw clearly the immense power of living this truth. The pebble seemed to throb and pulse in my hand. The warmth of her body passed from the pebble into my hand and seemed to warm my whole body, reinforcing our oneness. It was with profound reluctance that I heard Mari's voice calling me to leave the forest and return to the circle.

As I joined with the other women in the circle to raise a cone of power, I knew that what we desired and dreamed, all that we willed and visualized, could be brought to pass. We opened the circle and feasted. It seemed as if we had all been on long journeys as we sat sharing tales of our adventures. I was confident that the insights I had gained in the ritual would stay with me beyond the bounds of the circle. I also knew, from past experience, that I could, and would, re-enter the world of ritual and magic many times in the future as I sought to create a space for enchantment in my life. Like the protagonists of medieval romance, I had journeyed to a magical world, where I had faced fears and challenges and come to a deeper understanding of myself and of my personal and spiritual goals.

Conclusion

This essay has argued that spiritual feminist ritual is both a development and an enactment of medieval romance. That is, the central motifs of medieval romance literature, incorporated into the basic mythic structural framework, are pivotal to the development, self-understanding and expression of contemporary spiritual feminist ritual. In these rituals, spiritual feminists simultaneously remember and 're-member' – recall and reconstruct – the story told in romance tales: the story of a sacred quest for self-knowledge.

An analysis of the romance of *Sir Gawain and the Green Knight* identified two key themes: magic and female power or agency. These were also seen to be central to the spiritual feminist ritual celebration of the full moon. In their ritual 're-membering', spiritual feminist women are creating a tradition which: reflects the empowering journeys of the romance literature of the Middle Ages; recreates and allows access to the sense of wonder and enchantment that is fundamental to medieval romance; uses magic as a tool for personal and communal enrichment; and provides a safe 'otherworldly' space within which women can explore and develop their own female power.

Notes

1   My argument could also be illustrated by medieval romances such as *Sir Perceval of Galles, Sir Launfal, Sir Degaré, Thomas of Erceldoune and the Queen of Elf-Land*, and by other spiritual feminist rituals such as the dark moon, the major sabbats, the solstices and the equinoxes. For an analysis of the role of *Sir Perceval of Galles* in spiritual feminism, see Rose (2001).
2   Marion Zimmer Bradley's *Avalon* series; Mary Stewart's *Merlin* trilogy and her *Arthurian* saga; the *Guenevere* trilogy and the *Tristan and Isolde* novels by Rosalind Miles.

3   See http://www.fordham.edu/halsall/medfilms.html for a complete listing.
4   The web site http://groups.msn.com/ThingsMedievalInTheModernWorld is an example of this trend.
5   Movies like *Robin Hood: Prince of Thieves* and *First Knight* where medieval dirt, hunger and illness are ignored in favour of well nourished protagonists, clad in elegant attire, living in orderly villages or spotless castles.
6   Graham Harvey (1997, p.183), *Listening People, Speaking Earth*, Wakefield, Kent Town, suggests that '[e]very generation finds new ways to tell the tales of King Arthur', and names two significant influences on paganism today: Marion Zimmer Bradley's novel *The Mists of Avalon*, and John Boorman's film *Excalibur*.
7   Caitlin and John Matthews' extensive writings on the Arthurian tradition have introduced this material to a wide audience, and explored the literary and legendary links between Arthur and the Goddess.
8   Leonora Carrington (1976), *The Hearing Trumpet*, St. Martin's, New York; Marion Zimmer Bradley (1982), *The Mists of Avalon*, Sphere, London; Diana Paxson (1988), *The White Raven*, William Morrow, New York; Candida Baker (1991), *Women and Horses*, Pan Macmillan, Sydney.
9   A search of the Internet using the terms 'King Arthur, pagan, Goddess, books' found over 9,000 sites.
10 Spiritual feminists also use tales from other traditions, as well as fairy and folk tales, as resources for their mythologizing and ritualizing. See, for example, Starhawk (1990), *Truth or Dare*, Harper, San Francisco; Starhawk and Hilary Valentine (2000), *Twelve Wild Swans*, Harper, San Francisco.
11 W. R. J. Barron, chapter 1, summarizes the nature of romance.
12 Roger Sherman Loomis (1927), *Celtic Myth and Arthurian Romance*, Columbia UP, New York; John Bayley, 'Correspondence re *Sir Gawain and the Green Knight*', *Scrutiny* 1950, vol. 17, no. 2, pp.128–130; C. S. Lewis, 'The Anthropological Approach', in N. Davis and C. L. Wrenn (eds.), (1962), *English and Medieval Studies Presented to J. R. R. Tolkein on the Occasion of his Seventieth Birthday*, Unwin, London.
13 John Speirs (1971), *Medieval English Poetry: The Non-Chaucerian Tradition*, Faber, London, first published 1957; Jessie L. Weston (1957, p.173), *From Ritual to Romance*, Doubleday, New York.
14 Some 'classics' which opened this issue to a wide readership: Merlin Stone (1978), *When God Was a Woman*, Harvest, San Diego; Mary Daly (1978), *Gyn/Ecology*, Women's Press, London; Carol P. Christ and Judith Plaskow (eds.), (1979), *Womanspirit Rising*, Harper, San Francisco; Naomi Goldenberg (1979), *Changing of the Gods*, Beacon, Boston; Charlene Spretnak, (1982), (ed.), *The Politics of Women's Spirituality*, Anchor, New York.
15 Kathy Jones (2001), *The Ancient British Goddess*, Ariadne, Glastonbury, also explores the positive role models that a number of Arthurian female characters provide for women in contemporary Goddess religion.
16 Joseph Campbell was one of the leading proponents of this approach to myth. In *The Hero with a Thousand Faces* (1990), Princeton UP, Princeton, first published 1948, he examined mythological stories from diverse cultures to support his thesis that myths function primarily as frameworks, or guides, for human self-understanding.

17   Numerous scholars have classified medieval romances according to themes, motifs, archetypal patterns, etc. See Edmund Reiss, 'Romance', in Thomas J. Heffernan ed. (1985), *The Popular Literature of Medieval England*, Tennessee UP, Knoxville. This present study will focus only on those motifs that are influencing spiritual feminism.
     Pagans from outside spiritual feminism are also reading medieval romances, seeking insights into myth and magic. See David Marley 'Thomas the Rhymour', in *Quest for the Magical Heritage of the West*, 10, pp.92–222.
18   See also Anne Wilson (1988), *The Magical Quest: The Use of Magic in Arthurian Romance*, Manchester UP, Manchester.
19   Starhawk (1989); Zsuzsanna Budapest (1980, pp.229–231), *The Holy Book of Women's Mysteries*, Wingbow, Berkeley, CA; Cynthia Eller (1993, pp.92–103), *Living in the Lap of the Goddess*, Crossroad, New York.

References

Barron, W. R. J. (1987), *English Medieval Romance*, Longman, London.

Daly, M. and J. Caputi (1987), *Websters' First New Intergalactic Wickedary of the English Language*, Beacon, Boston.

Davies, B. (1997), *Shards of Glass: Children Reading and Writing Beyond Gendered Identities*, Allen and Unwin, Sydney.

Davis, N. (ed.), (1967), *Sir Gawain and the Green Knight*, Clarendon, Oxford.
     Frye, N. (1976), *The Secular Scripture*, Harvard UP, Cambridge, Mass.

Grey, M. (1993), *The Wisdom of Fools? Seeking Revelation for Today*, SPCK, London.

Irigaray, L. (1993), *Sexes and Genealogies*, trans. Gillian C. Gill, Columbia UP, New York.

Lewis, W. H. (1966), *Letters of C. S. Lewis*, Harcourt, New York.

Markale, J. (1986), *Women of the Celts*, trans. A. Mygind, C. Haugh and P. Henry, Inner Traditions, Rochester.

Matthews, C. and J. (1992), *Ladies of the Lake*, Aquarian, London.

Orenstein, G. F. (1990), *The Reflowering of the Goddess*, Pergamon, Sydney.

Raphael, M. (2000), *Introducing Thealogy: Discourse on the Goddess*, Pilgrim, Cleveland.

Rose, P. (2001), *The Role of Medieval and Matristic Romance Literature in Spiritual Feminism*, PhD Thesis, University of Queensland.

Sammons, M. (1988), *A Better Country*, Greenwood, New York.

Sjöö, M. and B. Mor (1987), *The Great Cosmic Mother: Rediscovering the Religion of the Earth*, Harper, San Francisco.

Speirs, J. (1982), 'A Survey of Medieval Verse and Drama', in Boris Ford (ed.), *The New Pelican Guide to English Literature*, vol. 1, part 1, *Chaucer and the Alliterative Tradition*, Penguin, Middlesex.

Starhawk (1989), *The Spiral Dance: A Rebirth of the Ancient Religion of the Great Goddess*, Harper, San Francisco.

Wittig, M. (1971), *Les Guérillères*, trans. David LeVay. Avon, New York.

Chapter 3

The Goddess Tour: Spiritual Tourism/ Post-modern Pilgrimage in Search of Atlantis

Bob Hodge

This chapter explores interconnections between tourism, post-modernity and spirituality. Tourists are often seen as irredeemably superficial and secular, yet in some cases they have much in common, in a post-modern way, with old-style pilgrims. Post-modernity is often dismissed on the grounds that it is a kaleidoscope of contradictions, detached from the past, incapable of real spirituality. Spirituality in turn is often viewed as out of place and out of date in the contemporary world. This chapter will put these three categories together in a dynamic, creative, tripartite relationship, and explore the complex new object that results: spiritual tourism/post-modern pilgrimage.

Within this framework, there is one kind of tourism that can be seen as one strategy in a contemporary search for (re-)enchantment. Many tourists leave their disenchanted everyday world seeking places where there is still some magic. In this respect tourism is an escape. Yet tourists usually return, with photos, memories, stories, souvenirs and a sense of the overwhelming and inexpressible meaning of what happened on the trip, material and non-material objects with which to re-enchant their everyday life.

I use a case study approach to ground these issues in the story of a single instance, my own 'Goddess Tour', built around the idea of Atlantis and the Deep Past, visiting a series of A-list sites with my partner, Gabriela Coronado on what was for us also a kind of second honeymoon (itself a category of tourism which overlaps with 'spiritual tourism'). We returned, like so many others, with photos and cheap momentos, and a sense that we had sanctified and renewed our common life. This outcome is too private and personal to talk about easily in an academic work, yet it is too basic and important to this phenomenon to be left out.

'Spiritual Tourism' in a Post-modern Age

No-one has captured the paradoxes of modern tourism better than Dean MacCannell (1989). His description of the core practice of tourism today, 'sight sacralization', sounds like a post-modern parody of religion, in which postcards and momentos can create the 'aura' of a site. But he also defends tourists, tracing their lineage back to very ancient ritual practices. He sees a structure of feelings and practices transmitted undiminished from the deep (pre-pre-modern) past. The post-modern tourists' world is linked by a string of sites they are drawn to by an obscure compulsion:

> Tourist attractions are an unplanned typology of structure that provides direct access to the modern consciousness or 'world view' … tourist attractions are precisely analogous to the religious symbolism of primitive peoples. (1989, p.2)

From this perspective tourism is an illuminating practice precisely because it is so contradictory and paradoxical. Tourism is old yet new, an *experience* of the folding of the pre-modern into the modern, dismantling its linear logic and static surfaces. It is 'post-modern', a phenomenon of late capitalism that recognizes the co-presence of modern and pre-modern in the kaleidoscope of the present. From this point of view the experience and practice of tourism are able to contain both a spiritual journey and a search for history, reconstituting a contemporary self by profound contacts with real traces of an unknowable deep past.

The Goddess of Atlantis

MacCannell points out that 'authenticity' is crucial for tourists, even if absolute authenticity can never be guaranteed. In my case, before I could set off on a Goddess tour, I needed to believe there is and was a Goddess. Before I could look for her in Atlantis, I had to believe in Atlantis. Not that I had to wait till I absolutely knew. If so, I would never have gone. But I had to do the best research I could. I believe that being a scholar and a tourist are not incompatible, as so many claim. Yet there is often a tension. Both Atlantis and the Goddess are made to seem impossible or scandalous in modernist (binary) scholarship, which categorizes Atlantis firmly as myth, and the Goddess as a feminist fiction. Scholars today do not believe in Plato's Atlantis (Vidal Naquet, 1992), and attack anyone who toys with the idea with unscholarly ferocity (see Hodge, 2002). But scholarship that incorporates post-modern logic can be better scholarship than this, not distorted by binarism, by a need to decide prematurely between faith and reason, male and female, goddess and god.

My search for Atlantis and the Goddess included scholarship, classical and post-modern, directed at Plato. The Atlantis story is found in two of Plato's last and best attested works (Taylor, 1926). He reports it as Solon's story not his own. Solon says the story isn't his, either, but told to him by Egyptian priests in 600 BC. Solon was a famous thinker ancestor of Plato. The story of the transmission is credible. True, the text contains some incredible things, as do all texts that old (including the Bible). Yet modern scholarship (see Vidal-Naquet, 1992) decrees it must be all true or all myth then opts for myth.

Two things are lost with this, and only one of them is Atlantis. If Plato's text was what he claimed, a priceless record from 600 BC of a deep past before 9600 BC it contains a buried history of the Goddess, which complements Marija Gimbutas' history of the goddess religion of Old Europe, overthrown around 5000 BC she says by patriarchal Indo-Europeans (1999). The Goddess myth continued into classical Greece but debased and devalued, in disguise (Baring and Cashford, 1993, p.xiii) The twists and turns of this new history question Weber's Disenchantment thesis (1976), that the 'iron cage' of capitalism was the inexorable consequence of 'ascetic Protestantism' in the sixteenth century, suggesting new strategies for a 're-enchantment' project (Hillman, 1996, Moore, 1997). Plato's text contributes to these debates, as a rare voice from an almost silent past. It raises crucial historical questions. When did disenchantment begin? How does a re-enchantment project position itself in time and space? How far back does 'post-modernism' go?

As with the Goddess generally (Engelsman, 1979) the Goddess in Atlantis has to be recovered from Plato's text, by a post-modern 'reading against the grain'. In his account, the god Poseidon, who married a mortal, 'Cleito', founded Atlantis. She bore him ten sons and disappeared from history. But Cleito means 'the famous one'. What was Cleito famous for, who is known only as the mother of Atlas, the one who carries the world? Like many other mortal women who became consorts of male Gods in classical Greek myths, Cleito probably was the Great Goddess, the truly 'Famous One'. Greek myths about male gods of Olympus who marry, rape or father mortal women usually record a patriarchal takeover of a major shrine of the Great Goddess.

Cleito is the daughter of two mortals, Evenor and Leukippe. Both were dead by the time Poseidon arrived. The story has the typical form of myths of a 'sacred marriage' between the Great Goddess and Her consort. And Cleito is not the only Great Goddess in Atlantis. 'Leukippe' means 'White Mare'. One important form of the Goddess was a mare. Epona of the Celts and Demeter, 'Divine Mother', were mare goddesses. White is Her special color (Graves, 1961). Cleito is 'the Maiden' Persephone, daughter of Demeter, central figures in the mystery religion of Eleusis in classical Greece, derived from Egyptian rites of Isis (Kerenyi, 1967).

'Atlantis' connects with the Goddess in another way. In Greek cosmology Atlas carries the cosmos on his shoulders. 'Atlantis' is the place he does it from, or the Goddess he once was. In Egypt the Goddess's name was Nut, Neith, in Greek Athena. The names and functions of the Goddess converge, Athena and Atlantis, Sky and Serpent Goddess, Goddess of Life and Death, Above and Below, pillar of the Universe. In an evocative phrase Peter Berger (1969) talked of the 'sacred canopy' as the enchanted world lost by modernism. 'Atlantis' (Nut) integrated the sacred; underworld, column and sky.

Mircea Eliade (1959) calls this principle the Axis Mundi (Cosmic Pillar), found in all ancient religions. Plato's Atlantis was an Axis Mundi society, worshipping at a central pillar, in a temple on a sacred island surrounded by concentric circles of water, image of a cosmos as a spherical World Mountain in an ocean. 'Atlas' was the Cosmic Pillar, so Atlantis means in effect 'Place or Goddess of the Axis Mundi'.

The Axis Mundi principle is as important to post-modern spirituality as it was to ancient religion, then as now the centre-piece in sacralization strategies. Wherever its two grand forms were placed or found, columns or concentric circles, the place was sanctified, becoming an image of the sacred world. The Axis Mundi strategy underpins MacCannell's process of 'site sacralization', where places lend their aura to objects that are connected with them, which reflect back their symbolic power onto the places.

In this sense, Atlantis as 'the place of the Axis Mundi' is the object of every spiritual tour, every sacralization practice, and the Goddess of Atlantis in all her disguises is always there, at the end of the journey, and all along the way.

'New Age Tourists' as 'Unreliable'

Modernism insists on strict boundaries and unilinear categories. There is only one approach to the only truth: scholarship is good or bad, and tourism is something else. And then, in their own category, are writings called 'New Age', a convenient label with which to dismiss them all. Post-modernism allows for a range of ways of reading for a range of kinds of truth, not in order to abandon truth but the contrary, to develop richer ways of approaching it. For instance, literary criticism uses the idea of 'unreliable narrators', whose meanings come not from the truths they tell, but from the pattern of distortions and discrepancies in what they say. In practice, even 'objective' scholars are to some degree 'unreliable' in this sense. 'New Age' writers are more evidently so. Far from that making them useless guides for spiritual tourism, it gives them a role. As 'unreliable tourists', 'unreliable scholars', they are provocative, creative, suggesting new angles and possibilities.

I illustrate the value of 'unreliable (New Age) tourists' with Barbara Hand Clow's *Signet of Atlantis*, which was channeled, she claims, by the Pleiadians, in an intense burst after an eclipse of July, 1991, to meet a publishing deadline of mid-1992. It begins:

> It is summer solstice 1989 at the ancient temple of Knossos on the isle of Crete. I pass through a narrow, blood-red temple entry door, just tall enough for my head... My knees weaken as sobs well up from the center of my heart... I rush quickly into the first courtyard of Knossos, oblivious of the tourists. I remember the labyrinth. (Clow, 1992, p.3)

Then she is Aspasia, a fourteen-year-old girl initiated into the Cretan labyrinth in 1569 BC, just before a volcanic eruption destroyed Knossos, which some believe was Plato's Atlantis. Then she is Alcior, male scientist of Atlantis in 11,000 BC, about to be part of the terrible scientific mistake that destroyed it. How can I take any of this seriously? Doesn't it confirm all the worst suspicions of conventional scholars about Atlantis?

Her history irrupts into the present, conflating tourism and spirituality, ecstasy and history. It is obviously not 'good scholarship'. Yet her version of Atlantis is closer to Plato's than most 'good scholars'. She distinguishes between the Cretan disaster and Atlantis. Her history has a large place for the Goddess, who is eliminated from most histories of civilization. Sir Arthur Evans and the other 'discoverers' of Knossos gave the ancient Minoans a male 'King', and some decorative women. Nanno Marinatos, a good scholar without assistance from the Pleiadians, comes to the same conclusion as Clow: the Minoans worshipped the Goddess with women's rituals in dark, enclosed spaces (1984).

As Gabriela and I stand in the palace of Knossos, at the start of our Goddess Tour, we do not find Clow's fantasies or enthusiasms ridiculous, as responses to this sacred place, as myths that make a kind of sense of a history that no-one today knows: invitations to spiritual tourists to look and feel with soul as well as mind.

The Role of Experience

The category of 'experience' is crucial in tourism. In spiritual tourism it allows knowledge, emotion and spirituality to meet and interact, where the 'pre-modern' can be felt as a powerful presence in the post-modern touristic present. An example for me is the Cave of Dicte on Crete, where Gabriela and I continued our Goddess tour. Ancient Cretans were proud of the history of the Goddess on their island. According to Diodorus Siculus in the first century BC, they claimed that most Greek Goddesses were associated with Crete. Demeter had her origins here. Her mysteries originated in Crete, they said. Zeus himself was born here, in the Cave of Dicte.

It was only 3 pm in the afternoon when we arrived at the cave, but the sun was low in the sky. This was yet another place sacred to the Great Mother taken over by patriarchal Olympians. Zeus's mother was called Rhea, which Graves (1960) thinks comes from *era*, an archaic word for 'earth'. Lions were her sacred animals, and so were doves, as they were to Aphrodite, Goddess of love. I wondered if the root of the Greek word for sexual love, *Eros*, came from the same root.

Rhea, mother of Zeus the Father of the Gods, was obviously very powerful. Dicte probably comes from *Di*, 'divine' and *tikto*, 'give birth'; where the God Zeus was born or more likely the Goddess who gives birth to all things.

At Dicte this meaning hit us in the face. The cave is high up on a hill but goes almost straight down, deep into Mother Earth, its shape hard to misinterpret. I almost felt embarrassed to be with Gabriela as we walked past clusters of pubic trees around the entrance and entered the labial folds of this great vaginal slash in the mountain. The experience was intense as I clambered down the winding path. Suggestive shapes loomed in the darkness below, like strange beings waiting to be born.

It was like being reborn myself, stripping off layers of maturity to reach a state of helpless dependency, like a fetus in the womb. Gabriela was deeply affected too. We stopped half way down. I knew she didn't want to go deeper. I had to support her on our way up, and when we reached the surface she clung to me for some minutes to recover.

When I was back in the light of day I felt strange, different, transformed. It was a powerful, disturbing experience, to connect with the Great Mother and the Deep Past.

'I felt I was inside my own womb,' whispered Gabriela. I just held her.

A Post-modern Pilgrimage to the Goddess

Part of the power of spiritual tourism is that it involves body as well as mind, repeating ancient actions in ancient places in the modern world. There is always a clash between present and past. The modernist perspective resolves the clash in only one way: by deploring the present as a debased intrusion into the (lost) purity of the past. This habit of thought is so powerful that it can inscribe the Weberian narrative of disenchantment onto any modern scene or practice. Post-modern spiritual tourism has other options, arising out its tolerance for the co-existence of contradictions.

As an instance, Gabriela and I went straight from Crete to modern, highly polluted Athens. In Plato's time, Athens still celebrated the Goddess in their major ritual, the Thesmophoria, one of the reasons for the existence of the Parthenon, sacred to Athena, Goddess patron of patriarchal Athens. This procession, for women only, began at Klepsydra ('hidden waters'), a cave at the foot of the Acropolis. It passed a large statue of 'Demeter and Child', now lost, to reach Eleusis by sunset, and commence the rituals of the Goddess. The road still exists, now paved in bitumen, still called 'the sacred way'. We could have lamented the loss of the road, but it is equally valid to celebrate the miraculous survival of the name. Gabriela and I took this route, in the next stage of our post-modern pilgrimage: on foot for a kilometer, by car through a modern urban sprawl.

Modern Eleusis could be experienced as another kind of disappointment: mere ruins on a bare hill. The sacred cleft where once devotees communicated with the Goddess is no longer visible. But to me it still had an aura, a sense of the Goddess. Her hidden meanings hover in names and stories. Myths say the name came from King Eleusis, son of Daeira, daughter of Oceanus. Graves (1960) argues this genealogy encodes an esoteric meaning. Eleusis never existed, he says. 'Eleusis' is Greek for 'he has come', like Latin 'Advent' used for the coming of Christ. In the Eleusian mysteries this word announced the coming of the Divine Child, Horus.

These are the same ceremonies as Clow fantasized about in Knossos. Here they certainly happened. I imagine ghostly, long-dead women still inhabiting this still sacred place.

Daeira like Cleito is otherwise unknown. Graves believes she is Aphrodite, Goddess of Love, born of ocean foam. Myths give Eleusis a father, Ogyges. Graves doubts this name, too. It simply indicates where he came from: Ogygia, mentioned by Homer as the island of Calypso, also unknown except as Goddess of this island where Odysseus found refuge. Like Cleito's, her name encodes a subtext. Calypso is 'Hidden One'. It's the same root as *Kleps* of Klepsydra, hidden spring, where our walk to Eleusis began. It's not a name but a title of the Goddess of the Mysteries, here connected with an island in the Atlantic. According to Homer Calypso was a daughter of Atlas. That means that in Greek, she and her island were 'Atlantis': the same as Plato's island.

Our goal in this stage of our pilgrimage was Delphi, the most famous shrine in ancient Greece. The Goddess and Her suppression are both close to the surface here. Homer's *Hymn to Apollo* describes how the god killed Python, once the Goddess as serpent. In spite of his status as Olympian he did penance for eight years, returning to Delphi as master of the shrine in the ninth year, number of the Goddess. Even then there were limits on his powers. Oracles came from Python through her priestess, whose incomprehensible words were translated into ambiguous Greek by male priests. Men controlled the shrine and its wealth, but the complex method of divination was a constant reminder that power and prophecy came from the Goddess, controlled by male priests of the male god, not initiated by them.

Delphi after 2800 years still has power. I felt it standing there, gazing south across the luminous sea, or back to the hill in which the shrine nestles. There were many other tourists here, on package tours, but that did not spoil the experience for me. On the contrary, they like me are witnesses. We all in our way add to the force of the sacred, giving as well as taking. The crevice through which the Goddess spoke is lost, but I felt Her presence. Gabriela felt it more strongly. Before she came, she told me, she'd had a physical pain in her breast, near her heart. Now it was gone. Delphi was famous for oracles not healing, but maybe the priests of Apollo did not know the full power of this place of the Goddess, still sacred, still able to connect with post-modern pilgrims like us.

The Layered Past

Modernist time is linear, but post-modern time bends and plays strange tricks. This may be a source of problems for modernist scholars, but for spiritual tourists it is one of the most profound and satisfying of experiences. Perhaps nowhere on earth is it so powerful and rich as in the next stop in our post-modern pilgrimage, the south of France, part of the territory of Atlantis according to Plato. The soft green hills hide marvelous caves and murals from before 10,000 BC, not known to Plato nor to others for thousands of years, only rediscovered in the twentieth century. But were the Great Caves really forgotten? The medieval village of Magdalene, after which stone age 'magdalenean culture' is named, is half cave, half town. This landscape is a palimpsest, which speaks of a continuous tradition over 45,000 years. It is almost impossible to imagine so many layers of time, over 45,000 years of human history, but I try. Surely Plato's Atlantis lived on here under other names, a continuous chain of transformations.

We begin at the beginning of Deep Time, with the Great Caves. We visited many caves, images of the womb of the Goddess (Bahn, 1997, p.200). Paintings are found at the end of long, dark winding passages, a journey into the womb of the Goddess, full of images of the life that only She creates, mostly horses and bovines, male and female. These carefully guarded places were sacred to the Goddess, whose effigies date back to 35,000 BC (Gimbutas, 1991).

Scholars mostly doubt that Celtic Druids who lived in this same area connected back to megalithic or cave societies, or forward to Celtic Christianity, or Cathar heretics of southern France (see, for example, Rutherford, 1993). I wonder how not. All these secret traditions were famously tenacious in keeping and passing on knowledge, worshipping a Goddess who was the same even in the time of Atlantis.

For me the mysterious Cathars are one connecting thread, Gnostic heretics who flourished from the eleventh century in the south of France. Their ideas echoed the esoteric Hermetica, in a family of secret traditions whose branches and histories can no longer be reconstructed, which often went underground to escape persecution, mainly known through texts written by enemies. They were brutally suppressed by Pope Innocent III at the beginning of the thirteenth century. Most histories say the suppression was total, leaving no traces. But de Rougemont (1956) argues the Cathars did survive, influential beyond all expectations.

Their doctrine of the pure love of Sophia, Wisdom, (Matthews, 1992) inspired the songs of the troubadours, the invention of Romantic Love and the selfless service of the Lady. It influenced St Francis of Assisi, himself almost condemned for heresy by a later Pope, and Dante, greatest writer of his age, poetizer of his beloved Beatrice, his *Donna di Virtu*. Some suppression!

Our quest followed traces of the Cathars, from France to Italy. We had our private theme: the angel Gabriel whom Gabriela was named after. In the Koran he is God's main mediator with Muhammad, like Thoth/Hermes the sage in the Hermetica. We found many representations of him in Italy. Tuscany, formerly Etruria, part of Atlantis according to Plato, was flooded with his image, from the thirteenth century to the sixteenth, from the suppression of the Cathars till the High Renaissance. Annunciations were the third most popular theme of the Renaissance, after the Crucifixions and the Madonnas. By a nice irony, Cathar doctrine was expelled from France, and finished up in churches all over Italy.

The Bible describes the annunciation, but its iconography comes from elsewhere. A winged, feminine Gabriel comes from the left. The virgin usually has a book, sometimes open on her lap, sometimes with her finger in it to mark a place. God the father is sometimes depicted, above centre, with lines flowing towards the womb of the Virgin, signifying divine fertilization. The annunciation by Gabriel is the act of incarnation, when the 'word became flesh'. The book is key to this iconography. As Gabriel's words enter her ear, God's seed enters her womb, and she reads a Word as Logos, the Logos of the Hermetica. She is a gnostic, hermetic, Cathar Sophia. Gabriel, Gabriela, hermaphrodite angel and servant of the Goddess, kneels before her like a knight before his lady in the chivalric tradition. Each Annunciation is a palimpsest, like the hills of southern France: an image from the present carrying traces of a very long history, probably from earlier than Plato. As we gaze at the form, we peek into the shimmering vortex of Deep Time.

The focus of our pilgrimage was an Annunciation by Fra Angelico, the 'angelic friar', in San Marco's convent in Florence. We stood in front of it for hours, coming back on other days to gaze some more. Surprisingly it lacks many conventional motifs: no book for the Virgin, no lilies for Gabriel, no God the Father sending his seed from above. The hermaphrodite angel kneels, humble in front of the Virgin, who is anxious yet eager, her blue robe open to reveal the red of the womb which will receive the seed: like two vulnerable humans playing out their destined role without iconographic aids.

But the scene is framed by three columns, three images of the Axis Mundi, and in the space above the central pillar, exactly where the image of the Father normally is, a sphere is carved into the stone, surrounded by a circle, the feminine cosmos of Atlantis. Behind the Virgin a barred window reveals a garden, image of the womb of the Goddess, the 'book of nature' seen through a grid. White flowers grow behind Gabriel, in place of his lilies. Fra Angelico incarnated Cathar themes so perfectly they are hard to see, re-enchanting the act of love and the relation of lover to beloved, like the troubadours, like St Francis, like Dante. Enchantment was not a taken-for-granted fact of their pre-modern world, soon to be lost with the coming of Protestantism. It was heresy, an irruption from the deep past, as dangerous but possible then as now.

Post-colonial Goddess

The Goddess has survived 5000 years of patriarchy; still a living force in many forms in many places for many people, but that struggle, then and now, has always been political, leaving traces of power on images and beliefs, creating ambiguous images and ambivalent feelings for spiritual tourists. We saw this in the next part of our pilgrimage, across the ocean to what Plato called 'the opposite continent', the Americas, identified by Plato 2000 years before Columbus.

The Goddess was displaced in this offshoot of Atlantis as in Europe. Mexico had powerful goddesses, rulers of death and source of life, revered and feared, but a mostly male pantheon. For instance, Huitzilopochtli, Chief God of the Aztecs, was conceived miraculously by Coatlicue ('serpent skirt'), whose 401 other children were jealous and cut off her head. But Huitzilopochtli leapt from her womb, fully grown with sword in hand (like Athena born from Zeus' head), killing his brothers, dismembering his sister, scattering the pieces down the sacred mountain. Coatlicue was a frightening goddess. One famous statue shows her decapitated, with snakes writhing from her neck like Medusa. She wears a coat of snakes like Athena, at her breast an owl-faced monster, Tecolote. She parodies Athena at so many points it seems clear she is the same goddess.

Feminists often feel uneasy at these goddesses, powerful yet angry and debased, a judgement that is complicated by a post-colonial perspective. The Spanish came to the New World, where they massacred Indians and tried to eliminate their gods. Native Mexicans still suffer in their own land. But this attempted cultural genocide had a paradoxical result, as is shown by the story of the Virgin of Guadalupe, patron saint of America, revered today by all Mexicans. Legends say Her image was miraculously painted by Herself, given to a poor Indian, Juan Diego, ten years after the conquest. The French scholar Lafaye (1985) sees the story as a Franciscan fraud that went wrong. Some Franciscans constructed an object of worship that Indians would accept, he says, Christian but incorporating native beliefs. According to the legend, the Virgin has many qualities of Xochiquetzal ('flower-quetzal'), goddess of love and beauty, child-birth and weaving. She appeared on a mountain, site of a major Aztec shrine of Tonantzin, Goddess of the Sun, now in Mexico City.

Lafaye discusses 'Guadalupe', name of a place in Spain with its own Virgin tradition. It comes from Arabic *guada al upe*, covered or hidden water, for a place where a secret statue of a secret Goddess was found. The Guadalupe Virgin was Calypso, the Hidden One, Goddess of Atlantis, through a fraud perpetrated by Franciscans, whose founder was deeply influenced by the Cathars.

The miraculous image is housed in a basilica on the shrine, the huge plaza in front always full of pilgrims from all over Latin America, come to worship their Goddess. Gabriela and I joined this throng. The image can be seen from anywhere in the church, but those who want to worship it descend to a cave-like crypt behind the altar. Four ramps transport worshippers past the image at the rate of three 'Hail Marys' per transit. Each time I passed the luminous image the emotion grew more overwhelming. Tears came to my eyes, and I could not speak.

This Virgin can be tracked to the Bible, to St John's woman 'clothed with the sun, and the moon under her feet, and upon her head a crown of twelve stars' in *Revelation*. St John's mystic vision comes not from St. Paul and the Church Fathers but the Wisdom tradition (Griffiths, 1994), out of which grew Gnosticism, the Hermetica, neo-Platonism and the Cathars. Even more than the Annunciations she is a palimpsest. The Virgin is surrounded by rays of the Sun, Tonantzin, robed in stars, like Egyptian Nut. She is *morena*, a Brown Virgin, standing on a black moon: five goddesses in one image, drawing on cultures from both sides of the Atlantic: sixteenth-century post-modernism. The moon is supported by a young brown angel: Juan Diego, Gabriel, Thoth, Hermes, messenger of the gods, supporting the Goddess of the moon and sun who is the Axis Mundi, her cloak the heavens. He is a small Atlas. She is the cosmic pillar, Atlantis.

The brown faces and black moon connect with a heresy, which Graves (1965) calls 'Gipsy Mary', a Black Goddess ('I am black but comely' she says in *Song of*

Solomon). This heresy challenges the loaded binaries of western patriarchy: black versus white, evil versus good, female versus male, and its racist shadow, dark skinned races against whites. Surely the Guadalupe was co-constructed by Indians and Friars. Each recovered the same Goddess buried in their own traditions, weaving the two halves into a glowing new whole that had seemed lost on both sides of the Atlantic. The politics of the colonial past are transformed in a post-modern present.

Island of the Goddess

A pilgrimage needs a climax. For ours it was Plato's lost island. I believe this was Tenerife, in the Canary Islands, off the coast of Africa, on the Canary current Columbus followed in his famous voyage. Tenerife means 'bright one' in the language of the Guanches, the 'white aborigines' of the Canaries conquered by the Spanish in the fourteenth century, their culture apparently eliminated like the Cathars.

The Guanches are vital links in a chain back to Atlantis. Archeologists believe they came to the island around 500 BC, not Plato's Atlanteans, but from the mainland part of the empire of Atlantis, inhabited in 450 BC by people Herodotus (1965) called 'Atlantes'. Guanche means 'people of Achinech', their name for Tenerife. Achinech comes from *A-ti-ne-te,* a word that Wolfel, the major authority on Guanche language, cannot interpret (1996, p.11, pp.718–20). I am struck by its phonetic resemblance to A-the-na, Libyan goddess who was also Neith, Nut, Atlantis. Guanche means 'people of Atinete', Atinetians, Athenians. They are also people of the Axis Mundi, the world mountain, Atlanteans.

Until the conquest Guanches guarded a Goddess culture in which women priestesses served the Goddess of the Axis Mundi. When Catholicism came to the island, Guanches adapted and adopted the cult of the Virgin with the same facility as the Aztecs, even using the same trick. They too had a miracle, the 'Virgin of the Candelaria', statue of a black Virgin who legends say was washed ashore on Candlemass Day, found by Guanches in a cave on a day sacred to their Goddess. Guanches said, of this virgin, they 'serve and honor her because she is the mother of the one who supports the earth and the sky'. This translates the Guanche prayer: 'the mother of the one who is the supporter of the sky and earth, and for this reason she is queen of both' (Tejera, 1992, pp.16–17). The image is now in a basilica nearby, but the cave is still there, open to the sea to the east, full of the presence of the Goddess, illuminated by strange light from the ocean, echoing with the low roar of water on the pebbled beach outside.

It is one of the two most sacred places of the Goddess on the island. The other is the sacred Volcano, Teide, the world mountain, from *Eheide* Hell: the two aspects of the Goddess. The Guanches feared and worshipped Her, giver of death and life. I wanted our pilgrimage to finish on the peak of Teide, so we drove there. The last part of the ascent was by cable car. But a notice told us it was closed for a month: precisely the month of our stay on Tenerife.

We bought a terracotta image of the Goddess, replica of a Guanche statue from before the conquest. The basic shape is woman as cross, as Tree of Life. Her arms are two short stumps, breasts far apart, two mounds like the mound of her head: three heads, three breasts, three mounds. This Goddess is a mountain. Her dress rises from a round base like a volcano. Her hair radiates from her head, with zigzag lines inscribed on it. In many artistic traditions, zigzags signify running water, the element of the great goddess: the sea the Virgin of the Candelaria came from, and Greek Aphrodite, Sumerian Tiamat. The wheel shape She stands on is round, like the disk of the sun, which is also herself, the fire below as above, and also the waters around the Cosmic mountain.

This is an image of the Goddess of Teide, the Sacred Volcano. I see the liquid flowing from her head as lava flowing from the volcano, liquid rock that flows like water, like milk, and burns with fire, that comes from the depths of the earth and falls from the sky, in which the fire above and below, the sun and the volcano, meet in a single contradictory deity. Every time I gaze at this marvelous image I feel I understand something supremely important about the Goddess.

The Post-modern Sacred

The journey now is over, but the pilgrimage continues to exist in the space–time matrix of the Goddess. William Faulkner said: 'The past is not dead. In fact, it's not even the past'. To which I add: '"There" is not absent. In fact, it's not even there'. It was important our pilgrimage moved in real space and time, to places irradiated and sanctified by Her presence, indicated through scholarship. Those times and places now fold over into everyday time and space, affecting where and how and why we live as we do, in seemingly pointless moments and acts in a seemingly unenchanted world. The Volcano Goddess of Tenerife has a shrine in our front room. Fra Angelico's *Annunciation* is above our bed. There is a small image of Guadalupe in our car, a larger one in our bedroom: the One who took the tricks of conquerors and conquered, uniting and transforming the best that each remembered and preserved from very ancient times, from the time of Atlantis.

This mixture of times, cultures and places could be labeled post-modern, the eclectic collection of a serial tourist, which I also am, as is Gabriela. But the Goddess is not fragmented into multiple images nor squeezed into a single unity, in past or present. She is everywhere, yet She is in specific places. We worshipped the Goddess of the Americas in Her shrine, in Her church, in Her city, and I believe She protects us in Australia, where we worship Her in Her incarnations there, empowered by our pilgrimage in space and time, more able to believe because of what we know, more able to learn because of what we believe. As the pilgrimage showed, in the Goddess binaries co-exist, and problems that come from binary thinking are resolved, for men and women, women and men.

References

Bahn, P. (1997), *Journey through the Ice Age*, Weidenfeld and Nicolson, London.

Baring, A. and Cashford, J. (1993), *The Myth of the Goddess*, Arkana Penguin, London.

Berger, P. (1969), *The Sacred Canopy,* Anchor Books, New York.

Clow, B. Hand, (1992), *Signet of Atlantis*, Bear & Company, Santa Fe.

De Rougemont, D. (1956), *Passion and Society*, Faber and Faber, London.

Eliade, M. (1959), *The Sacred and the Profane*, Harcourt, Brace, New York.

Engelsman, J. (1979), *The feminine dimension of the Divine*, Westminister Press, Philadelphia.

Gimbutas, M. (1991), 'The Monstrous Goddess', in J. Campbell (ed.) *The Goddess in all Her Names*, HarperCollins, San Francisco.

___(1999), *The Living Goddess*, University of California Press, Berkeley.

Graves, R. (1960), *Greek Myths*, vols 1 & 2, Penguin Books, Harmondsworth.

___(1961), *The White Goddess*, Faber and Faber, London.

___(1965), *Mammon and the Black Goddess,* Cassell, London.

Griffiths, J. (1994), *The Reclaiming of Wisdom,* Avon Books, London.

Herodotus, (1965), *Histories*, trans. A. Selincourt, Penguin, Harmondsworth.

Hillman, J. (1996), *The Soul's Code*, Random House, New York.

Hodge, B. (2002), 'Feral Archaeology and the Problem of Atlantis', *Cultural Studies*, vol. 16, no. 3, pp.351–364.

Kerenyi, C. (1967), *Eleusis*, Schocken Books, New York.

Lafaye, J. (1985), *Quetzalcoátl y Guadalupe*, Fondo de Cultura Economica, México.

MacCannell, D. (1989), *The Tourist*, Schoken Books, New York.

Marinatos, N. (1984), *Art and Religion in Thera*, Mathioulakis, Athens.

Matthews, C. (1992), *Sophia Goddess of Wisdom*, Aquarian Press, London.

Moore, T. (1997), *The Re-enchantment of Everyday Life*, HarperCollins, New York.

Rutherford, Ward (1993), *Celtic Lore*, HarperCollins, London.

Taylor, A. (1926), *Plato's Timaeus* Oxford University Press, Oxford.

Tejera, A. (1992), *La Religión de los Guanches*, Centro de la Cultura Popular, Tenerife.

Vidal-Naquet, P (1992), 'Atlantis and the Nations', *Critical Inquiry*, vol. 18, no. 2, pp.300–326.

Weber, M. (1976), *The Protestant Ethic and the Spirit of Capitalism,* ed.T. Parsons, Allen & Unwin, London.

Wolfel, D. (1996), *Monumenta linguae Canariae*, trans. M. Sarmento Pérez, Direccíon general de Patrimonio Historico, Tenerife.

Chapter 4

Discworld and Otherworld: The Imaginative Use of Fantasy Literature among Pagans

Graham Harvey

It is tempting to consider fantasy fiction as a popular challenge to the rationalist denigration of mythology and popular story-telling traditions. Fantasy fiction approaches 'myth' as empowering stories which carry a sense that something true is being said about the world, relationships, behaviour and life. Fantasy is, by definition, about imagined worlds, which seem unlike everyday reality. It touches on the matter of myth: the elusive proximity of an otherworld or otherworlds to and from which it is possible to travel with care or dangerous folly. Some mythic otherworlds are afterlife destinations (heaven, hell, the land of youth). Others are realms where mysterious persons dwell, such as dwarves, elves, goblins and trolls. However, the contrast with the everyday is often merely superficial. Beyond the *seeming* difference there is commonly a rich engagement with more ordinary matters, events and entanglements. That is, fantasy stories offer various mirrors to reality: some are celebratory, others critical. So as well as providing entertainment, fantasy may also invite us to reflect on alternative possibilities that might alter our vision and understanding. None of this is to say that particular writers or story-tellers of fantasy fiction take seriously the existence of the otherworlds they create. Yet some Heathens and animists do; and it is their belief in the existence of these otherworlds and their inhabitants that has prompted me to write this chapter. I will argue that such Pagan worldviews exemplify an enchantment of one's life, and that such worldviews can be carefully explored in relation to works of fantasy.

Until recently most scholars interested in Paganisms have focused attention on Wicca, Druidry and the more feminist Goddess-centred 'paths'. New interest in Heathenry (Harvey, 1997: pp.53–68, Blain, 2002, and Wallis, 2003) portrays it as a reconstruction and contemporary evolution of religious traditions originating in Northwest Europe and involving at least some of the following: polytheistic reverence towards Norse, Germanic and/or Anglo-Saxon deities; respect towards a wider community of 'other-than-human persons'[1] such as dwarves and [other] land-wights; the use of runes for meditation, healing, magic and the quest for knowledge; exploration of the cosmology encoded in references to Yggdrasil, the cosmic World Tree that connects all realities, and a dynamic interconnecting web that is named Wyrd; attempts to work out the implications of all these in daily life; and (particularly in the work of Blain and Wallis) various shamanistic practices which seek health and wisdom, especially through trance and through dialogue with other-than-human persons. Many Heathens, like many other Pagans, do not all give priority to deities in their religious rituals or discourse, nor in their everyday concerns. Those who are deeply involved with specific deities from the pantheon rarely deal with them to the exclusion of other persons: ancestors, land-wights, animals, birds, plants and so on.

If 'Heathenry' (or its cognates Heathenism, Ásatrú, Norse Paganism, Odinism and Northern Tradition) labels a fairly well-defined style of Paganism, there are as yet no organizations specifically for self-identified 'animist' Pagans. However, the term 'animist' is used by an increasing number of Pagans to refer to that part of their lifestyle or practice that attends to participation in a wider community of life. It indicates the importance of the diversity of species not only as a context in which human life occurs (as 'environmentalism' sometimes implies) but as a community of persons with value, agency, rights, needs and desires. Contrary to Tylor's use of 'animism' as a label for the original form of religion, defined as 'belief in spirits' (Tylor, 1913), the new animists are those who act towards the world as if towards a community of persons, only some of whom are human (see Bird-David, 1999, and Harvey, 2004). Animism may be seen among all kinds of Pagans, especially those who are more environmentally actively activist. Typically, animists might consider deities to be just one more group of persons, certainly worthy of respect for their power and/or wisdom, but no more important to the ecology and community of life than persons encountered by everyone in more everyday circumstances. Thus, animists are therefore just as likely to offer gifts and respect to particular trees, rocks or animals as they are to deities. Their religious rites are likely to be on a continuum between the respectful but almost casual stroke of a leafy branch and the attempt to mitigate the impact of human living on the wider community. If Paganism may be considered an acceptance that the world speaks (see Harvey, 1997), animism might be about actively trying to listen. Many of the Pagans who engaged in eco-activism and eco-drama challenging the UK government's road-building programme in the 1990s were motivated by an animist concern for the well-being of this wider community of persons (human and otherwise). Their actions engaged not only with trees and badgers but also, so some say, with elusive beings more typically (but not necessarily correctly) represented in mythology than in ecology books (see Letcher, 2001a, 2001b).

Among some Heathens and animists, as among many other Pagans globally, fantasy fiction is immensely popular. This chapter focuses on two of the most popular series in fantasy fiction today: Terry Pratchett's *Discworld* and Robert Holdstock's *Mythago Wood*. I will begin by examining elements in these two series which feature prominently in Heathen and animist readings, and will then offer some thoughts about the enchantment evident in these alternative worldviews.

Pratchett's *Discworld*

Terry Pratchett's ever-growing *Discworld* series includes at least 33 books in various formats. There is also a host of spin-offs, such as computer games and miniature figurines. The stories take place on a flat, circular world turning on the backs of four elephants which, in turn, stand on the shell of an enormous turtle swimming through space. According to Pratchett:

> This is one of the great ancient world myths, found wherever men and turtles are gathered together; the four elephants were an indo-European sophistication. The idea has been lying in the lumber room of legend for centuries. All I had to do was grab it and run away before the alarms went off (http://www.terrypratchettbooks. com/discworld/).

While it is unlikely that anyone has ever taken this cosmological image to be an empirically verifiable description of this or any actually existing world, there is something refreshing about a story that appeals to the everyday experiential sensation that we do indeed stand on a flat and circular world. Although Pratchett's *Discworld* is definitely not presented as our world, it speaks clearly to some people in ways that go beyond what the labels 'fantasy', 'fiction', 'imagination', 'comedy', 'entertainment' and 'recreation' are supposed to mean. Even as satire or parody (http://www.terrypratchettbooks.com/discworld/), it can still be taken as both a celebration and a re-enchantment of life. Pagans certainly do not mistake *Discworld* for a description of this world: they do not believe the earth is flat. Instead, *Discworld* for them is a scene for stories, entertainment and imagination which, by playfully engaging the possibilities of life in our world, resonate powerfully with Heathen and animist Pagan experiences. With the stories' insistence on the importance of magic, imagination and humour, the world is celebrated as a home we might get to know and enjoy better, and it is re-enchanted by the possibility of encountering beings (e.g. dwarves) and processes (e.g. magic) which are denigrated in the disenchantment that is modernity. The fact that the social dramas of *Discworld* involve a wider-than-human community (most of whose members take it for granted that 'strange things happen' by magic) is what makes such dramas appealing to Pagans.

One village on *Discworld*, Bass Ass in Lancre, is revisited in a kind of mini-series within the larger collection (Pratchett, 1987, 1988, 1991, 1993). This is the village inhabited by the witches Granny Weatherwax, Nanny Ogg and Magrat Garlick. These and other characters are enjoyed not only by Wiccans (who might be expected to recognize their own tradition more clearly here) but also by Heathen, animist and other Pagans. Some examples from the books will illustrate why. Pratchett typically takes a well-known theme, story or situation and sets it in the everyday life of characters in *Discworld*, often making it very clear that he is doing so. In *Lords and Ladies* (1993), for instance, as an episode in his use of Shakespeare's *A Midsummer Night's Dream*, Pratchett has a group of players perform something like (but not identical to) Shakespeare's play within a play. Pagan readers often say that the village's three witches are remarkably similar to self-identified witches who might be encountered in our world. This is often a compliment, but there are other witches in the series, comparison with whom might not be so welcome. Other facets of *Lords and Ladies* in which Pagans recognize familiar themes include a confrontation with otherworld opponents and a call on the ambiguous aid of a horned (and 'horny') God. The title of the book adopts a traditional Irish circumlocution that is gaining popularity especially among animist Pagans as an avoidance of naming those to whom it refers: Faerie or Elven folk who are far from being diminutive, cute, flower-dwelling beings with gossamer wings. As Pratchett writes:

> Elves are wonderful. They provoke wonder. Elves are marvellous. They cause marvels... Elves are terrific. They beget terror... No–one ever said elves are *nice*. Elves are *bad* (1993, pp.169–70).

In the story, as in Pagan understandings of this world and its otherworlds, such 'badness' is not the opposite of some divine or moral 'good'. Rather, it is a question of what is 'good' or 'bad' for particular people in particular situations. It is, for instance, 'bad' for people to be people to be treated as mere objects to satisfy the whims of others. 'They' (it is traditional not to name the 'lords and ladies' too many times) are simply not us. Their difference manifests itself in carelessness about what is 'good' for us. Just as we treat hedgehogs badly (casually and 'by accident' as we charge about in our cars), they treat us badly. They are an indigenous European version of the archetypal trickster who undertakes antisocial and dangerous activities. But if the pranks of some tricksters result in an increase of wealth or happiness, in *Lords and Ladies* the pranks of the 'lords and ladies' do not. They seek pleasure and power ('power-over' in the definition of Starhawk 1990) by being abusive. While there is something adolescent and even petulant about the Queen of the Faeries, and something severely maladjusted in the behaviour of her people towards all other persons (humans and bees in particular), their kin in Lancre's own mysterious otherworld show that they can act differently. They may never be 'nice', they may never care for anyone but themselves, but they *can* act differently – even if they have to be compelled to behave decently by an angry witch carrying the traditional iron that they hate. This struggle continues in two of the most recent *Discworld* books (Pratchett, 2003, 2004).

These evocations of witches and otherworld visitors, indeed the whole book as well as the entire series to which it belongs, are enjoyed by Pagans from many different traditions who enjoy the playful centrality of magic, the satirizing of power and pomposity, the sheer enjoyment of life, and the sense that ordinary people and events are themselves worthy of celebration. In these regards, Pratchett's *Discworld* may be seen as a carnivalesque celebration of the everyday and the ordinary. In addition to the perceptive observations that *Discworld* makes about our (real) world – sometimes with love, sometimes with biting parody – and in addition to all its colourful and amusing characters, *Discworld* is enchanting because it subtly encourages respect for, and even delight in, pluralism and animism. All manner of life is here. Readers emerge with the sense that the whole thing (these worlds and life itself) only works because there is a diversity of life. While a somewhat clichéd kind of animism (more like a projection of human-likeness onto inanimate artefacts) is evident in characters such as the Sentient Luggage (who appears several times), the *Discworld* series tends to be pervaded by a more down-to-earth animism, as the following passage illustrates:

> One of the recurring philosophical questions is: 'Does a falling tree in the forest make a sound when there is no one to hear?' Which says something about the nature of philosophers, because there is always someone in a forest. It may only be a badger, wondering what that cracking noise was... (Pratchett, 1992, p.6)

Badgers, squirrels, trees and many other living beings are presented as worthy of consideration and respect in *Discworld*. This satirical fantasy and comic fiction has serious implications. Pratchett's reference to philosophical questions might have been different if he were aware that the personalist philosopher Erazim Kohák (1993) makes a similar point in asking what a 'philosopher and a tree might converse about'. A development of these thoughts would contribute to challenges made against Cartesian mind/body dualisms and broader modernist culture/nature dualisms.

A paragraph from the Pratchett website not only summarizes the nature of the series, but also ends with a reference to global change, which might contribute further to a consideration of disenchantment and re-enchantment in this world:

> *Discworld* stories aren't parodies, according to Pratchett. They're 'resonances.' The people of Ankh-Morpork go to war with those towel-headed villains in neighbouring Klatch, and pretty soon characters are acting so pigheadedly that you might think they were real. Vampires who wish to be accepted in human society join the League of Temperance (you can suck, but you mustn't impale.) Witches tend to be good (they'll give you what you need) and fairy godmothers tend to be bad (they'll give you what they think you ought to want). A continent-wide system of semaphore towers is changing society. (http://www.terrypratchettbooks.com/discworld/)

If, as I am arguing, Pratchett's fantasy world and characters addresses issues in our world and can contribute to its re-enchantment, especially when read by Pagans (more especially by animist Pagans), a similar case may be made for other examples of the genre. In the following section, therefore, I consider the animate, life-filled, larger-than-human world portrayed in Robert Holdstock's *Mythago Wood* series.

Holdstock's *Mythago Wood*

The labelling of Holdstock's 'Mythago Wood' series (1984, 1988, 1991a, 1991b, 1993, 1994, 2002) as a 'cycle' might be precisely what Pratchett initially set out to parody about the fantasy genre. Like the *Discworld* series, *Mythago Wood* is not Pagan in the sense of being written by or for Pagans. Nonetheless, both are evocative of a world with which some Pagans claim to interact – one that is alien to scientistic philosophers and noisy anthropocentrists. The series is set in our world, but imagines that in particular places and in various ways other realities impinge upon and sometimes engulf the unwary and the overly bold. It is predicated on the idea that something within humans interacts with something in some ancient woodland to generate or re-generate mythic or archetypal forms. Although *Mythago Wood* is more sinister than *Discworld*, the possibilities it allows are recognisable to some Pagans. (The nature of these 'somethings' are the elusive and, at times, frightening mystery at the heart of the Mythago cycle.)

Let me begin with a brief summary of how the series starts. A young man leaving his family home for the Second World War tears a page out of estranged father's notebook. It contains an enigmatic reference to weird happenings in nearby ancient woodland. On returning from the war he finds that his brother, like his father before him, has also become enchanted or enthralled (in ways that are considered negative) by something about the wood. Through tentative exploration the young man begins to discover the wood's true hidden nature. His casual attempts to enter the wood usually result in disorientation, and he finds himself heading back out into the fields. Only after long, careful and painful probing does he learn how to go deeper into the wood. However, the depth of the wood is matched by deepening mental or psychic phenomena: first the traveller's peripheral vision and then all of his senses are affected by something about the wood. The deeper he penetrates into the wood, the further back in history (of a mythic sort) he travels.

The cover blurb of *Mythago Wood* (the first book in the series) quotes reviewers who describing it as 'haunting' and 'enchanting', clearly intending to mean that it is disturbing. The world portrayed in the series is not a 'nice', gentle or romantic place. Its vibrant life refuses to accede to humanity's prevalent wish to dominate, control and order the world to its benefit. This is a world that hinders human aspirations, one where humanity's inner demons and heroes refuse to make life easy. Holdstock's 'mythagos' are not autonomous agents, persons in their own right, but products of the human mind – even if they are given material substance by the leaf-mould and other elements of the wood. They are 'mythic' in that they are, finally, unreal.

While Pagans might want to resist this rejection of the ontological reality of 'tree spirits' and so on, there are elements of the series' thesis that resonate with Pagan worldviews. The title of another of Holdstock's books, *The Fetch* (1991a), written in-between two of the Mythago Wood books) is suggestive here. *The Fetch* uses the idea that part of every human is more or less detachable (somewhat like the 'soul' in other cultural or religious traditions). In both the *Mythago Wood* series and *The Fetch* some part of humans engages with the world in ways that are exceptional, unusual, and not everyday. In Holdstock's telling there is frequently something disturbing and dysfunctional about the way the 'fetch' and the human unconscious operate. The plots of books in the series work towards some resolution, especially peace-making between parents and their children, and between siblings. But the chief interest and pleasure of the series, for Pagans, is that it encourages a reading that celebrates and intimates something of the richness of their enchanted worldview.

Re-enchantment through Otherworlds

Animists, Heathens and Pagans celebrate life. Their goal is not to transcend, redeem or reject it. While sharing much of the worldview of their secular, scientifically-informed neighbours (especially ecologists), their notion that the world is shared with other significant persons, most of whom are not human and many of whom have been relegated to the status of myth and fiction, makes their world enchanted. It is a world made meaningful by relational engagement with those who might otherwise be treated as resources or scenery. It offers a considerable challenge to modern notions of de-traditionalization, dis-location and alienation.

For many Pagans, an enchanted world is most easily conveyed in works of fantasy fiction such as the two series discussed here. Many similar works are also regularly cited by Pagans, including those by Pagan authors such as Gerald Gardner (1949) evocative elaborations of regional folklore such as Alan Garner's *Weirdstone of Brisingamen* (1995 [1960]). The Discworld and Mythago Wood series exemplify the playful and imaginative ways in which Pagan readers engage with the genre as a whole. For example, because *Mythago Wood* is (at least theoretically) locatable on maps of the UK, proximate to the everyday world, means that it is close to the sense of 'otherworld' in Heathen and animist discourse. There are places and times at which it is possible to enter otherworlds. Indeed, Blain (2002) discusses the Heathen shamanic practice of 'seidr': willful and skilful journeys into otherworlds. Seeking knowledge or wisdom, entranced seidr-workers 'travel' among the nine worlds embraced by the 'World Tree'. These places are seen (i.e. understood, envisaged and visually experienced) as real places with scenery and ecology. Travellers seek inhabitants of these realms (including the ancestors who dwell in the place to which we will all go after death) to ask questions of importance to people in this-world.

There is a tradition reiterated by many Pagans that on the festivals of Beltain and Samhain (the beginnings of summer and winter respectively), the 'veils' between this-world and the otherworld are thin – the 'gates are open'. Following the ethnographic example of Edith Turner (2003), Jenny Blain (2002) and Robert Wallis (2003), I assert the veracity of this tradition. I too have been to the otherworld. One Beltain eve, before my handfasting (Pagan wedding), I spent the night on West Kennet long-barrow. Ancient burial mounds are commonly depicted in folklore and Paganism as the gateways to and from the otherworld. In the early morning mists I saw the barrow open and was invited into the feast-hall that lay within. It is also a tradition that whoever spends the night on a barrow on Beltain night will, by morning, either be dead, mad or a poet. I claim no poetic expertise so leave the reader to judge for themselves. It may, of course, be unfair that I am not going to say what I saw within. My point, however, is simply that for Pagans of all sorts of traditions, otherworlds are important. Heathen trance-practitioners may journey to theirs; animist Pagans may anticipate encounters with those who travel the other way, from the otherworld to here.

The significant point for this discussion of re-enchantment is that the everyday world dominated by humanity is not far removed from other realms. It is certainly not that this-world *only* gains meaning or value from the otherworld. Paganisms are all about celebrating 'nature', this-world's physical, daily being and acting. They are about ways of engaging with the life of the world in which all humans live (wherever they may go after death). The duality 'transcendent/immanent' has little role in Paganisms: the world is not made meaningful by another place that transcends it. However, the centrality of 'nature' requires consideration of what 'nature' means. In Heathenry and animist Paganisms 'nature' *includes* the otherworld. There is nothing un-natural or supernatural about the otherworlds encountered in trance, ritual, or story-telling. It could even be said that space between this-world and an otherworld is the space between one ecosystem and another. If geographers and biologists have not yet negotiated that boundary, Pagans may assert that they could. Animist eco-Pagan reflections and activisms may, thus, be of importance to improved consideration of what 'nature' means and how humans engage with it (see Letcher, 2003).

If this-world is meaningful and valued in and of itself, regardless of the possible existence of otherworlds, this might enhance the process of re-enchantment. The possibility of a nearby otherworld accessible through, for example, an ancient woodland or a barrow-mound, may further enhance the value of an already valued world. It is, of course, possible to become obsessed with other places and mysterious persons and to neglect the concerns and problems of this world. However, the sense that otherworld persons (the faeries, elves, dwarves and others) could be included in ecology books (in the same way that humans should be) rather than mythology books is significant. Like the principal setting of *Mythago Wood*, the otherworld is part of this Earth. It is not some distant, alien place. Thus, the re-enchantment of celebrating the otherworld should not be a romantic distraction from either radical or everyday engagement with this-world. It should be part of an argument that just as there are woods, fields, lakes, rivers, mountains and other life-filled environments in this-world, so there are other locations, otherworlds, with yet more diversity of life. If Descartes was wrong in asserting that animals are unable to think in ways he considered distinctively human (see Bekoff et. al. 2002), maybe the whole disenchanted construction of modernity has dangerously erroneous foundations. If so, re-enchantment is not a backwards step but a radical reconsideration of the foundational myths of modernity. In the dappled light of Pagan readings of fantasy literature, re-enchantment is not about mistaking imagination for reality but about achieving a more adequate view of a dynamic world shared with a wider community of living persons. Re-enchantment is, then, about finding appropriate ways to live as full members of that community, in contrast to disenchantment in which humanity has claimed a unique and lonely position.

Fantasy literatures often touch on Pagan perceptions of otherworld realities by popularizing some of the names of those who inhabit, and travel from, these places. They allow people to talk about dwarves and others 'as if they were there', which is, for some people, true. However, it is also important that such discourses and literatures are 'imaginative', 'creative' or 'fictional': Paganisms rarely treat any discourse as dogma. They are happy to narrate significant events as 'may be' possibilities and as entertainment. Pagan 'truths' are, usually, far better conveyed in storytelling than in any other mode of discourse, and fantasy literature takes precedence here. It is not that Holdstock or Pratchett is Pagan, nor that their otherworlds are pagan, but that there is a resonance between their stories and those that Pagans tell around festival bonfires and other venues.

A recent interview with Terry Pratchett about his book, *The Wee Free Men* (2003) provides a useful example of such resonances with which to conclude.

> [Interviewer:] In *The Wee Free Men*, Tiffany comments that where she lives there are 'a lot of people with a lot to do. There wasn't enough time for silence.' Would this be as fair a comment from you about life for us all today as it is for Tiffany in the Chalk?

> [Pratchett:] More so, I think. We've banished silence from our lives. We seem to fear it. We fill the world with noise. I'm sure it makes us ill.

> The silence up on the Chalk that I mention in the book – well, we get that where I live. It doesn't mean no sound at all, though. You hear the buzzards and the wind in the hedgerows and tractor sounds a long way off, and all of this gives the silence a kind of texture, makes it richer somehow. (TerryPratchettBooks website)

Realizing that 'silence' here refers to listening more attentively to what Heathen and animist Pagans might consider to be voluminous acts of communication resonates with an invitation to re-enchant the world by acting differently towards the ever-present community of life. This is made more straightforward by the fact that far from being a rationalized world, we actually live in one in which fantasy fiction is immensely popular. Along with indigenous storytellers (see Sarris, 1993, Stover, 2001), it is possible for us all to counter the attempt to make the world more rational, less diverse, less dialogical and less enchanted. Knowing that it is possible to visit an otherworld may greatly enhance the pleasure and responsibility of living in this-world.

50 *Popular Spiritualities*

Note

1   A phrase drawn from the work of Irving Hallowell and his Ojibwe hosts, see
    Hallowell 1960.

References

Bekoff, M., Allen, C. and Burghardt, G. (eds), (2002), *The Cognitive Animal*, MIT
    Press Cambridge, MA.
Bird-David, N. (1999), '"Animism" Revisited: Personhood, Environment, and
    Relational Epistemology', *Current Anthropology* vol. 40, S67–S91. Reprinted
    in G. Harvey (ed.), (2002), *Readings in Indigenous Religions*. Continuum,
    London, pp.73–105.
Blain, J. (2002), *Nine Worlds of Seid-Magic*, Routledge, London.
Gardner, G. (1949), *High Magick's Aid*, Atlantis Bookshop, London.
Garner, A. (1995 [1960]), *The Weirdstone of Brisingamen*, HarperCollins, London.
Hallowell, A. I. (1960), 'Ojibwa Ontology, Behavior, and World View', in S.
    Diamond (ed.), *Culture in History*, Columbia University Press, pp.19–52.
    Reprinted in G. Harvey (ed.), (2002), *Readings in Indigenous Religions*,
    Continuum, London, pp.17–49.
Harvey, G. (1997), *Listening People, Speaking Earth: Contemporary Paganism*, C.
    Hurst, London.
___(2004), *Animism*, C. Hurst, London.
Holdstock, R. (1984), *Mythago Wood*, Gollancz, London.
___(1988), *Lavondyss*, Gollancz, London.
___(1991a), *The Fetch*, Warner, London.
___(1991b), *The Bone Forest*, Grafton Books, London.
___(1993), *The Hollowing*, Harper Collins, London.
___(1994), *Merlin's Wood*, Harper Collins, London.
___(2002), *Gate of Ivory, Gate of Horn*, Earthlight, London.
Kohák, E. (1993), 'Speaking to Trees', *Critical Review* 6, pp.371–88.
Letcher, A. (2001a) 'The Role of the Bard in Contemporary Pagan Movements',
    Unpublished PhD thesis, King Alfred's College, Winchester.
___(2001b). 'The Scouring of the Shire: Fairies, Trolls and Pixies in Eco-Protest
    Culture', *Folklore*, vol. 112, pp.147–161.
___(2003) '"Gaia told me to do it": Resistance and the Idea of Nature within
    Contemporary British Eco-Paganism', *Ecotheology*, vol. 8, no. 1, pp.61–84.
Pratchett, T. (1983), *The Colour of Magic*, Gerrards Cross, Smythe.
___(1987), *Equal Rites*, Gollancz, London.
___(1988), *Wyrd Sisters*, Gollancz, London.
___(1991), *Witches Abroad*, Gollancz, London.
___(1992), *Small Gods*, Gollancz, London.
___(1993), *Lords and Ladies*, Gollancz, London.

___(2003), *The Wee Free Men*, Doubleday, New York.

___(2004), *A Hat Full of Sky*, Doubleday, New York.

Pratchett website: http://www.terrypratchettbooks.com/discworld/

Sarris, G. (1993), *Keeping Slug Woman Alive: A Holistic Approach to American Indian Text*, University of California Press, Berkeley.

Starhawk, (1990), *Truth or Dare*, Harper & Row, New York.

Stover, D. (2001), 'Postcolonial Sun Dancing at Wakpamni Lake', *Journal of the American Academy of Religion*, vol. 69, no. 4, pp.817–36. Reprinted in G. Harvey (ed.), (2002), *Readings in Indigenous Religions*, Continuum, London, pp.173–93.

TerryPratchettBooks website: *http://www.harpercollins.com/catalog/pratchett/site/books/interview.asp?isbn=0060012366*.

Turner, E. (2003), 'A Visible Spirit Form in Zambia' in G. Harvey (ed.), (2002), *Readings in Indigenous Religions*, Continuum, London, pp.149–72.

Tylor, E. 1913 (1871), *Primitive Culture*, 2 volumes, Murray, London.

Wallis, R. (2003), *Shamans / Neo-Shamans*, Routledge, London.

Chapter 5

Superheroes and the Development of Latent Abilities: A Hyper-real Re-enchantment?

Adam Possamai

Without doubt, contemporary Western culture is facing the return of spiritual/magical thinking in everyday life that can, among other things, produce a sense of the mysterious, the weird and the uncanny (e.g. Maffesoli, 1996; Tacey, 2000). This is both a response to the disenchantment of modernity and a consequence of the rise of consumer and popular cultures.

One way to understand the impact of popular culture on the spiritual/magical dimensions of social life is to use Baudrillard's (1988) notion of the hyper-real. He proposes that modern society is a social world constructed out of models or 'simulacra' which have no foundation in any reality, except their own. For example, theme parks represent Hollywood movies or Mickey Mouse cartoons rather than 'reality'; television viewers relate to characters in soap operas as if they were 'real' people; and popular news broadcasts are more focused on entertainment than facts.

Hyper-reality is structured via signs and symbols in such a way that it becomes difficult to distinguish the real from the unreal, which in turn encourages people to seek spectacle rather than meaning. In this hyper-real world, fictions offer a library of narratives which can be borrowed and used by anyone ready to consume them for identity purposes. Indeed, the mass marketing of narratives – and lifestyles, for that matter – has re-located identity within the domains of choice, individuality, aesthetics and consumption. For example, some people involved in alternative spiritualities use works of fiction such as Star Wars, Star Trek, the Lord of the Rings and H. P. Lovecraft as sources of inspiration to express their spirituality (see Hume, 1997; Luhrmann, 1994; Possamai, 2002a, 2002b, 2003a). In Australia there is evidence that Jediism constitutes a hyper-religion – that is, a simulacrum of a religion created out of popular culture that provides inspiration for believers/consumers at a metaphorical level (Possamai, (2003a). It could be argued that hyper-religions constitute a source of re-enchantment consisting of a simulacrum created out of, and partly carried by, popular culture.

This chapter will assess the contribution of popular culture to the development of post-modern re-enchantment tropes.[1] A case study of superhero comics is used as a source of popular culture and hyper-real moments. These comic narratives are re-enchantment narratives and, importantly, they situate the superhero as an archetypal expression of greater human potential. The idea that New Age culture encourages the development of latent human qualities or abilities is relevant here. The following extract, found in a New Age magazine on the Internet, offers an example of how the consumption of superheroes may be linked to the ethics of New Age culture:

> When I was a young boy, I recall playing superheroes with my younger brother, in our back yard. We would declare our powers and use them to our benefit, of course; and it all seemed "real" in a sense... even if it were in our imaginations. Funny thing is though, now that I am older and have come to terms with certain gifts I have; actually that we all have; I have come to realize that with these powers comes a decent amount of responsibility and compassion.
>
> In comparing the gifts I have become familiar with and comfortable using, it is the empathic one that still remains the hardest to adjust to. Everyone is born an empath and continues throughout life utilizing empathic abilities. What we call hunches, a vibe, a gut feeling, and in some cases even when we simply rely on instinct; all of these stem from empathy. Defined, empathy regards the ability to share in another person's emotions, thoughts, and feelings. In a spiritual sense however, we all do this. It is a natural born gift. I am sure we have experienced a moment when we accuse someone of bringing our spirits down or up. This can be accredited to an empathic ability...
>
> ...Who would have guessed that the ability to become a superhero is innate in us. All we have to do is acknowledge it, trust it, and then utilize it.[2]

Is there an affinity[3] between superheroes in comics and the development of latent abilities? Could such an affinity be part of a hyper-real re-enchantment process? If this were the case, then it would have important ramifications for both our understanding of popular culture and the development of religious sensibilities in the New Age.

The Human Potential Ethic and Alternative Spiritualities

Alternative spiritualities (such as New Age, Neo-Paganism, non-traditional Esotericism and Occultism) and westernized Eastern practices (such as Zen meditation and Est) are part of what Bauman (1998) calls post-modern religions, and more specifically, consumer religions. Spiritual actors consume products for gathering and enhancing spiritual sensations, and one of their central characteristics is a belief in what could be called the 'human potential' ethic (Possamai, 2001a). This potential includes greater self-insight, more body awareness, and enhanced communication with others. It leads to personal growth and the development of latent abilities. People who believe in this ethic find in the soul something similar to, or even identical with, divine reality; and they discover this through an inner adventure that leads to a spiritual mutation and/or the development of latent personal qualities.

This inner adventure is not literally a search to become a god or a super human. It is best understood as the realization of a 'higher' self – similar in some ways to the Westernized Buddhist quest for Enlightenment. By understanding one's body/mind/spirit, and by working on the self through meditation, preventive healing, or other praxes, it is possible to develop one's latent abilities. This reflects a heuristic spectrum that at one end might involve the quest for instrumental forms of development through techniques the individual uses to better himself or herself so as to become more effective and efficient in worldly pursuits (e.g. use of crystals for healing). At the other end, it is a search for illuminational development – that is, a quest for a direct inner personal experience of the divine or for a greater individual potential (e.g. use of meditation to reach a higher stage of being).

The human potential ethic permeates mainstream and popular culture (Possamai, 2003b). Ross (1991, p.27) argues that these 'alternative' orientations are found in mainstream talk shows such as the Oprah Winfrey Show, which, without presenting itself as *part* of the New Age, popularizes certain New Age *principles* such as spiritual growth and potential.

In popular culture, superheroes express the human potential ethic through a re-invented mythology that has been successfully commercialized in comics, cartoons, and mainstream films. The carriers of these new forms of spiritualities in Western societies in the 1960s to 1970s belong to the baby boomer generation (see below). One might well ask if such processes of re-enchantment have socio-cultural repercussions – a question I shall attempt to answer through a case study of superheroes in comics.

Superheroes in Comics

The Golden Age of comics in North America began with the debut of Superman in 1938. As a cultural artefact, the Superman character gained an enormous audience, not only in comics but also in other media such as animated cartoons, radio and television. It also established the norms and conventions for other super-heroic characters. Readers were keen for further stories and characters. Comic artists were obliged to follow the demand, and as a result the superhero market boomed. Despite the fact that the superhuman theme first appeared in North American science fiction around the beginning of the twentieth century, it was not until the arrival of the Superman character that the genre became popular. Prior to this 'the message of the superman stories [was] always the same: whether saviour or destroyer, the Superman cannot be permitted to exist' (Andrea, 1987, p.125). One reason for this was that the Superman was seen as glorifying Aryan racial superiority. Another was that in a world dominated by a Christian ethos, the belief in becoming a god was considered blasphemy.

So why did Superman, the comic book creation, in contrast to other supermen from pulp fictions, become a cultural icon? Andrea suggests it was because:

> ...he is the embodiment of society's noblest ideals, a "man of tomorrow" who foreshadows mankind's highest potentialities and profoundest aspirations but whose tremendous powers, remarkably, pose no danger to its freedom and safety (Andrea, 1987, p.125).

By the 1940s, comic books were being published in greater quantities, and new superheroes were constantly appearing. Superheroes had virtually taken over the Anglo-Saxon comic book medium due to the economic success of the Superman mythos (McAllister, 1990, p.58) and were firmly established when the first baby boomers started to read comics.

The connection between comics and religion has been addressed by scholars of both the Superman (Reynolds, 1992) and the Silver Surfer (Gabilliet, 1994) stories, with particular reference to biblical imagery. Savramis (1987) goes further into the religious analysis of Superman and discovers, Christian elements aside, references to suprasensible forces that are found in occultism and that have a strong affinity with the human potential ethic (Faivre, 1992). Schechter (1979) makes reference to some aspects of popular culture that serve a 'magico-religious' function and suggests?] there might even be a submerged spiritual significance in superhero stories that has some parallels with pre-industrial mythological narratives.

It could be argued that the transformation of superpower figures from pre-industrial mythologies to the medium of commercial comics had unintended consequences in Western consumer culture: that of being in affinity with, and popularizing, the human potential ethic. In other words Superman, as the first character in popular culture with positively stigmatized superpowers, generated an 'imaginary doxa' – that is, a general desire grounded in everyday-life fantasies which has been articulated by works of fiction. Examples of 'imaginary doxa' might include wanting to be as beautiful and wealthy as a character in a soap opera, as sexually active as a character in a pornographic movie, or as skinny as a magazine model. The 'imaginary doxa' carried by the superhero mythos is one people attempt to use, consciously or not, to acquire and/or achieve 'super' powers for themselves. The function of this 'doxa' is not to make people cultural dupes; writers and producers of these superhero stories did not consciously set out to produce or to re-enforce this human potential ethic.[4] The argument here is not simply one of emulation, but more of a metaphysics of transformation in the reader's mind. The 'doxa' is rather part of a 'fantasy collective', in a similar sense to Durkheim's notion of *conscience collective*, where works of fiction make it possible for people to dream and wish for some out-of-world outcome that might to some extent influence their everyday life. In Elliots's words: 'as directors of our own self-narratives, we draw upon psychic frames of memory and desire, as well as wider cultural and social resources, in fashioning [ourselves]' (Elliot, 2001, p.2). In this 'imaginary doxa', then, the evolution of superheroes in comics and the popularization of the desire to imagine a 'super' self (i.e. a human potential ethic) are in affinity and might lead to a re-enchanted sense of life.

The Human Potential Ethic and Superheroes in Affinity: Three Arguments

Works of art also support and render plausible a discourse on the human potential ethic (Faivre, 1992; Henderson, 1987), but they mostly remain within the boundaries of High Culture. However, it is also the case that popular/consumer culture is highly valorized among all strata of society, making superhero consumption open to a wider audience. There are three reasons why comic superheroes may be thought of as agents for popularizing the human potential ethic.

First, the character of Superman instigated a double non-problematic personality – a kind of benign Dr. Jekyll and Mr. Hyde in the form of Clark Kent/Superman – which became a model for future superhero characters. As Andrea (1987, p.132) notes: 'Superman differs from his predecessors in science fiction by being able to exist within society by disguising himself as the self-deprecating and mild-mannered Clark Kent'. That is, he was a middle class American white man to whom readers could relate. The superhero's double life allows him or her to be exceptional but not exceptional enough to be cast out by society. As Wedgwood (1930, p.139) writes, inspired by the excursus of Simmel (1991, pp.52–63) on ornamentation:

> In every individual there are two conflicting impulses: the one to resemble his fellows; the other to be different from them. Human beings are gregarious but they are also individualists. While everyone wishes to remain within the community, every normal individual desires to be in some degree outstanding in that community.

Superman became popular in comics because his powers were perceived positively; but just as importantly, his dual identity meant he did not need to give up his role in mainstream society.

Second, in the myths of pre-industrial societies, extraordinary powers were generally acquired by divine intervention – you were born a hero or a demi-god – or by the hero undergoing a harsh initiation to earn them (e.g. Ulysses, Hercules). In the post-industrial superhero mythos, 'superpowers' are acquired mainly by accident or by a non-ascetic self-transformation, as with Spiderman, the Fantastic Four,[5] and even mutants like the X-Men. The secular equivalent of divine intervention is transformed into contemporary technologies – chemicals, atomic energy, high-tech machines and so on – that are sometimes used willingly by, and at other times accidentally create, the superhero.

These non-ascetic and secular characters fit the Zeitgeist of a society of leisure that demands quick access to both material and spiritual goods. As Bauman (1998) argues, today's seekers of peak-experience *consume* sensations rather than follow the ascetic path of 'ordinary' seekers (e.g. through traditional Buddhist meditation and religious fasting). This provides a plausibility structure for the 'imaginary doxa' of quickly acquiring 'superpowers' without recourse to an ascetic path.

There are, however, exceptions. Not every superhero gains his or her powers quickly. Batman is an example of a superhero who acquires his abilities not by accident or divine intervention but by years of ascetic training, and mostly with the assistance of high-tech machines to facilitate his physical and mental development. Daredevil is another ascetic figure, but his super-sensibilities are gained by way of a 'secular' accident *before* he starts his training.

The third reason why comic superheroes may be thought of as agents for popularizing the human potential ethic relates to the importance of popular culture in the post-modern era. Prior to modernity there were other great heroes, some of whom had exceptional powers, who were agents of the human potential ethic:

> Tales of heroic endeavour have been popular from time immemorial, and some of the world's most influential narratives have invited readers and listeners to admire, emulate and/or measure themselves against the deeds, attitudes and beliefs of the great and famous. (Grixti, 1994, p.214)

There are long lists of heroes through the ages: Gilgamesh, Ulysses, Hercules, prophets and religious leaders, and political and military figures such as Che Guevara, Napoleon Bonaparte and Alexander the Great (Grixti, 1994). However, these heroes tended to be political leaders and in post-modern western cultures politics is not seen as a site for the expression of human potential and leadership. In our era, the rejection of external authority started in the counter-culture of the 1960s with young adults viewing scientists as a new kind of corruption (Roszak, 1969, pp.262–263). As Kellehear (1996, p.97) notes: 'The belief in the value neutrality of science is long gone, together with unconditional reliance on the local doctor, lawyer, teacher, and parson'. A growing scepticism toward institutional authority developed. The 'traditional' answers supplied by what Voyé (in Roof et al., 1995) calls the bearer of 'Grand Narratives' were questioned or ignored. Many of the educated young no longer accepted the 'set menu' of canonical knowledge.

Eco (1976, pp.37–39) argues that superheroes, given their abilities, should fight more for political and/or environmental issues rather than on the enforcement of justice in their own communities (e.g. Superman in Metropolis, Marvel heroes in New York). Indeed as Frank Miller, a writer and artist of comic books, says: 'It always struck me as odd, considering the strength of editorial cartoons in newspapers, that comic books were so meticulously apolitical, or even worse politically correct' (Salisbury, 1999, p.203). Apart from a few exceptions, such as Captain America during the Watergate scandal and other more recent DC and Marvel comics characters, superheroes tend to support the *status quo* and are not interested in changing society at a political level. If past heroes represented external authority, recent superheroes such as Superman are not role models of social and political leadership *per se*; and since they are not portrayed as part of any institutional authority, these new (super) heroes are consequently more popular with the contemporary general public.

The Human Potential Ethic and Superheroes

Comic book superheroes are not the only narrative form that has an affinity with the human potential ethic. Other genres such as fantasy, horror and science fiction also became commercialized and popularized in the late 1960s (Grixti, 1994). For example, even if the vampire has been popular since the nineteenth century, 'it has never had as pervasive an appeal in American popular culture as it has had in the past decade' (Schopp, 1997, p.232). According to Auerbach (1995, p.155), the character of the vampire, revised in the 1970s, aroused a longing for personal/spiritual/occult transformation. During this period, vampires were 'more frightened than frightening' and became 'at their worst, edifying, Superman-like rescuers'. In Jediism (Possamai, 2003a) there is evidence of people applying the code of conduct of Jedi Knights ('superheroes' from the Star Wars science fiction series) to their everyday life. However, as I have argued, Superman was the first popular character of a new brand of superhero, and laid down the norms and conventions of the superhero genre in a world no longer strictly dominated by Christian ethics.

There are, of course, exceptions to the argument that superheroes in comics are in affinity with the human potential ethic. The Hulk is a case in point. He cannot control his power and his double identity, but he is nevertheless a popular character. However, a stronger affinity with the human potential ethic can be found in the television version: Dr. David Banner transforms into the Hulk because he was trying to develop his hidden strengths with a machine of his invention (Daniels, 1991, p.176).

The best example of this affinity is Spiderman, an adolescent who acquires superpowers through a non-divine accident when he is bitten by a radioactive spider. One can see clearly that Spiderman creates an 'imaginary doxa' which allows readers to imagine a supra-human individual. This is made possible by Spiderman's alter-ego, Peter Parker, who is a 'typical' troubled adolescent – and now young adult. Indeed when Spiderman's creators, Stan Lee and Steve Ditko, launched their new character, they were aiming to provoke in their readers a sense of inspiration, rather than awe.

Most of the characters found in the superhero mythos express a strong sense of the human potential ethic. Indeed, particular comic universes often overlap and various superheroes meet each other. This is known in the trade as a crossover. Guest superheroes continue to carry the affinity with the human potential ethic outside their allocated magazine.

Conclusion

The human potential ethic has long been present in modern Western societies particularly among occultist and esoteric groups, but it only started to become popular from the 1960s when, amongst other factors, the development of latent abilities was popularized with the birth of Superman in comics. If this thesis is correct, it can be argued that superheroes contributed to the creation of the imaginary doxa of becoming a 'super' self. Popular culture provided an unintended pathway to the expression of the ethic, which resulted in a hyper-real re-enchantment of self and world.

The re-enchantment of parts of the contemporary world can take many forms, and this chapter has analysed a specific form based on the notion of the hyper-real; that is, a re-enchantment that is created out of, and largely carried by, popular culture. The affinity between the superhero in comics and the human potential ethic is only one aspect of this hyper-real re-enchantment; many more types inspired by other works of popular culture remain to be researched.

Notes

1   I would like to thank Bernard Caleo for his helpful comments and suggestions.
2   Yeldell, O. 'The Role of the Empath' OfSpirit.com: Healing Body, Mind & Spirit, Internet Site: http://www.ofspirit.com/omaryedldell1.htm.
3   By affinity, I refer to an intimate co-existence of these two elements and not to a relationship of cause and effect (see Weber, 1968).
4   Salisbury (1999) interviewed 14 leading comics scriptwriters, and only two made direct references to religion. The only specific comment that is connected to the thesis of this chapter is expressed by Grant Morrison: 'JLA ([Justice League of America] a group of superheroes) is full of mythological references and folk tale stuff, but nobody needs to know about it. If you do know about it, it will enrich your reading, but if you don't know about it you'll still get a rollicking good laugh' (Salisbury, 1999, p.212).
5   Even the identity of Thor, a Norse god, is given by accident to Donald Blake, an M.D. with a limp.

References

Andrea, T. (1987), 'From Menace to Messiah: The History and Historicity of Superman', in D. Lazere (ed.), *American Media and Mass Culture: Left Perspectives*, University of California Press, Berkeley, pp.124–138.

Auerbach, N. (1995), *Our Vampires, Ourselves*, The University of Chicago Press, Chicago and London.

Baudrillard, J. (1988), *Jean Baudrillard: Selected Writings*, Polity Press, Cambridge.

Bauman, Z. (1998), 'Post-modern Religion?', in P. Heelas (ed.), *Religion, Modernity and Post-modernity*, Blackwell, Oxford, pp.55–78.

Daniels, L. (1991), *Marvel. Five Fabulous Decades of the World's Greatest Comics*, Harry N. Abrams, Inc., New York.

Eco, U. (1976), 'Le Mythe de Superman', *Communications*, vol. 24, pp.24–40.

Elliot, A. (2001), *Concepts of The Self*, Polity Press, Cambridge.

Faivre, A. (1992), *L'ésotérisme*, Presses Universitaires de France, Paris.

Gabilliet, J. P. (1994), 'Cultural & Mythical Aspects of a Superhero: The Silver Surfer 1968–1970', *Journal of Popular Culture*, vol. 28, pp.203–213.

Grixti, J. (1994), 'Consumed Identities: Heroic Fantasies and the Trivialisation of Selfhood', *Journal of Popular Culture*, vol. 28, pp.207–228.

Henderson, L. D. (1987), 'Editor's Statement: Mysticism and Occultism in Modern Art', *Art Journal*, vol. 46, no. 1, pp.5–8.

Hume, L. (1997), *Witchcraft and Paganism in Australia*, University of Melbourne Press, Melbourne.

Kellehear, A. (1996), *Experiences Near Death. Beyond Medicine and Religion*, Oxford University Press, Oxford.

Luhrmann, T. (1994), *Persuasions of the Witch's Craft. Ritual Magic in Contemporary England*, Picador, London.

Maffesoli, M. (1996), *La Contemplation du Monde. Figures de Style Communautaire*, Editions Grasset & Fasquelles, France.

McAllister, M. (1990), 'Cultural Argument and Organizational Constraint in the Comic Book Industry', *Journal of Communication*, vol. 40, no. 1, pp.55–71.

Mondello S. (1976), 'Spider-Man: Superhero in the Liberal Tradition', *Journal of Popular* Culture, vol. 10, pp.232–238.

Possamai, A. (2001a) 'Not the New Age: Perennism and Spiritual Knowledges', *Australian Religion Studies Review*, vol. 14, no. 1, pp.82–96.

___(2001b), 'A Revisionist Perspective on Secularisation: Alternative Spiritualities, Globalised Consumer Culture, and Public Spheres', in C. Cusack and P. Oldmeadow (eds), *The End of Religions? Religion in an Age of Globalization*, Sydney Studies in Religion, vol. 4, University of Sydney, pp.200–215.

___(2002a), 'Secrecy and Consumer Culture: An Exploration of Esotericism in Contemporary Western Society Using the Work of Simmel and Baudrillard', *Australian Religion Studies Review*, vol. 15, no. 1, pp.44–56.

___(2002b), 'Cultural Consumption of History and Popular Culture in Alternative Spiritualities', *Journal of Consumer Culture*, vol. 2, no. 2, pp.197–218.

___(2003a), 'Alternative Spiritualities, New Religious Movements, and Jediism in Australia', *Australian Religion Studies Review*, vol. 16, no. 2, pp.69–86.

___(2003b), 'Alternative Spiritualities and the Logic of Late Capitalism', *Culture and Religion*, vol. 4, no. 1, pp.31–45.

Reynolds, R. (1992), *Super Heroes: A Modern Mythology*, B. T. Batsford, London.

Roof, W. C. Carroll, J. W. and D. A. Roozen (eds), (1995), *The Post-war Generation and Establishment Religion. Cross-cultural Perspectives*, Westview Press, Boulder and London.

Ross, A. (1991), *Strange Weather. Culture, Science, and Technology in the Age of Limits*, Verso, New York.

Roszak, T. (1969), *The Making of a Counter Culture. Reflections on the Technocratic Society and its Youthful Opposition*, Anchor Books, New York.

Salisbury, M. (1999), *Writers on Comics Scriptwriting*, Titan Books, London.

Savramis, D. (1987), 'Religion et Bandes Dessinées: Tarzan et Superman Sauveurs', *Social Compass*, vol. 33, no. 1, pp.77–86.

Schechter, H. (1979), 'Focus on Myth and American Popular Art', *Journal of American Culture*, vol. 2, no.2, pp.210–216.

Schopp, A. (1997), 'Cruising the Alternatives: Homoeroticism and the Contemporary Vampire', *Journal of Popular Culture*, vol. 30, pp.231–243.

Simmel, G. (1991), *Secret et Sociétés Secrètes*, Circé, Strasbourg.

Tacey, D. (2000), *Re-enchantment. The New Australian Spirituality,* Harper Collins Publishers, Sydney.

Weber, M. (1968), *The Protestant Ethic and the Spirit of Capitalism*, Unwin University Books, London.

Wedgwood, C. (1930), 'The Nature and Functions of Secret Societies', *Oceania*, vol. 1, no. 2, pp.129–145.

Chapter 6

Memorialization and Immortality: Religion, Community and the Internet

Margaret Gibson

When the afterlife fades in the face of the advances made by 'materialist' reason, it is quite simply because it has crossed over into life itself.
Jean Baudrillard (1988, p.144)

People used to be born into traditional societies, as they were into social classes or religions. Today even God himself has to be chosen.
Ulrich Beck (2000, p.164)

This chapter examines the status of self-identity, death, and community, in highly technological, spiritually hybrid, post-traditional (Giddens, 1994) societies. DIY (Do-It-Yourself) post-traditional spirituality includes 'denominational switching, church hopping (and shopping), institutionalized eclecticism and syncretism in the many congregations, and a growing variety of spiritual stimuli, ranging from recovery groups to New Age bookstores to angel books and spirit guides' (Wunthnow, 1998, p.40). Post-traditional societies are not devoid of traditions, religion or religious fundamentalism, just as forms of global culture and modern liberalism are part of many traditional societies. In other words, traditional and post-traditional societies are not mutually exclusive categories but contain elements of each other. In post-traditional societies, sacred rituals, beliefs and faith practices tend to be chosen in adult life. Inherited family religions are also maintained, or not, according to the criteria of what is meaningful or consistent with one's lifestyle, morality and sense of identity. Many sacred rituals or festivities have corresponding secular and consumer meanings and purpose. Furthermore, many individuals and families maintain religious observance in the spirit of family tradition, ritual and relationship maintenance rather than actual faith practice. In comparison to other globally-mainstream religions, the hegemony of Christianity in most Western, multicultural societies, has led to its greater integration into secularism and commodity/consumer culture.

Although the term 'spirituality' is used throughout this paper, it is not used uncritically; this is partly because it inscribes a dualism and, by omission, a hierarchy between the material and the spiritual. If the spiritual signifies a notion of the sacred or a transcendent otherness beyond the sensible and intelligible, then one has to ask what relation this has to material existence. It is my contention that the term spirituality either assimilates or excludes a dependent relationship on the material. Indeed, the privileging of spirit reiterates the traditional masculinist and culturally-Western flight from the material, the mortal and the body. From quite a different point of view, Slavoj Zizek questions the return of the 'deep spiritual' in the specific context of intellectual culture where, he says, 'Direct materialism is out [and] one is...solicited to harbor openness towards a radical otherness beyond the onto-theological God' (2003, p.487). The word spirituality, however, does signify a shift in religious culture whereby the sacred is not necessarily bound to a figuration of God within the context of organized religion. It also accommodates societal and global diversity in the many forms in which the sacred is understood, figured or experienced. Indeed the term spirituality can signify many ideas and experiences that locate the sacred in the ordinary material world without any sense of a mystical or transcendent beyond.

Slavoj Zizek has identified something else in contemporary culture amongst the intellectual classes of Europe and English-speaking countries: a general culture of silence and secrecy towards publicly admitting *any* belief. Even if the educated classes believe in some kind of radical otherness, answering a direct question such as 'Do you believe in some form of the divine or not?' is inevitably avoided (Zizek, 2003, p.487). In an anti-dogmatic and relativistic culture, belief itself, according to Zizek, has been made into 'a private obscene secret' (ibid.).

In this chapter, I am interested in the way a broad range of modern communication technologies enable the creation of sacred and transcendent *events* of community, particularly in relation to death. In terms of death, grief and memorialization, I use one main global 'event' as an example – the post-September 11 rituals of mourning that were reported, televized and recorded, in various media, over an extensive time frame across the world. I also briefly address Princess Diana's death and funeral. Both of these (particularly the former) represent and communicate the economic and symbolic privilege of First World lives as being worthy of collective identification and grief. They are also significant in revealing the continued presence of religion and collectivizing ritual in times of social and emotional crisis. As 'media events', they show the power of death in creating community (however fleeting) across divisions of time, space, language and nationality.

In this paper I suggest how the universal significance of death in creating community, both in this life and in imagined communities (that is, afterlife places and sites), is linked to communication technologies. Broadly, the paper argues that the technological transcendence of time and space barriers (part of modernity) has enabled new forms of spiritual, memorial and immortalizing practices. Community in life and death, as well as the sacred and memorial value of individual existence, are located in many major religions and in Western secularism. I argue that the decline in formal or traditional religions and practices does not mean a decline in or loss of ideas and desires for community (in life and death), nor does it temper the desire to sustain the memory of self and others. Rather, people who may once have looked to religion to find significance may now look to cyber-space to register a sense of the larger, the unbounded, and also meaning in anonymity. Furthermore, the paralleling and intertwining of religious and secular beliefs and practices in contemporary life has tended to expand rather than reduce the ways in which human beings try to record, archive and memorialize individual and collective life. While many people hold onto mystical ideas of immortal existence in otherworldly places, thoroughly secular individuals and societies use technologies such as the Internet to project and imagine ideas of community, immortality and existence beyond the body.

Death and Community

There will always be religious and/or spiritual cultures and practices while death continues to be part of the human condition. However, in post-traditional societies the ontological and teleological groundlessness of being is more acutely felt without 'the will of gods, which justifies your being' (Gauchet, 1997, p.206). Marcel Gauchet argues that a post-religious society is one in which inner unease rises to an unprecedented level as the individual faces existence without foundation in God/gods. Age-old questions about the meaning of existence, as well as more modern self-identity questions of 'Who am I?' and 'What am I supposed to be?', are difficult without God/gods and traditions which place the self in ready-made identities and roles (Gauchet, 1997, p.205). A post-religious society, according to Gauchet, is one that has moved beyond blind or unquestioning faith to a position where faith itself is experienced as an era, a historical memory (ibid.). The disenchantment of the post-religious society is experienced in the psychic or emotional oscillation between a desire for the 'soothing effects' of religious faith and an unwillingness to 'renounce the freedom to question' (ibid.).

While the thesis of death-denial has been prominent in philosophical literature about the role of religion (Heidegger, 1985; Becker, 1997), many aspects of new spirituality focus on the quality of existence on the way to and at the limit of death, rather than emphasize preparation for an existence after death. Priests and other religious persons do not have a monopoly on existential interpretations in contemporary society – they compete with other spiritual experts and often with secular experts such as counsellors and psychologists.

The nothing of death – the fact that it is not a *thing* – both creates and annihilates value and meaning. Death is the great equalizer because it is 'general equivalence' (Baudrillard, 1988, p.46). It creates community because it is *the* common existential truth and future that faces all human beings collectively and in their singularity. For Jean-Luc Nancy, death does not so much create community as is both the possibility and impossibility of community. I cannot self-consciously commune with others in my death; death undoes my being with, my communing with other mortals. At the same time, Nancy says: 'only the community can present me my birth, and along with it the impossibility of my reliving it, as well as the impossibility of my crossing over into my death' (1991, p.15).

As the void of signification (the empty place without meaning) but also the void enabling signification (the empty place to be filled with meaning), death is the wellspring of religion. Religion renders death meaningful when it could equally well be meaningless – or indeed outside this dichotomy altogether. In making death the threshold to another life, Christianity makes this life meaningful and purposeful in relation to another; the community of the living therefore crosses over into an other-worldly community – an afterlife. Death haunts existence as an inevitable and irreversible separation from those we love. Other-worldly communities express this desire to sustain contact with deceased loved ones. The desire for immortality is not just the egoism of always wanting to *be* but is also an expression of love – always wanting others to be and wanting always to be with others. Afterlife depictions of immortality are fantasies of renewed community after the breach and separation of death. Non-traditional forms of spirituality such as New Age beliefs and practices may or may not offer afterlife beliefs, and contemporary commodity and consumer culture certainly militates against a moral economy of asceticism, sexual repression, and other forms of denial and sacrifice that can purchase 'heaven'. Indeed the moral economy of Christian salvation is in direct conflict with Late Capitalism and its lifestyle ethos and imagery of hyper-consumption.

In post-traditional Western societies, the belief in immortality is much less integrated into an ethical framework of conduct. This does not mean that immortality is not desired or believed in, but rather that it is less tied to salvation as a moral economy of deferred reward and punishment. This is, in part, an effect of consumer society and its quelling of deferred gratification. In his 1911 essay on the relationship between the pleasure ego and the reality ego, Freud gives a brief psychological interpretation of the origin of reward in an afterlife. Freud's essay sets out to explain the shift from a self-gratifying, impulse-driven, morally-unrestrained pleasure ego, to the socially-adaptive, more morally-ordered and conservative reality ego. In the Freudian psychological economy, the deferral of immediate self-gratification (pre-eminently part of Christian asceticism) is not the absence of self-gratification. On the contrary, the deferral of immediate self-gratification leaves a kind of psychological effect which religious belief converts into the idea of a future reward. Of this economy, Freud writes:

> The substitution of the reality principle for the pleasure principle implies no deposing of the pleasure principle, but only the safeguarding of it. A momentary pleasure, uncertain of its results, is given up, but only in order to gain along the new path an assured pleasure at a later time. But the endopsychic impression made by this substitution has been so powerful that it is reflected in a special religious myth. The doctrine of reward in the after-life for the – voluntary or enforced – renunciation of earthly pleasure is nothing other than the mythical project of this revolution in the mind. Following

consistently along these lines, *religions* have been able to effect absolute renunciation in a future existence; but they have not by this means achieved a conquest of the pleasure principle ... (1986, p.514)

A series of interconnected economic binds is suggested in this passage. The deferral of immediate pleasure (self-denial now) is already caught up in the bind of self-interest (self-preservation later, in an afterlife) through a surplus trace. In psychological terms, this economic surplus is the mental impression that by sacrificing pleasure and immediate gratification, the greater reward will be gained of eternal life. In other words, there is no pure disinterested selflessness outside the moral economy of the reality principle: self-denial will be rewarded; the deferral of expenditure now is only a deferred gain. The deferred surplus effect (the endopsychic impression – this mental impression) becomes an investment (a saving/reserve) in the religious idea of a path beyond death, which death does not cancel.

The reward of an afterlife is a gamble many people are not willing to take if it limits self-gratification and the expression of desire too much. The 1960s counter-cultural movement in the West expressly rejected the containment of sexual experience, as well as the scripting of identity and lifestyle through religious traditions and dogma. Self-sacrifice through asceticism is anathema in consumer societies where individual identity is partly constructed, signified and sustained by consumption practices.

Symbolically-important deaths (however globally inequitable) also expose the force of emotion in creating collective and transcendent processes. While belief systems, faith and morality are fragmented, contradictory and often in conflict in contemporary Western societies, emotion emptied of these particularities can act as a collectivizing and spiritualizing force. This is a kind of modified Durkheimian thesis of the conscience collective and the role of secular and/or religious rituals in creating community. While media technologies make private the experience of public rituals of grief and memorialization, they also overcome space-time divisions on a global scale by enabling forms of virtual *communion* to be both televized and self-consciously registered by those within the visual frame and by those watching it. I use the word 'communion' because some events, such as Princess Diana's funeral, were watched with such emotional intensity and involvement that a collective (although not uniform) consciousness of emotion across the globe was brought into being. The atmosphere of this event was palpable with grief and emotion. Princess Diana's funeral was a transitory and transmitting event of symbolic global spiritualism. But perhaps even more telling is that this was a woman who achieved iconic, quasi-religious status without being sexually chaste. Diana's death showed the potential in contemporary society for a woman to transcend the authority of traditional religious sexual morality and overcome rigid dichotomies of sinner and saint. At the same time, it also showed the historical continuity of religious or spiritual investments in those who embody certain ideals or who harness, through their personalities and biographies, a high degree of collective identification. In the end, perhaps, Diana's quasi-religious status was grounded in her worldliness and the identifications this made possible. This paper does not consider this question in detail; suffice it to say that cyber-space technology, while perhaps a new god/new space for memory, memorialization, and fantasies of eternity, has shifted a sense of the spiritual into something less policed by traditional authorities. The continuous proliferation of sites and pathways through which individuals can globalize their world, inevitably changes the way in which people search for meaning and find communities beyond their immediate location in place and beyond time and space boundaries.

Modernity and Disenchantment

As a central theorist of religion and modernity, Max Weber traced the historical processes of industrial capitalism and the impact of Enlightenment thought. With the rise of science, rational systems of knowledge, and the secular democratic State, the institutional authority of religion became increasingly decentred, along with a decline in magical thinking (Weber, 1952/1991, pp.350–353). The 'de-magification' of the Western worldview was concurrent with emerging Protestant religions, systematic forms of calculation, empiricism, and inner-worldly rather than otherworldly asceticism. Weber described the increasing rationalization of everyday life that comes with rational systems of knowledge, bureaucratic institutions, and capitalist accounting. Weber's metaphor of the 'Iron Cage' was a particularly bleak thesis of modernity's foreclosure towards the freedoms of chance, unpredictability, otherness, and the incalculable. Weber was himself disenchanted by capitalist accounting and by the creation of value, including social values, according to what is economically measurable and profitable. The increasing colonization of everyday life – including art, self-identity and religion by modern capitalism and bureaucracy was Weber's perceptive prediction.

While modernity ushered in the authority of science and secular rites and institutions, religious beliefs and faith practices persisted. The unquestioned thesis of human progress through rational thought and technological development has also waned in late modernity (Giddens, 1994; Harvey, 1989). David Lyon suggests that the constancy of religion and the rise of new spiritual movements show the thesis of secularization to be over-stated (2000, pp.22–25). The thesis of secularization is also weakened by the recent growth of both Christianity and Islam, the continued and heightened existence of religious fundamentalism across the globe, and the rise of New Age spiritualities (Lyon, 1996, pp.14–15). The New Age movement, and its alternative therapies, actively breaks with the historical authority of traditional religions as well as the authority of scientific knowledge and skeptical realism. Aspects of New Age culture reinstate 'magical thinking' through beliefs in the healing power of crystals and in stories of alien abductions.[1] This process of re-enchantment is not just a question of identifying new social movements and trends; it also speaks of the presence of otherness, the incalculable, and the mystery of death, which form an enduring part of human existence and the search for meaning.

As a sociological counterpoint to Weber, Durkheim offered a thesis of religion as the transcendent expression of Society ([1915/1982). Durkheim's substitution of Society (a transcendental concept) in the place of a metaphysical Being was itself both a product and practice of modernist secularization. More recent social commentators of late modernity, such as Anthony Giddens, suggest that the Self and the project of identity now stand in this centrifugal place.[2] The concept of spirituality in relation to self-identity is complex and varied in contemporary societies. A range of social movements and discourses, particularly feminism and gay liberation, have politicized personal relationships, deconstructed essentialist ideas of identity, critiqued the anti-sensualism and the mind/body hierarchies of religion, and laid claim to legal and ethical rights against the conservatism and continuing authority of traditional institutions and ideologies. New forms of spirituality are contingently tied to these historico-political transformations.

One aspect of spiritual culture in contemporary societies concerns emotional well-being and 'quality of life' issues – the more materially-grounded strains of spirituality. The religious concept of the soul as an enduring metaphysical entity that survives death is reconfigured in post-modern culture through psychological discourses and self-help literature. The soul is less an innate, immortal entity and more a figuration of psychical well-being; one has to care for the soul in order to keep it alive and well. The concept of spirituality is part of a broader discourse of a holistic approach to life. Spiritual well-being, holistically approached, includes the nexus between personal relationships, work and the body. The concept of spirituality has become part of the discourse and practice of mainstream medicine and is actively cultivated (not without criticism or resistance) in recent management discourses and in workplaces (Ashmos, 2000; Butts, 1999; Conlin, 1999; Graber and Johnson, 2001; Hitchens, 2000). The rise of spirituality as a popular and meaningful concept in everyday usage is indicative of the new value placed on self-identity and self-fulfillment. This post-modern enchantment with the self is in contrast to the much more self-sacrificial values of traditional religions.

Communities of Grief

Virtual media technologies (including television) are a core aspect of spiritual access and religious community in contemporary societies. The voluntarism of Internet communities allows for flexibility of commitment and interest, which also enables religious rituals to take shape in the daily practice of logging into chat rooms or newsgroups. Cyber church sites, and other 'virtual temples' and 'cyber-deities', actively construct the Net as a spiritual forum or communication network (Lyon, 2000). Communication technologies have always been put to use as a means of recruiting, advocating and advertising religions and church membership (Bruce, 1990; Hoover, 1988; Horsfield, 1984). Through Cyber church, the Internet is a site of community in and of itself; it is also a contact and recruiting mechanism for localized, face-to-face church communities. Many sites such as http://www.gtm.org/cyberchurch/ use the image of a traditional church building, and entry into this particular site is through clicking on the church doors. Cyber churches are not always the churches or religions themselves but the host names that Internet service providers give to the web space they provide *to* churches and ministers. They offer, at a cost, packages for creating web sites so that face-to-face localized churches, religious messages and interactive forums (such as bible readings) can be put online. For example, http://www.cyberchurch.com/ advertizes its services as follows:

> Need an Interactive church website? ... We can help! Here's How!
> CAPTURE THE POWER of the Internet without the hassle and expense of traditional web sites.
> CyberChurch.com's easy to create and maintain Interactive Web Packages will revolutionize your church's communications.

The Net has a plethora of sites dedicated to spirituality: spirituality.com; beliefnet; eclecticspirituality.com; workplacesspirituality.com; amysticalgrove. com; druid.org; and many others. As a vast and growing archive of religious and spiritual sites available at the click of a button, the Net is a metaphor for the eclecticism of modern spiritual life. Quite literally, the Net operates through quasi-religious signifiers such as *searches, gateways* and *pathways* that potentially cultivate a sense of the mystical omnipresence of cyberspace (Dawson and Hennebry, 2003, p. 271). The labyrinthine and ultimately endless movement and expansion of the Net also conveys a sense of the infinite.

Virtual media technologies also feed into an enduring human desire for metaphysical experiences of disembodiment and for fantasies of immortality. With its various figurations of disembodied existence, cyber-culture also continues, rather than breaks with, mind/body dualisms and the human desire for immortality (Wertheim, 1999). As Wertheim demonstrates, Christian themes of immortality and resurrection abound in post-human discourses and cyberpunk fictions of downloading and uploading minds for later resurrection in living bodies (1999, pp.261–269). Thus while we tend to view new technologies as signifiers of an ever-growing secular and scientific worldview, what we often find is the projection of age-old ideas and desires mediating the perception, imagination and use of technologies.

In *The Elementary Forms of the Religious Life*, Durkheim suggests that death disturbs community in pre-modern, small-scale societies in quite particular ways. The disturbance is partly the effect of a role loss within a structure of role-interdependency (1915/1982).[3] In the highly-urbanized, mass populations of nation-states, most deaths are those of strangers, and these go unnoticed at the level of individual knowledge and concern. These deaths have little or no economic or emotional impact on a population, which is not a self-contained unity/community but rather a fragmented flux of lives criss-crossing without emotional or sustained biographical intertwining. But it is precisely in the post-modern social conditions of fragmentation, impersonal economic relationships, and anonymity, that death can create community through the mediations of communication technologies which, literally and symbolically, collect and interface people in response to 'significant' global deaths. Significant global deaths include the deaths of global identities or media personalities and the deaths of individuals whose value derives from the economic and symbolic privilege of their nation-state or class.

Mass deaths such as those that occurred in New York on 11 September 2001 are a case in point. The people who died are memorialized in a way that would not have been possible if they had died individually in more ordinary circumstances. This kind of mass death gives deceased citizens of the First World international public recognition as their deaths are mourned in services and anniversaries involving large numbers of people who did not know them personally. The deceased is absorbed into a national and international culture of grief and memorialization, whilst maintaining his or her identity *as an individual*. 'In modern societies nationalist ideologies have often been successful in transforming the meaning of individual deaths into heroic acts that sustain the fictive immortality of particular social groups, bonded together in an imagined community' (Seale, 1998, p.3).

With an entire nation behind them, the personally bereaved from September 11 have an ongoing public recognition of their bereavement and may be able to show their grief more publicly in the long term. This is because individual bereavement has converged with national identity and its collective ritualization. In the case of everyday, ordinary circumstances of bereavement the public display of grief usually has an unspoken time limit. Addressing the Oklahoma bombing and September 11 memorial practices, Frank Furedi argues that these represent a shift from 'a bereaved community to a community of bereaved'. In both cases an 'individualizing imperative is at work' not just for the dead but survivors too (2004: 14). Oklahoma survivors had their names on the memorial while New York September 11 survivors and bereaved families have enormous input into the design aesthetic and moral reasoning of the public memorials.

Writing about the extensive public mourning of Princess Diana, Richard Johnson suggests that a transference of grief occurred through Diana's death: it was a vehicle for grieving over other deaths that had not been properly mourned (1999, p.31). The public concealment of grief as a lived reality in many people's lives can find expression or an emotional outlet in monumental public deaths and 'communities of mourning' (Kear and Steinberg, 1999, p.6). The significance of collective rituals of mourning, like other forms of collective ritual, enables 'collective sentiments [to be] renewed' in the assembling of a group (Durkheim, 1915/1982, p.399). The rituals of a nation-state are crucial in this regard; and in the case of the funeral services and mourning rituals for Princess Diana and the victims of September 11, Christian symbols came to the fore, serving (and being asserted) as collective representations within culturally and religiously diverse nation-states.

Net memorials for September 11 continue the Christian cult of memorializing and remembering the dead. The dead and their mourners are thus like a virtual community. The Net is a metaphysical space that mimics our metaphysical experience of the dead as being neither here nor there but somehow everywhere yet nowhere in particular. One of the striking uses to which the Net has been put is to proliferate, in a global community essentially made up of strangers, acts of memorialization to the dead. These memorial web sites often imitate graveyard headstones with the wording, 'In Memory of…'. On many web sites one finds oneself looking at the spatial layout and memorial sentiments of a virtual graveyard. The dead are also amongst other dead on or in sites that give them a kind of presence in the public arena and archive. Indeed, a sense of individual permanence is achieved through the variety of ways lives are traced and documented by writing and memory technologies.

A Google search of September 11 memorials' called up 117,000 sites. On these sites, there are thousands upon thousands of Internet memorials to strangers, from strangers, around the world. Lynne Desplender has commented on the significance of the Internet in disseminating information about September 11 survivors and as a means to 'identify and commemorate the dead' (2003, p.88). Grief rituals, she argues, were forged through the Internet in the widespread ritual of logging on, reading other people's messages or stories, and writing one's own messages or stories (ibid.). It is also notable that people logging onto grief sites made choices about which September 11 victims they would personally remember and incorporate into their lives through prayers and sometimes anniversary rituals:

> I will always keep you in my prayers even though I never knew you. Toya – submitted 5/11/2002.

> You will always be in my thoughts. Carol – submitted 5/21/2002.

> Hello Gordon! May God Bless You! I'm sure the right always beats what's wrong, so please rest in peace, because the whole Nation will fight for you and give you back the RIGHT. Submitted 9/10/2002. (http://www.sept11thmemorial.com).

Through these Net memorials, and in the promises made to remember the dead, individuals also authorize and record their own existence as a trace that will probably survive their death. The growth in practices of memorializing represents as well as reinforces the universal value placed on individual life in liberal democracies. It is also part of the contemporary global economy where individual lives in the First World have the greatest symbolic, memorial and media value. The Net enables the practice of actively incorporating global events into biographical practices and annotations. For example, wherewereyou.org/ has over 2,500 mini-stories from people recounting where they were and what they were doing when the news of the attacks on the Twin Towers and the Pentagon reached them. The site presents itself as an archive capturing history in the making – not just any history, though: American history. The cultural-political imperialism in the site's self-justification is explicit:

> This site exists to gather the thoughts and emotions of everyday people to the events on and after September 11, 2001. Why must we record these thoughts? Wouldn't it have been wonderful to have known what everyday people felt when Pearl Harbour was bombed or what the nation was thinking when the word Vietnam was first introduced into our nation's psyche or when Kennedy was assassinated, and how those views changed as the events afterwards unfolded? It would be a great historical resource. The media records everything, true, but those records get lost and aren't compiled like these fresh ongoing thoughts from people of all backgrounds.

In Christian mythology, God, as a figure who protects against absolute annihilation from forgetfulness and de-materialization, is the ultimate memory-bank. In the September 11 narrative, it is the omnipotent media that 'records everything' – but of course it does not. What is interesting about this site is the tension between its obvious American-centrism and the democratization of history *as* the thoughts and emotions of 'everyday people' from 'all backgrounds':

#5 | Saturday, September 15th, 2001
 I remember looking at the clock on my computer and seeing 11:59pm. The phone rang, and mum and I both said at the same time that it had to be my sister, she's the only one with the guts to call so late. Then my mum picked up the phone, said hi etc. and then she swore and ran into the lounge room and I was just thinking, 'oh shit what's happened?' she told dad to switch to channel 7 and the first image I saw was of the two towers standing, and the first one with smoke absolutely pouring out of it. Then my mum repeated off the phone, 'America's been attacked by terrorists!' It was crazy... (nikole/16/Australia)

#87 | Wednesday, September 19th, 2001
I was laying in bed, being ill, trying to get some sleep, when my mobile phone rang. It was my girlfriend, telling me that there was something terrible happening. The rest of the days after I watched CNN and visited websites. (Michiel/29/ Netherlands)

#213 | Monday, October 22nd, 2001
I was sitting having a Coke with my friend Elke. We were in Jaime III road in Palma City, sitting outside a café by the road. I can remember looking at my clock at 15:04 (Spanish time). Now I think about it, that was the time the second plane hit the building. Even thinking about it maked [sic] me shiver. God bless America.....and good luck... (Dale Hosford | 17 | Spain)
(http://www.sept11thmemorial.com)

The events of September 11 caused shock and anger not just because the deaths were horrible, but because the most powerful nation in the world was rendered vulnerable both literally and symbolically to itself and the wider world. Part of the shock was the 'collision' between fundamentally different ways of valuing the individual life. The terrorist, suicide culture represents a more traditional sacrificial economy of individual life. In post-traditional, highly individualist societies such as America, the status and sacred value of individual life is a fundamental aspect of collective and individual consciousness. The sacrificial economy of most theistic religions 'saves' the essential (the soul) and morally-accumulative value of an individual existence until after death.

In most (though not all) post-traditional societies a deity is not a universal anchor, guaranteeing and rallying collective belief and action. While America still anchors itself politically to the authority of God, evidenced by President George Bush's speeches demanding 'a war on terrorism', the rest of the Western world is much more secular politically and culturally. In the Western world, the sacrifice of an individual life requires considerable social debate and consensus before a war can be waged and carried out. While the existence of armies means that the sacrifice of the individual is already accepted, individual life, especially from the point of view of a specific individual, is more sacred than death. Lyon argues that post-modern spirituality 'reveals a trend towards the more general sacralization of the self' (2000, p.18). This sacralization of the self creates a tension in relation to death. In the context of nationally significant deaths (but also on the smaller scale of the interpersonal), the sacralization of individual life is represented by and materialized through memorials that remember and archive the individual. The increasing importance of memorialization in contemporary post-traditional societies signifies the groundlessness of post-modern mortality in absolute forgetfulness and non-distinct materiality (an individual body finally merging with the earth to become indistinct matter). Western societies, especially since modernity, have been preoccupied with recording and archiving human history. On the other side of the coin, there is the recognition that many individual histories/biographies disappear, are subject to oblivion. When 'God' has been sentenced as dead (the Nietzschean proclamation) there is a desire, perhaps even a psychological imperative, to pursue some sense of permanency. Technologies that record and store information, including memories, enable individuals to archive themselves beyond the grave. The immortalizing practices of post-modern, technological societies are precariously grounded in the microchip.

Notes

1   The literary and filmic genres of science fiction have crossed over into everyday life. The belief in alien life forms (which also forms part of scientific research), and particularly stories of alien contact, expresses the desire to have 'other worlds'. These stories are about bridging the relationship between this world and other-worldly existence as part of the experience of life rather than of death. Similarly, the vast literature on near-death experiences also raises the question of the status of death in contemporary post-traditional societies. The operative word is 'near', expressing proximity to something that in fact eclipses

consciousness and therefore experience. There is a form of fetishism in this concept of nearness, because it creates a sense of spatial proximity to death as if it is a thing.

2   For Durkheim the concept of an immortal soul is not ultimately a form of egoism nor an aspect of death denial; rather it expresses the immortality of society within the individual: 'the belief in the immortality of the soul is the only way in which men were able to explain a fact which could not fail to attract their attention; this fact is the perpetuity of the life of the group' (1915/1982, p.268).

3   Role–interdependency refers to the situation, especially in the context of small societies and kinship groups, where each person has a specific role that is depended upon by others in an integrated system.

References

Ashmos, D. P. and Duchon, D (2000), 'Spirituality at Work', *Journal of Management Inquiry*, vol. 9, pp.134–146.

Baudrillard, J. (1988), *Symbolic Exchange and Death*, trans. Ian Hamilton Grant, Sage Publications, London.

Beck, U. (2000), 'Living Your Own Life in a Runaway World: Individualization, Globalization and Politics', in W. Hutton and A. Giddens (eds), *On the Edge: Living with Global Capitalism*, Jonathan Cape, London, pp.164–174.

Becker, E. (1997), *The Denial of Death*, Free Press, New York.

Bruce, S. (1990), *Pray TV: Televangelism in America*, Routledge, London and New York.

Butts, D. (1999), 'Spirituality at Work: an overview', *Journal of Organizational Change Management*, vol. 12, pp.328–331.

Conlin, M. (1999), 'Religion in the Workplace: The Growing Presence of Spirituality in Corporate America', *Business Week*, November 1, pp.151–58.

Dawson, L. L. and Hennebry, J. (2003), 'New Religions and the Internet: Recruiting in a New Public Space', *Cults and New Religious Movements: A Reader*, Blackwell, Oxford, pp. 271–291.

Despelder, L. A. (2003), 'September 11, 2001 and the Internet', *Mortality*, vol. 8, no. 1, pp.88–89.

Durkheim, E. [1915] (1982), *The Elementary Forms of the Religious Life*, Allen & Unwin, London.

Freud, S. (1986), *The Essentials of Psychoanalysis*, trans J. Strachey, Penguin Books, London.

Furedi, F. (2004), *Therapy Culture: cultivating vulnerability in an uncertain age*, Routledge, London and New York.

Gauchet, M. (1997), *The Disenchantment of the World: A Political History of Religion*, trans. O. Burge, Princeton University Press, New Jersey.

Giddens, A. (1991), *Modernity and Self-Identity: Self and Society in the Late Modern Age*, Polity Press, London.

___ (1994), 'Living in a Post-Traditional Society', in Urlich Beck, Anthony Giddens and Scott Lash (eds), *Reflexive Modernization: Politics, Tradition and Aesthetics in the Modern Social Order*, Polity Press, Cambridge, pp.56–109.

Graber, D. R. and Johnson, J. A. (2001), 'Spirituality and Healthcare Organizations', *Journal of Healthcare Management*, vol. 46, no. 1, pp.39–52.

Harvey, D. (1989), *The Condition of Post-modernity: an enquiry into the origins of cultural change*, Blackwell, Oxford.

Heidegger, M. (1985), *Being and Time*, trans. J. Macquarie and E. Robinson, Blackwell, London.

Hitchens, C. (2000), 'God at Work', *Free Inquiry*, Spring, pp.5–6.

Hoover, S. M. (1988), *Mass media Religion: The Social Sources of the Electronic Church*, Sage, New Delhi.

Horsfield, P. G. (1984), *Religious Television: The American Experience*, Longman, New York and London.

Johnson, R. (1999), 'Exemplary differences: mourning (and not mourning) a princess', in A. Kear and D. L. Steinberg (eds), *Mourning Diana: Nation, Culture and the Performance of Grief*, Routledge, London and New York, pp.15–39.

Kear, A. and Steinberg, D. L. 'Ghost Writing', in A. Kear and D. L. Steinberg (eds), *Mourning Diana: Nation, Culture and the Performance of Grief*, Routledge, London and New York, pp.1-14.

Lyon, D. (1996), 'Religion and the Post-modern: Old Problems, New Prospects', in K. Flanagan and P. C. Jupp (eds), *Post-modernity, Sociology and Religion*, Macmillan, London, pp.14–29.

___ (2000), *Jesus in Disneyland: Religion in Post-modern Times*, Blackwell, Oxford.

Nancy, J-L. (1991), *The Inoperative Community*, Peter Connor (ed.), University of Minnesota Press, Minneapolis and Oxford.

Seale, C. (1998), *Constructing Death: The sociology of dying and bereavement*, Cambridge University Press, Cambridge.

Weber, M. ([1952]1991), *From Max Weber: Essays in Sociology*, H. H. Gerth and C. Wright Mills (eds), Routledge, London.

Wertheim, M. (1999), *The Pearly Gates of CyberSpace: A History of Space from Dante to the Internet*, Doubleday, Australia and New Zealand.

Wuthnow, R. (1998), 'Morality, spirituality, and democracy', *Society* vol. 5, no. 3, pp.37–43.

Zizek, S. (2003), 'A Symptom–of What?', *Critical Inquiry*, vol. 29, Spring, pp.486–503.

PART 2

Queer Enchantment and Religious Borderlands

Chapter 7

Enchanting Camp: A Case Study of Queer Politics through the Medium of Ritual Performance

Michael Carden

This chapter explores how sacred imagery and ritual are used by lesbian, gay, bisexual and transgender people (hereafter LGBT or queer) in their struggles against homophobia and heterosexualism. Specifically, I reflect upon my own experiences in the queer community at the University of Queensland (UQ) in Brisbane during the 1990s and consider how this community employed ritual and the sacred, often in satirical and burlesque forms, to consolidate itself and to sustain itself in a time of crisis. My analysis highlights how, in contemporary social movements for political and cultural change, the boundaries between 'religious' and 'non-religious' can become blurred, and particularly how movements such as those of LGBT people that aim at creating community through identity-based politics can develop a quasi-religious character. I also demonstrate Beckford's point that religion can nowadays be conceptualized more as a 'cultural resource…than as an institution' (1992, p.171), even when, as in this case, the sacred motifs belong to religious traditions typically regarded as hostile to LGBT people. The chapter discusses the meaning and function of 'camp' in LGBT subcultures and gives a brief historical background of the LGBT communities in Brisbane and the University of Queensland. My own experiences in the University of Queensland's LGBT community are presented under the themes of marking sacred space and using ritual and performance. It is my contention that while these activities might have been seen by outsiders as irreligious and mocking, the community saw them as affirming its religious and spiritual worth in the face of rejection by the mainstream. Part of that affirmation came from the playful irony inherent in the 'camp' sensibilities integral to LGBT subcultures. Finally, I argue that the use of sacred imagery and ritual, ostensibly parodic or lighthearted, in fact marked and 'enchanted' otherwise heteronormative space as queer, thus sustaining commitment to and solidarity in promoting personal and social transformation.

The lesbian and gay movement, as Mary Bernstein observes, is 'the quintessential identity movement' (1997, p.532). To promote the acceptance of homosexuality, same-sex relationships and gender variance, LGBT movements have constructed identities to mobilize and empower existing communities of non-heterosexual people and to create new ones where none existed. The movements have sought not only political change but 'cultural change...facilitated by the movement of transformed individuals through social networks' (Neitz, 1994, p.145). In fact political 'wins' have depended in large part on the broader cultural changes already brought about through the creation and mobilization of communities based on minority sexual identities. Important to the success of these LGBT movements is that they have been fluid and structureless; there is no LGBT equivalent of the Communist Party or the Roman Catholic Church that seeks to lead or control. Instead, LGBT communities are marked by a wide variety of organizations – political, social, cultural, commercial and religious. The importance of these organizations lies in the fact that they provide LGBT people with circumstances that are favourable to them forming and maintaining their 'new' identities (Greil and Rudy, 1990, p.227). LGBT movements as a whole – not their constituent organizations individually – are movements of identity transformation whose success depends on individuals identifying their goals and interests with those of the movement. Cultural change takes place because 'individuals carry with them symbols and practices of a social movement...even when they are not active in an organization' (Neitz, 1994, p.129).

Identity transformation, commitment, cultural change and fluidity have been identified with the phenomena of quasi-religions. The term 'quasi-religion' refers to 'activities and organizations that involve expressions of ultimate concern or organizational dynamics similar to those of religious organizations narrowly defined...but that do not involve a belief in the supernatural or super-empirical' (Greil and Rudy, 1990, p.220). Neitz's analysis of Wicca (1994) highlights how cultural movements do not need to have the structure of religious organizations to be considered quasi-religious. This (quasi) religious dimension can be seen in many aspects of the LGBT community's life: the celebrations of Pride and Sydney's Gay and Lesbian Mardi Gras, the energy invested in 'coming out', the symbolism of rainbows, the labrys, pink triangles, the variety of dress codes and so on – all of which were means by which marginalized communities built and sustained individual and collective identity in the face of a hostile mainstream. Indeed, dress codes and rainbow jewellery represent forms of implicit religion, providing 'affirmation and reinforcement' at individual and communal levels for LGBT people (Barker, 2001, p.64).

This quasi-religious nature is evident in another feature of LGBT movements: like all movements for social change, they tell 'participants what is wrong, what can be done to fix it, and why they should be involved' (Williams, 2002, p.249). This critiquing of the status quo existing order is what Williams identifies as a 'devastatingly effective...constitutive component' of religion (Williams, 2002, p.251). Lewy points out that religion 'involves transcendent moral standards which define an ideal against which human performance can be measured. Hence those who are dissatisfied...may find in religion strong support for their attack upon the status quo' (1974, pp.583–4). And Smith argues that the utopian impulse to correct perceived flaws and shortcomings in daily existence is implicit in the origins of all religions and persists as a subversive subtext (1974, p.166). A major characteristic of religions is that they enable access to alternate reality through ecstasy, ceremony and other means, thus reinforcing the utopian dynamic by virtue of the fact that such alternate reality 'is a realm where power hovers' (Goodman, 1992, p.47). Access to such power enables people to resist and challenge the *status quo*. Religions can provide the means whereby we 'can work on ourselves and invent, I do not say discover, a manner of being that is still improbable' (Foucault, cited Stone, 1997, p.147). Religions even can provide perceptual frameworks and ensuing technologies for structuring the body: ritual is a physical as well as spiritual practice, as are meditation, asceticism, and healing.

So in addition to communal identity-building phenomena such as Pride, Mardi Gras and 'coming out', the quasi-religious dimension of LGBT experience is reinforced by the commitment of LGBT movements to social change. It is largely this commitment that motivates the struggles to forge LGBT identities. The Stonewall riots in New York in June and July of 1969, in which LGBT people fought back against police repression, dramatically illustrate this quasi-religious dimension. A display of public resistance, the riots have been used to mark the beginnings of gay liberation and are celebrated in annual Pride Day festivities around the world.[1] The Stonewall story is an exceptional example of a foundational myth or religious story providing models and themes that people can look to and draw upon.

These observations might strike many people, heterosexual and LGBT alike, as incongruous, particularly the suggestion that an event like the Sydney Gay and Lesbian Mardi Gras has a religious function. This sense of incongruity might arise in part from the fact that LGBT cultural expressions are known for being outrageous, over-the-top, parodic and light-hearted. These qualities have marked the 'camp' sensibility uniquely associated with LGBT subcultures from long before Stonewall. Esther Newton identified three themes characteristic of 'camp' – incongruity, theatricality, and humour (1993, p.46) – and added that 'camp' depends upon creating or perceiving 'incongruous juxtapositions' (1993, pp.46–7) which can include 'high and low status, youth and old age, profane and sacred functions or symbols, cheap and expensive articles' (1993, p.47). If something is declared 'camp' it is because of the tension between it 'and the context or association' (ibid). From incongruity comes theatricality, because, as Newton observes, 'camp' shifts focus 'from what a thing *is* to how it *looks*, from *what* is done to *how* it is done' (ibid, italics in original). 'Camp', then, is a style of exaggeration that is consciously performative and that recognizes the theatrical role-playing nature of human behaviour. Furthermore, 'camp' recognizes that this role-playing is *play*; it is an act or show. The necessity to play at life, living role after superficial role, should not be cause of bitterness or despair… The actor should throw himself into it; he should put on a good show; he should view the whole experience as fun, as a camp (1993, p.49, italics in original).

'Camp' is fun and therein highlighting the role of humour. Newton declares 'camp' a '*system* of humour…laughing at one's incongruous position instead of crying' (ibid, italics in original).

Some of these qualities were recognized by Susan Sontag in her seminal essay on 'camp'. She noted that 'camp' is both 'playful, anti-serious' and has a 'new, more complex' relationship to 'the serious' (1966, p.288). She also identified 'camp' as 'a mode of enjoyment of appreciation – not judgment. Camp is generous. It wants to enjoy' (1966, p.291). Bergman (1993), however, argues that Sontag portrayed 'camp' merely as a form of consolation for the homosexual and failed to grasp the political implications of 'camp' in its playful relationship to the serious. Nevertheless, before Sontag, Christopher Isherwood, in his novel *The World in the Evening* (1956), had already observed:

You can't camp about something you don't take seriously. You're not making fun of it; you're making fun *out* of it. You're expressing what's basically serious to you in terms of fun and artifice and elegance (cited Bergman, 1993, p.4, italics in the original).

'Camp' is playful and 'anti-serious' but works by enabling a temporary detachment from that with which one has fervent involvement 'so that only…after the event, are we struck by the emotional and moral implications' (Babuscio, 1993, p.28). This temporary detachment facilitates 'the re-imagining of the material world into ways and forms which transform and comment upon the original' (Bronski, 1984, p.42). As Newton points out, the humour of 'camp' has a transformative role, being a 'continuous creative strategy for…defining a positive homosexual identity' (Newton, 1993, p.50). Bronski concurs, arguing that camp is political because 'it contains the possibility of structuring and encouraging limitless imagination – to literally create a new reality' (Bronski, 1984, p.43).[2]

'Camp', in this light, is a creatively transformative strategy for sustaining identity positively in the face of social proscription. As cultural practices, camp and religion/quasi-religion have elements in common and share some characteristic traits. Most strikingly, both employ incongruous juxtaposition. There is no more incongruous a juxtaposition than declaring a man divine and then declaring a wafer to be his flesh and a cup of wine his blood. That wafer and wine 'become' flesh and blood only through the performance of an elaborate ritual highlights another trait that 'camp' and religion share: theatricality. In this regard they differ only in mood: religion is reverent and serious; 'camp' is ironic, humorous and playful. Nevertheless, because the 'camp' moment of playful ironic laughter relies on an underlying fervent involvement, religion is constantly invested with 'camp' potency. This potency, as Mark Jordan observes, is grounded in the 'simultaneity, the inseparability of reverence and ridicule... lifting the curtain once again to giggle – and then dropping it solemnly back into place' (2000, p.182). I would suggest that when religion loses this 'camp' potency it risks falling into soul-destroying fundamentalism, arid triviality and vacuous kitsch.

Case Study: the Queer Community at the University of Queensland

These theoretical perspectives on both religion/quasi-religion and 'camp' are well illustrated in the way the University of Queensland's queer community used ritual and the sacred to consolidate their group identity and cohesion from 1992 onwards. But first, a brief historical background. For Queensland's LGBT communities the victory of the Australian Labor Party in the 1989 State election marked a significant turning point, ending several decades of conservative National Party rule. In the 1970s and 1980s, under the Premiership of Joh Bjelke-Petersen, the National Party had become overtly and virulently homophobic; and it allied itself with and gave encouragement to various fundamentalist Christian morals organizations. Gay films and magazines were regularly banned, and in 1985 the government passed laws to close down (unsuccessfully) gay bars by making it an offence to knowingly serve 'deviants, perverts, drug dealers and child molesters' on licensed premises. The government's response to the HIV/AIDS crisis was particularly vicious. In 1984 the deaths of four babies due to infected blood transfusion was used by the Health Minister to launch a public hate campaign against gay and bisexual men. The State government refused to fund, or even acknowledge, the Queensland AIDS Council, because it was a community organization born of the LGBT community; it even refused to participate in national AIDS policy meetings of federal and state governments because it did not want to engage with any other AIDS (LGBT) community organizations, whose working relationships with the federal and other state governments were in fact strong. It also refused to countenance homosexual law reforms to facilitate education programs amongst gay and bisexual men. The Queensland Government's attitude, in short, seemed to be that the crisis would be resolved if all the 'perverts' were driven south of the border. In response to scandals concerning police corruption, Bjelke-Peterson was removed by his colleagues in December 1987 and replaced by the reformist Mike Ahern. Ahern initiated a process of engagement with the queer community but was himself removed by more conservative forces in mid-1989. The ALP came to power at the end of that year with a policy supporting homosexual law reform, yet they were reluctant to enact it without first holding a parliamentary inquiry. The inquiry found in favour of the decriminalization of homosexuality. Despite this, the reform was implemented with difficulty and with the inclusion of differential age of consent provisions with the intent of preventing male-male sex before age 18 in contrast to the general age of consent of 16. Anti-discrimination laws were then introduced banning discrimination in a variety of areas including lawful sexual activity.

The queer community at the University of Queensland campus first organized itself as Campus Camp in the very early 1970s. Since that time, and with several name changes, it operated as a club affiliated with the Students Union, which provided limited funding and other resources. Various campaigns to establish a Union Department for LGBT people culminated in 1990 in a failed referendum. One of the goals of these campaigns was to acquire a queer space on campus as a drop-in centre for LGBT students. In 1991, empowered by the State law reforms, club members occupied the Union President's office demanding that an unused room in the lower level of the Union complex be made available to them. The conservative Union executive agreed, on the proviso – because of the 1990 referendum result – that the room not be called a lesbian/gay area. The club accepted; but in a very camp spirit of irony they named it the Rona Room, after the leading fundamentalist Christian morals campaigner, Rona Joyner (http://www.angelfire.com/id/ronajoyner/).

The Rona Room transformed LGBT campus life. For the first time LGBT people had a place where they could meet socially and be themselves; the room served as a retreat from the heteronormativity of the campus and outside world. Most of the people who frequented it were young, a year or two out of school, and had grown up in the homophobic climate of the Bjelke-Peterson regime. Even many of those who were older had not had much to do with Brisbane's LGBT subculture. It was important, then, to adorn – 'redecorate' – the room with images affirming LGBT people. ACT UP and AIDS posters, posters of LGBT icons and movies, banners, rainbow flags and stickers soon covered the walls. This redecoration meant that the room quickly became affirmatively and unashamedly LGBT space. In 1993, a new progressive Student Union encouraged the club to expand into some adjacent unused inner rooms. The intervening walls and partitions were quickly tore down, and the empty rooms with bare concrete walls and floors became a new canvas but not so much for posters and stickers as for graffiti. Most of the written graffiti were slogans and jokes, as well as lines from poetry and songs that had or could be given a queer slant. The artistic graffiti consisted mainly of queer political and cultural symbols, though some of it was more personal and even consciously spiritual; on the floor of one room was painted a huge mandala, with esoteric and queer symbols. Much of the written graffiti also adopted religious themes, but in playfully ironic 'camp' ways. For example:

Luscious lesbian love goddess

In the beginning god created the world
Then god created women and men
To stop them going crazy god created queers

It must be pointed out that these inner rooms could only be accessed from the original room, not directly from the outside, and this gave them a sense of privacy, almost of sacred space. They served to establish the Rona Room as a shrine proclaiming difference in a perceived ocean of heterosexual normalcy.

In 1995, redevelopment of the Union Complex meant that the old warren of rooms constituting the Rona Room was replaced by a new, more open, large single room. However, in the spirit of the old room, the group requested that the walls and floor of the new one be left bare. Once again the walls became adorned with posters, art and graffiti, and on the floor was painted a central mandala with a yellow brick road leading to it from the entrance. The yellow brick road deliberately evoked *The Wizard of Oz*, a film long possessing iconic status in LGBT subcultures (see Doty, 2000, p.71). In the mid-90s the club changed into a Queer Collective of the Students Union and the resultant increased funding meant that it could acquire a small, but not cheap, mirror ball to hang in the room. This was referred to playfully as the 'queer cultural artefact'. For several years one person also made available their Barbie and Ken doll collection, which people would dress and display in playful ways. Through these means, members took personal ownership of the space, investing it with queer symbolism to affirm and sustain individual and collective LGBT identity against the heteronormative mainstream. This collective identity was further grounded by the physical continuity with the past that the Rona Room provided through the artefacts and adornments left behind by those who had since graduated and left campus life. That a great deal of this adornment was in the form of graffiti and artwork gave an added personal dimension to this continuity.

The room helped develop a new sense of queer community on campus. Some people found it an invaluable haven, even staying there overnight to escape the pressure of family or residential college when they were 'coming out'. To reflect this change, the club changed its name in 1993 to Queer Tribes. This sense of tribalism was strengthened by the use of performance and ritual. Some members developed a 'coming out' ritual – since most members were young, 'coming out' issues were inevitably a major concern – which was eventually performed at the 1994 National Queer Collaborations conference in Brisbane. There was, however, a marked preference for less scripted, more informal events. From very early in the room's history, a tradition had begun of holding parties there known as spontaneous gatherings. It wasn't long before the parties included drag and other performances, which served as very personal 'coming out' rituals for the performers. By 1995, these activities evolved into very public 'coming out' events known as Camp-Ins that were held during lunch hour in the university's most public space: the Great Court. Participants would assemble in the Rona Room, many of the men wearing dresses and make-up because the Camp-In was meant to be very out/rageous. With a ghetto blaster playing the Petshop Boys' 'Absolutely Fabulous', everyone would then process from the Rona Room to the Great Court, where they would dance, cuddle, kiss and generally have fun. The purpose of the Camp-In was to make a very public statement of LGBT identity and solidarity. Participants were empowered because the Great Court is a very popular lunchtime venue for students; thus, for some, Camp-Ins were very public 'coming out' statements. It was empowering also to see strangers being moved to join in and then return to the Rona Room in the closing procession. Indeed, the recruiting of new members was one of the Camp-In's goals. The Camp-In also served to extend temporarily the aura of queer space beyond the confines of the Rona Room; and thus, for short periods of time, public heteronormative space collapsed in the face of a resistant and celebratory queer reality.

In 1996 the campus LGBT community faced a crisis to which it responded by deliberately employing ritual and celebration in acts of resistance and mutual support. The political ascendancy of conservatives at both state and federal level in that year was mirrored in the Students Union. The conservatives in the Union were unsympathetic if not hostile to the Queer Collective and instituted various administrative and financial restrictions. Their long-term goal, it was feared, was to abolish both the Area and the Rona Room. In rallying against this threat LGBT people consciously appropriated and redeployed mainstream religious imagery and themes. They decided to hold a very public exorcism on Maundy Thursday, to rid the Union of the 'boringly beige' demons of conservative homophobia. A procession made its way from the Rona Room through the Union complex, circling the Union administration block while people chanted, 'Out demons! Out!' Some consciously evoked church ritual by wearing clerical vestments and sprinkling water along the route. The procession then entered the office of the Union newspaper, now under very conservative and unimaginative editorship, and people strewed confetti and glitter around it to 'exorcise the beige' before returning to the Rona Room. The following night, Good Friday, a Disco Jesus party was held there. Above the room's entrance a sign declared 'Passover, passunder, passout', and in one corner a confessional was erected where people could kiss and make up. The high point of the night was a Passion Play that commented on and satirized the crisis over the conservative-controlled Union. The performance was followed by a queer communion. The communion was offered with the phrase 'queer as fuck', to which each recipient responded 'Amen'. After communion, the party resumed and continued late into the night.

What is notable about these events is that the community drew on the symbols and motifs of Christianity. Western homophobic ideologies draw much of their power from reading strategies that link biblical texts condemning same-sex desire and gender transgression, with biblical texts promoting reproductive sex and male priority and authority. Such religious ideologies are used to condemn LGBT people as intrinsically disordered or hell-bound signs of divine wrath. Consequently, LGBT people are invested by the phobic imagination with all manner of pathology and menace. Western religion, overtly or covertly, manifests what Eve Kosofsky Sedgwick describes as the mainstream culture's 'desire that gay people *not be*' (1993, p.164). Some might see the events recounted above as irreligious or perhaps as an attack on the most important symbols of Christianity. I would argue, however, that the exorcism gave the LGBT people a sense of their collective power to withstand a perceived threat; the Passion Play functioned as a ritualized liberation interpretation of the Easter myth applied to represent and explain a specific community crisis; and the communion served to build community cohesion in the face of a threat by uncompromisingly affirming LGBT identity and solidarity. By appropriating and radically reinterpreting myths and rituals associated with the ideological buttress of homophobia, Christianity, the community affirmed its own spiritual and religious agency and worth in the face of mainstream religious denunciation. Performed with a sense of festive irony and playful humour, these rituals further validated and grounded LGBT identity by combining mainstream religious motifs with the 'camp' sensibility integral to queer cultures.

I would argue, further, that these events could only take place because of the quasi-religious nature of LGBT movements. By 1996, the LGBT community at the University of Queensland had become accustomed to consciously employing ritual forms in celebratory and affirming ways to sustain its tribal identity. Crucial to this development was the existence of a space, the Rona Room, which had been established as both a safe haven and a shrine for sexual difference. It served as a point of physical continuity with the past, providing a collective memory or tradition in which to ground identity and community. It had become an enchanted queer space in a heteronormative world. Through ritual, performance and celebration the community maintained this queer space and on occasion expanded it, pushing back the boundaries of heterosexualist space. By these means members of the community were able to confirm their own worth, accept their own sexuality and acknowledge those 'deepest feelings' (Brass, 1999, p.133) that had been negated or denied by mainstream heterocentric society. Consequently, at a time of crisis, this community felt empowered to daringly appropriate and reinterpret through ritual the central myths of the homophobic mainstream world in order to sustain itself. This fact illustrates Beckford's argument that religion 'has come adrift from its former points of anchorage but is no less potentially powerful as a result' (1992, p.170). The appropriation by this LGBT community of religious symbols and motifs normally associated with the 'opposition' showed that they remained a 'potent cultural resource' to be employed as a 'vehicle of change (and) challenge' (ibid). As Foucault pointed out: 'It's not only a matter of integrating this strange little practice of making love with someone of the same sex into pre-existing cultures; it's a matter of constructing cultural forms' (cited Stone, 1997, p.148). This construction of cultural forms is a process of transformation, initially of LGBT people, ourselves, and of our communities, and finally of the broader society in which we live. The transformative role of LGBT movements gives them a quasi-religious character in which distinctions between 'sacred' and 'secular' are blurred. As movements of personal and cultural change, they represent forms of re-enchantment and spiritual empowerment in response to the disenchantment of the mainstream homophobic social and religious order.

Notes

1 Sydney's Mardi Gras began in 1978 as a Stonewall Day commemoration. In that year it was held in June; later it was moved to its current time as an end of summer event.
2 This continuing role of camp also demonstrates that identities are not created *de novo* but draw on existing (sub)cultural repertoire.

References

Babuscio, J. (1993), 'Camp and the Gay Sensibility', in David Bergman (ed.), *Camp Grounds: Style and Homosexuality*, University of Massachusetts Press, Amherst, pp.19–38.
Barker, E. (2001), 'A Comparative Exploration of Dress and the Presentation of Self as Implicit Religion', in W. J. F. Keenan (ed.), *Dressed to Impress: Looking the Part*, (foreword by David Martin), Berg, Oxford & New York, pp.51–67.
Beckford, J. A. (1992), *Religion in Advanced Industrial Society*, Routledge, London and New York.
Bergman, D. (1993), 'Introduction', in D. Bergman (ed.), *Camp Grounds: Style and Homosexuality*, University of Massachusetts Press, Amherst, pp.3–16.
Bernstein, M. (1997), 'Celebration and Suppression: The Strategic Uses of Identity by the Lesbian and Gay Movement', *The American Journal of Sociology*, vol. 103, no. 3, pp.531–65.
Brass, P. (1999), *How To Survive Your Own Gay Life: An Adult Guide to Love, Sex, and Relationships*, Belhue Press, New York.
Bronski, M. (1984), *Culture Clash: The Making of Gay Sensibility*, South End Press, Boston, Mass.
Doty, A. (2000), *Flaming Classics: Queering the Film Canon*, Routledge, London.
Goodman, F. D. (1992*)*, *Ecstasy, Ritual and Alternate Reality: Religion in a Pluralistic World*, Indiana University Press, Bloomington, Ind.
Greil, A. L., and Rudy, D. (1990), 'On the Margins of the Sacred', in T. Robbins and D. Anthony (eds), *In Gods We Trust: New Patterns of Religious Pluralism in America*, Transaction Publishers, New Brunswick, N.J., pp.219–33.
Isherwood, C. (1956), *The World in the Evening*, Avon, New York
Jordan, M. (2000), *The Silence of Sodom: Homosexuality in Modern Catholicism*, University of Chicago Press, Chicago & London.
Joyner, R., *Rona Joyner's Issues & Information Site*, http://www.angelfire.com/id/ronajoyner/.
Lewy, G. (1974), *Religion and Revolution*, Oxford University Press, New York.
Neitz. M. J. (1994), 'Quasi-Religions and Cultural Movements: Contemporary Witchcraft as a Churchless Religion', *Religion and the Social Order*, vol. 4, pp.127–49.

Newton, E. (1993), 'Role Models', in D. Bergman (ed.), *Camp Grounds: Style and Homosexuality*, University of Massachusetts Press, Amherst, pp.38–53.

Sedgwick, E. K. (1993), *Tendencies*, Duke University Press, Durham.

Smith, J. E. (1974), *Experience and God*, Oxford University Press, London, New York.

Sontag, S. (1966), *Against Interpretation: And Other Essays*, Dell Publishing Co, New York.

Stone, K. (1997), 'Biblical Interpretation as a Technology of the Self: Gay Men and the Ethics of Reading', *Semeia*, vol. 77, pp.139–55.

Tacey, D. (2000), *Re-Enchantment: The New Australian Spirituality*, HarperCollins, Pymble, N.S.W.

Williams, R. (2002), 'From the 'Beloved Community' to 'Family Values': Religious Language, Symbolic Repertoires, and Democratic Culture', in D. S. Meyer, N. Whittier and B. Robnett (eds), *Social Movements: Identity, Culture, and the State*, Oxford University Press, New York, pp.247–65.

Chapter 8

Entheogens, Elves and Other Entities: Encountering the Spirits of Shamanic Plants and Substances

Des Tramacchi

Since the early 1990s a new paradigm has been gaining currency among psychedelics enthusiasts. Increasingly, the category *psychedelics* is being subsumed under the rubric *entheogens* – substances that purportedly facilitate experiences of divinity. Among entheogen users a nature-valuing or *organophilic* ethos generally prevails, often coupled with a professed deep reverence for indigenous peoples and their ethnopharmacological knowledge. The entheogen user seeks to engage with 'plant-teachers' or 'chemical allies'; to grow spiritually; to encounter magical forces; and to enter alternate worlds.

The evolution of entheogenic worldviews and philosophies can be reconstructed from key texts including 'cyberdelic' and 'techno-shamanic' web sites, a number of 'underground' publications such as *Notes From the Underground*, and periodicals such as *The Entheogen Review* and *Eleusis*. These sources provide orientation in a network of enchanted realms. Each of these visionary geographies is accessed through the use of a specific substance. For example, 'DMT hyperspace' is accessed through n,n-dimethyltryptamine; 'the K hole' is accessed *via* the anaesthetic ketamine, and 'Salvia Space' is accessed through the use of the herb *Salvia divinorum*. Apart from the vivid narratives of neo-shamanistic peak-experiences, such as those presented here, what is remarkable about these accounts is the high incidence of convergence between them. Continuities in the various accounts indicate that different substances have their own distinctive inhabitants. Some travellers in DMT hyperspace report 'Mantis-beings' and a presiding intelligence called 'Lord DiMiTri'; while some ketamine users report a presence they call 'Lady K'. My own experiences with the herb *Salvia divinorum*, which I discuss below, impel me to sympathize with this 'fundamentalist' interpretation; however, a compelling impression of reality is no guarantee that one's senses are correctly calibrated (to whatever criteria one may wish to apply), so it is useful to present some other, equally plausible explanations for entheogenic 'close encounters'. To this end, I include a discussion of theories of imagined beings drawn from works of Carl Jung and Charles Cooley.

The Psychedelic and Entheogenic Movements

During the late 1950s and 1960s the use of psychedelics contributed to significant changes in Western understandings of the mind and consciousness, changes that were to have important social and political consequences. Initially psychedelics were used in experimental psychiatry, but substances such as mescaline, psilocybin and especially LSD – popularized by Aldous Huxley, Timothy Leary and others – were soon in wide use by university students, artists, mystics and radicals. Even in the early years of the psychedelic movement, religious frameworks such as those found in Western representations of Tibetan Buddhism and various shamanisms were invoked as a means of navigating the profound alterations of consciousness induced by psychedelics. The criminalization of many psychedelics in most Western countries, effective from the early 1970s, led to a deregulated and greatly expanded black-market trade, as well as broader experimentation with new substances and with non-drug alternatives such as holotropic breath-work, yoga and meditation. The raves and acid-house parties of the late 1980s can be seen as a revival of the sociality of the 'be-ins' and happenings of the earlier psychedelic movement, with LSD still widely used but now supplemented by the very popular *empathogen* (empathy enhancing substance) MDMA or Ecstasy. The liminal wonderland of rave culture, like other islands of existential *communitas*, proved difficult to sustain in material terms. The transformation of the rave party into an economically viable venture often resulted in a formula for the anticlimax and stimulant-fuelled weekend insomnia.

The term *entheogen* – a substance that gives rise to a sense of divine immanence – was first proposed by Ruck in 1979 (Ruck et al., 1979), but popular interest in entheogens and associated ritual burgeoned only in the 1990s (Jenks, 1997). Ott recommended the term when discussing shamanistic substances and he provided the following definition:

> *Entheogen[ic]* was proposed as a name for a subclass of *psychotropic* or *psychoactive* plants (and, by extension, their active principles and derivatives "both natural and artificial"), as a broad term to describe the cultural context of use, not specific chemistry or pharmacology; as an efficient substitute for cumbersome terms like *shamanic inebriant, visionary drug, plant-sacrament,* and *plant-teacher.* (Ott, 1996, p.205)

Users of entheogens could perhaps be described as *entheogenists* to distinguish them from other kinds of psychonauts.[1] Many publications address the interests of post-modern plant-shamanists (for examples see: De Korne, 1994; Ott, 1994; Pendell, 1995; Trout, 1999; Pendell, 2002), as well as periodicals such as *The Entheogen Review* and *Eleusis*. The sincerity of many *entheogenists* is, I have little doubt, genuine; for these individuals, to grow or harvest their sacred plants and fungi[2] is to invite divinities into their homes and daily lives. Our society has thus far been unable accommodate the legal use of controlled substances by religious users (Boire, 1994). While there exists a general consensus that the use of entheogens constitutes a *bona fide* element of religious practice among groups with distinctively non-Western ethnic identities, social commentators and legislators have often been extremely reluctant to extend this legitimacy to cultural dissidents in the West, especially to the constituencies of renegade pharmacological subcultures displaying significant cognitive divergence from material realist sensibilities and aesthetics ('a bunch of hippies').

The reader may be wondering precisely how the entheogenic experience differs from other kinds of inebriation. The continuities with psychedelic experiences are quite strong, in particular the experience of the dissolution of the ego; however this experience is not necessarily the object of entheogenic practice as it is for some forms of psychedelic practice that aim at *nirvana* or 'non-dual', 'not-I' modes of awareness. Two aspects of entheogenic experience are quite distinctively shamanistic in character. Firstly, entheogenic narratives frequently speak of entering a visionary landscape. Secondly, this landscape is often inhabited by spirit beings that may interact with the psychonaut. In the entheogenic worldview, as in many shamanistic worldviews, these interactions are highly significant and may form the principal object of the 'trip' or 'journey'. The metaphor of the shamanic journey or 'trip' to another world is widely applied to the effects of entheogens. For example, Kensinger (1973) reports that the Cashinahua of Peru describe inebriation by *ayahuasca* (a potion compounded from the vine *Banisteriopsis caapi* with various admixtures) as *Nixi paewn en bai wai pe*, which he translates as 'Vine drunkenness-with I trip good'. The word *bai*, according to Kensinger, conveys the idea of 'a sight-seeing tour' with 'house calls'. The journey is far from being a drunken imbroglio. Rather, subjects frequently report enhanced sensory acuity, complex ideation, great coherence of meaning, and transcendent emotion, the whole orchestrated to a minute level of detail.

Hyperspace and Beyond

The experiences described in the next two sections are 'trip-reports' I recorded between January 2001 and July 2003. During this time I also conducted fieldwork, interviews and conversations with entheogenists in eastern Australia and participated in the entheogenic community. In addition to this 'hard data' I also present a personal account of an entheogenic experience, along with some reflections and interpretations.

Contemporary entheogen use represents a psycho-spiritual *terra incognito*, and the responses to these 'alien' realms provide fascinating insights into the workings of the religious and para-religious mind. Entheogens are often used by communities of psychonauts, and some of the new visionary realms have already become culturally codified. Prominent among these shared visionary worlds are 'DMT hyperspace', a bustling spirit world usually accessed through smoking n,n-dimethyltryptamine; the 'K-hole', an exhilarating realm of flowing, disembodied gnosis that draws enthusiasts of the dissociative anaesthetic ketamine back for more and more and more again; 'Tussin-space', the bizarre continuum attained through the unlikely portal of Robitussin DM, a cough syrup containing the potent dissociative dextromethorphan or DXM (White, 1997); and 'Salvia-space', the peculiar and enchanted realm of 'Sylvia' or 'Ms D' or some other name for the holy and inimitable *deva* of the shamanic herb *Salvia divinorum*. The communities that use these substances are all well represented on the Internet.

'DMT hyperspace' is perhaps the most celebrated and thoroughly described of these 'corroborated' entheogenic spaces. Peter Meyer (Meyer, 1992) has already discussed the enigma of the 'Apparent communication with discarnate entities induced by dimethyltryptamine (DMT)' and offered a number of explanations for the phenomenon. Within the first minute after smoking a high dose of DMT – and often within seconds – consciousness may become dissociated from the body (to use a Cartesian idiom). This has been described as a sense of transcending time and space. In the absence of some somatic reference point, subjects may experience a wide range of impressions including formless vibration, strange plant-like forms, alien machines, intelligent entities, and otherworldly music and languages (Gracie and Zarkov, 1985). After several minutes ordinary perceptions resume, although a sense of euphoria or relief may persist along with residual visual effects:

> At the end of the 'flash' of the visions you will have an after-vision of circular interlocking patterns in exquisite colors. It has been described as looking at a vaulted ceiling or dome. If you did not 'breakthrough' to the levels described above, this 'chrysanthemum' pattern, as we call it, is all you will see. It is worth the trip, too. (Gracie and Zarkov, 1985)

'Fritillated' Environments

Patterns of contrasting coloured tiles are commonly associated with psychedelic and entheogenic substances. These 'hallucinatory form constants' were described in 1942 by Heinrich Klüver (1966) who hypothesized that they were caused by irregular activity of retinal structures. This common syndrome appears to lack a technical term; perhaps 'fritillation' from the Latin for 'chequerboard' would be appropriate. In the course of researching DMT visions I have spoken with a number of people who reported entering tiled or chequered environments during their DMT trance. For example, I gave a ride to a middle-aged male hitchhiker near Nimbin, Australia, who told me that about twenty years ago he had experimented liberally with synthetic DMT, with consistent results. During the 'trip' he would travel rapidly upwards and arrive in a room with a chess-board-like floor where he would interact with entities whose nature he was not easily able to articulate. An informant in Melbourne, with whom I spoke earlier this year, explained how during his only experiment with DMT he had travelled to a chequerboard-like realm where the vivid landscape of valleys and plains was composed entirely of black, white, and violet octagonal tiles. Here he beheld tentacles that produced resonant tones by stroking the sides of a bowl-shaped declivity. As the intensity of the vision abated these tentacles became coterminous with billowing curtains in his familiar, physical world.[3]

Visionary Ecologies

According to numerous accounts 'DMT hyperspace' is inhabited by a whole ecology of creatures: some resemble the 'Greys' of extraterrestrial lore (thin, diminutive, grey-skinned, humanoid aliens, with two large almond-shaped eyes set in an inverted pear-shaped cranium); others are insectoid or mantis-like; yet another class of beings has been described by Terence McKenna (McKenna, 1992) – whose many books and public-speaking engagements did much to popularize DMT and psilocybin-containing mushrooms – as 'self-transforming machine elves'. Indeed, although the sighting of elves is probably rare, elves were nonetheless disproportionately represented in accounts of DMT from the 1980s. The decline in elf-sightings could be the result of any number of rational or super-rational factors. For example, DMT experiences seem to have a remarkable plasticity – one informant emphasized this protean quality with the words, 'It's whatever you want it be', in a tone that conveyed that this was to be taken in the broadest and most literal of senses. Perhaps the mind can tune into any number of experiences during DMT inebriation depending in part on prior social cues, just as one can tune into any number of radio stations although the choice may be influenced by social factors including taste or fashion. The following account of elves is typical:

> ...a gaggle of elf-like creatures in standard issue irish (*sic*) elf costumes, complete with hats, looking like they had stepped out of a hallmark cards 'happy saint patrick's (*sic*) day' display, were doing strange things with strange objects that seemed to be a weird hybrid between crystals and machines. (Gracie and Zarkov, 1985)

During the period January 2001 to July 2003 I collected more than fifty accounts of DMT use, primarily from Australian informants. I should emphasize that not all DMT users report 'contact experiences'. Many DMT psychonauts who do undergo 'contact experiences' initially report being extremely surprized and sometimes very frightened; but the fear usually gives way to ecstasy and sometimes to a peculiar sense of recognition or *déjà vu*. Some psychonauts identify DMT hyperspace with 'the Death Zone' and Near Death Experiences (NDEs).[4] This zone beyond physical embodiment is characteristically both awe-inspiringly mysterious and strangely familiar:

> ...I was aware firstly of the whispering of many beings and entities almost whispering 'you've always wondered, you've always known you would come...' (http://dmt.lycaeum.org/reports/reports/orlando.txt)

The following account is very similar:

> ... I realized: THIS IS JUST LIKE THE LAST TIME...I concluded I had broken out of time and space and WAS experiencing either my 'normal' pattern of dying, or was connected to a time in the future when, once again, I will experience, THIS IS THE TIME I WAS IN BACK THEN NOW. Awed, and slightly confused, I stored this thought for recall... (http://dmt.lycaeum.org/reports/reports/ivdmt.txt)

Plant-Teachers and Chemical Allies

Some of the entities encountered during entheogenic travels were interpreted by my informants as the personifications of entheogenic organisms and substances. The idea of psychoactive plants as teachers is a concept of key importance in many forms of South American and Mexican shamanism. For example, in some forms of Peruvian shamanism that incorporate the entheogenic potion *ayahuasca*, the medicine itself may be considered a 'Doctor' with its own consciousness (Luna, 1984; Luna, 1986) and powerful plants are thought to possess powerful spirit 'Mothers' (Luna and Amaringo, 1991). Many Western entheogen users are familiar with the concept of 'plant teachers'; indeed, the idea has been part of the psychedelic counterculture since Carlos Castaneda popularized 'Mescalito' and other 'plant allies' in his now infamous 'Don Juan' novels. The accessibility of internet forums and the increased circulation of previously obscure organisms, compounds and information has also resulted in the greater prevalence of this model of 'plant-teachers' as opposed to 'psychoactive drugs'.

The spirits of entheogens are frequently alleged to convey practical information about substances and their use. Indeed, some renowned South American shamans claim to have learnt most of their healing craft from the communications they receive when they ingest entheogens (Luna and Amaringo, 1991). The subjective quality of entheogenic encounters makes them highly ambiguous. Those who meet otherworldly beings are often unable to determine whether these entities are aspects of their own unconscious imagination or fully autonomous beings from a 'parallel dimension':

> ...One has the impression of entering into an ecology of souls that lies beyond the portals of what we naively call death. I do not know. Are they the synesthetic embodiment of ourselves as the Other, or of the Other as ourselves? Are they the elves lost to us since the fading of the magic light of childhood? Here is a tremendum barely to be told, an epiphany beyond our wildest dreams. (McKenna, 1993, p.258)

Reflections on My Own Experiences with *Salvia Divinorum*

I became intrigued by the entheogenic approach to substances as 'teachers' over a decade ago, although I remained unconvinced that the contact experiences reported by others were more than psychological or poetic. However, as I explored entheogens the evidence of my senses began to weigh heavily against my scepticism. At a particular point in my investigations the pendulum of my evaluation swung emphatically towards provisional acceptance of the autonomy of plant spirits, as a consequence of an experience that, from a subjective perspective, was most palpable. This happened in 1998 when, after smoking the dried leaves of the herb *Salvia divinorum*, I encountered the spirit of the plant. The spirit seemed to be present through the modes of sight, hearing and touch, and to communicate directly in a meaningful and coherent manner.

Salvia divinorum has a well-attested history of sacramental use among the Mazatec people of the Sierra Mazateca in Oaxaca, Central Mexico, who know the plant as *Ska Maria Pastora* and identify her with the Virgin Mary (Wasson, 1963; Valdés et al., 1983; Valdés, 1994). The plant has been widely used in the entheogenic community in recent years. During this time it has become evident that *Salvia* is non-addictive. Its effects (for those sensitive to them) are usually disconcertingly strange, uncomfortable (one informant suggested 'not intolerable', although his facial expression suggested otherwise).[5] *Salvia* experiences seem essentially introverted. Generally *Salvia* is taken alone or in small groups, although in 2001 I attended a very interesting *Salvia*-leaf chewing workshop, held at night around a large outdoor fire at a country resort in New South Wales, Australia, and attended by about 50 people. However, I found it very disconcerting to be around so much distraction. My main memory of the event is of trying to walk away from the group in a straight line to reach a more contemplative space but of finding that my body would always stagger to the left, while the earth beneath my feet took on the texture of a carpet sporting woven leaves and twigs, all being pulled counter-clockwise in the very direction I did not wish to go.

To return to my first encounter with the spirit of the plant: when I smoked *Salvia divinorum* leaf I had expected a remote and abstract experience but was instead surprized to find myself suddenly transformed – in a most tangible fashion – into the hem of a black, green and purple velvet gown, flared at the base where it merged into a large, revolving vinyl record. I distinctly recall my dread at the thought of being dragged under the stylus. Above me towered the gown's occupant: a pale, stern woman with large dark eyes, her black hair a coiffure of three large ringlets arranged as an upright triangle. What most shocked me was that she was singing a country and western song about the displeasure that goddesses feel when they are invoked at whim by reckless experimenters. I knew that she was singing just for me, and my panic intensified. Part of my mind became aware that in another sense I was lying on a bed and was very close to rolling onto a hapless cockroach. It took all my powers of concentration to reverse my inertia in order to spare the insect. The vision began to abate and I regained my orientation, although

I was still in a state of shock and rapidly sought the support and interaction of my partner, who was babysitting at a neighbour's house.[6]

To compound my subsequent bewilderment, it soon became clear that many others have had remarkably similar experiences with this plant. Numerous anecdotes from informants, internet discussion groups and *The Entheogen Review* (Aardvark, 1998) testify to encounters with a being variously known as 'Ms D', 'Sylvia', 'Aunt Sylvia' and 'Sally'. My reading in the area had made me aware of contact phenomena as a characteristic feature of both Mazatec use in Mexico and Western use. Subsequently I had to ask myself, 'Was I somehow "programmed" at an unconscious level with the expectation of seeing a divinity?' Perhaps my vision of 'Sylvia' was an effect of what Tanya Lurhmann (1989) has called 'interpretive drift', whereby one's scheme for attributing meaning gradually changes as a result of socialization. Perhaps the reports I had read had built up an expectation that my unconscious mind fulfilled. Or maybe Sylvia *does* exist autonomously. After all, when we go to the cinema to see a movie we do not say that we saw particular content because the program or review built up an unconscious expectation. Is the existence of human-like spirit beings so implausible, considering the precedent of the existence of humans themselves on Earth, unlikely as we are? The worlds of spirits and of the social sciences have proved extremely difficult to bridge. Edith Turner (1993; 1994) has reviewed the major anthropological attitudes to spirits. For Turner, Levi-Strauss's emphasis on rational structural regularities and Joseph Campbell's 'myth as metaphor' are overly intellectual and hence reductionist, while positivist approaches to culture evade the problem altogether:

> But we eventually have to face the issue head on, and ask, 'What are spirits?' And I continue with the thorny question: 'What of the great diversity of ideas about them throughout the world? How is the student of the anthropology of consciousness who participates during fieldwork to regard all the conflicting spirit systems in different cultures? Is there not a fatal lack of logic inherent in this diversity?' (1993, p.11)

Carl Jung, Charles Cooley and 'Entheogenic Hyperspace'

Encounters with 'imaginary entities' have been grist for theoretical mills for some time, and a number of interesting hypotheses have been brought forward. Carl Jung's idea of the *complex* provides a useful perspective on some of the psychological aspects of entheogenic experience, while Charles Cooley's concept of *imaginary friends* allows for an analysis of visionary entities at the level of social interaction. A brief discussion of each of these perspectives follows.

Carl Jung's analysis of medium-ship as a system for integrating numerous 'part-souls' or 'autonomous complexes' is directly applicable to the challenge of explaining the vivid 'disincarnate entities' frequently encountered during entheogen-induced trance. In Jungian thought, a complex is a set of relationships between an individual's ego with its own highly personal experiences and an agglomerate of shared, universal archetypes (Samuels, 1985). Complexes are said to determine an individual's feeling-state and can be projected onto others: 'when people of ancient and medieval times spoke of possession by a demon, or of loss of soul, they were referring to possession by, or repression of, a complex' (Samuels, 1985, p.49). Complexes are thought to interact with other complexes as well as with the ego and are thus fully autonomous psychic entities that exhibit a personal ego-character (Jacobi, 1959; Jung, 1960).

From this perspective, the beings encountered through entheogens can be seen as vivid representations of complexes, independent 'splinter psyches' arising from the relationship between an individual's unique 'ego position(s)' (which may be culturally mediated) and archetypes such as the persona, the syzygy (anima and animus), the shadow and the self. If it is the case that entheogens facilitate immersion into the world of autonomous complexes, then their therapeutic use may constitute a most direct and efficacious technique for regulating the psyche, improving the integration between archetypes, and enhancing emotional outlook and psychosomatic health. This view of entheogenic trance, while useful, does however leave us in the unsatisfactory state that Marie-Louise von Franz describes as the final phase of the 'recollection' of a 'psychic projection' where we wonder 'how such an overpowering, extremely real, and awesome experience could suddenly become nothing but self-deception' (von Franz, 1980, p.10).

The interactionist sociology of Charles Horton Cooley (1956) is of special relevance to problems of the ontology of entheogenic entities. Cooley begins with the observation that children often have 'imaginary playmates' and arrives at the conclusion that there is no concrete distinction to be made between 'real' social interactions and 'imaginary' ones:

> ...thought and personal intercourse may be regarded as merely aspects of the same thing: we call it personal intercourse when the suggestions that keep it going are received through faces or other symbols present to the senses; reflections when the personal suggestions come through memory and are more elaborately worked over in thought. But both are mental, both are personal...The mind is not a hermit's cell, but a place of hospitality and intercourse. (Cooley, 1956, p.97)

According to Cooley, identity is rooted in inter-subjectivity. Indeed, even in the absence of exterior beings, the self can interact with itself to produce reflective awareness or internal dialogue. Ego-less, content-less, and dissociative modes of consciousness *are* well-attested, but these form an outer horizon of human experience requiring their own special consideration, whereas we are presently concerned with the densely populated 'spirit world' that interfaces and relates to the individual ego and is so theologically central to shamanism and entheogen use.

Now, to return to the peculiar problems of DMT hyperspace and the K-hole. Soon after the entheogen is ingested, the signals of the body disappear or are diluted by competing impressions. The senses can no longer track the ordinary social environment. Emotions may range from terror through ecstasy, wonder and absolute indifference. The sense of self may be entirely lost, at which point the universe may be perceived as 'formless vibration'. Very soon however entities appear, first as objects, but presently as interacting agents. As social interaction involves reference to the self, it is at this point that the routine functions of the self re-emerge. That is to say, 'others', however fantastic those others may be, are the prompt for the concretization of the 'self' and the self is the nucleus of routine consciousness. As one becomes an actor, rather than a disembodied observer, the visions start to fade. Comparative studies in the phenomenology of other trance states (dreaming, delirium, guided meditation, comas *et cetera*) might help to ascertain whether interaction with visionary entities is a common mechanism for return to routine consciousness. If so, this may suggest novel clinical or psychotherapeutic applications for visionary contact scenarios (entheogen-assisted or otherwise), especially for the interruption of illnesses characterized by chronic entrancement.

Summarizing the Known and the Unknown

In raising these issues and relating some of my own experiences, it has not been my intention to assert that these encounters are 'real' in the same sense that, for instance, Max Weber or Elvis Presley were 'real', historical personages. For one thing, these historical personages had greater stability, whereas the entheogenic entities are only apprehended for a short while before routine perception terminates the trance. But what they lack in durability of form they often make up for in the meanings and feeling-tones they evoke, and these impressions can be persistent and life altering, affecting personal priorities and schemes of attribution. Perhaps these entities are not an appropriate topic for the social sciences and need to be exiled from rational debate. I hope not, but if we are to bid them farewell, we might at least try to understand precisely *what* we are banishing and to assess what we may lose in the process.

The conundrums associated with entheogenic 'close encounters' remain stubbornly unresolved. The models developed by Carl Jung and Charles Cooley represent possible theoretical 'handles' on these problems but require considerable expansion. A closer study of visionary 'interactions' may also yield clinically valuable knowledge. The entheogenic contact scenario has parallels with other enduring problems in the field of religious phenomenology. Conditional acceptance of non-verified or contested worlds and entities is a characteristic feature of most religions. Beliefs in the illusory or partial nature of routine experience are also associated with many forms of shamanism in which entheogens are theologically central; for example, in Mazatec shamanism the world accessed through entheogenic mushrooms is considered more real than our everyday world because in the world of mushrooms all things have already happened and all things are known (Wasson, 1974). Similarly, in some Colombian shamanisms the day-to-day world is considered a pale echo of the world accessed through the potion *yajé*

(Reichel-Dolmatoff, 1975). Many non-entheogenic religious worldviews also claim that all or most entities are relative or illusory. For instance, in classical Indian thought the world is said to be *maya* or 'illusion'; and in some religious schemas, beings are said to be manifested in or by some ultimate condition or deity, as for example when features of the world are said to be formed in 'the dreamtime' or to be a product of the dreaming of a god such as Rudra (Doniger O'Flaherty, 1982). In these respects a natural affinity exists between entheogens and the broad sweep of religious ideas.

Notes

1 *Psychonaut* was coined by Ernst Jünger (1970) in *Annäherungen: Drogen und Rausch* to describe those who use psychoactive materials to achieve a subjective sense of excursion or inner exploration. It is roughly synonymous with the popular informal term *tripper*.
2 Within the entheogenic community there are contending attitudes towards artificial compounds such as ketamine, LSD, ecstasy and a wide range of psychedelic 'research chemicals' such 2–CB, 2–CT–7, and 5–AcO–DIPT. Many entheogen users eschew artificial compounds and exhibit what Ott has called 'organophilia' (1985, p.52*ff*). There is an analogous debate between proponents of perfumery and aromatherapy, indicating that different philosophies of health may be the more central issue. In any case, the notion that natural entheogens are more 'pure' than artificial ones is widespread. This is particularly evident in the case of the deep mistrust with which the 'entities' of the artificial anaesthetic ketamine are sometimes described.
3 Chequered pavements feature in the rituals of a number of initiatory systems, including Golden Dawn ceremonial magick and Freemasonry where they represent polarity: 'The "mosaic floor" of black and white tiles refers to the bipolar nature of earthly existence: the chimera of light and darkness, agens and patiens, form and matter. It leads to the holiest of holies containing the eternal spirit-fire of Jehovah, which no mortal can see.' (Roob, 1997, p.223).
4 Both DMT and ketamine have been proposed as models for explaining the endogenous basis for NDEs. DMT and related substances appear to be normal constituents of human cerebrospinal fluid (McKenna and Towers, 1984), and Rick Strassman has suggested that during *extremis* the pineal gland may secrete active quantities of DMT, giving rise to NDEs (Strassman, 2001). Karl Jansen's 'ketamine model' asserts that the phenomenology of NDEs and ketamine are similar (Jansen, 1989; 1997). These similarities have also been described by Rogo (1984) and that an endogenous ketamine-like agent may be involved in certain natural body responses that function to reduce brain-trauma, but that also produce compelling hallucinatory episodes.
5 In 2002 *Salvia divinorum* was scheduled by the Australian Therapeutic Goods Association (TGA) as a dangerous substance with a high abuse potential; a move that generally foreshadows a substance's inclusion in the Drugs Misuse Act. This was the first time that *Salvia divinorum* had been scheduled

anywhere in the world. The consensus among Australian entheogen users is
that Salvia is now effectively illegal. In Australia Salvia has been used almost
exclusively by serious entheogenic practitioners who treat it with great
reverence. Although there are thousands of people whose religious aspirations
are undermined by this scheduling, not one was consulted by TGA policy
makers when formulating the change.

6   My experience with Salvia, in a mundane setting and primarily motivated by
     curiosity, contrasts strongly with Kathleen Harrison's (2000) account of an
     encounter with the feminine spirit of *Salvia divinorum* during a shamanic ritual
     with a Mexican Mazatec healer. Whereas I experienced profound panic,
     Kathleen Harrison's premeditated and rigorously structured session resulted in a
     harmonious interaction with the spirit, and allegedly in tangible therapeutic
     benefits.

References

Aardvark, D. (1998), *Salvia divinorum and salvinorum A: The best of the
    Entheogen Review 1992–1998*, San Francisco.
Boire, R. G. (1994), *Accommodating Religious Users of Controlled Substances:
    Revisioning the Controlled Substances Act to Permit the Religious Use of
    Entheogenic Substances*, 1999, http://www.specmind.com/accomodating.htm.
Cooley, C. H. (1956 [1902, 1922]), *The two major works of Charles H. Cooley:
    Social organization* and *Human nature and the social order*, The Free Press,
    Glencoe, Illinois.
De Korne, J. (1994), *Psychedelic Shamanism: The Cultivation, Preparation and
    Shamanic Uses of Psychotropic Plants*, Loompanics Unlimited, Port
    Townsend, WA.
Doniger O'Flaherty, W. (1982), 'The dream narrative and the Indian doctrine of
    illusion', *Daedalus*, Summer, pp.93–113.
Gracie, A. Z. and Zarkov (1985), 'DMT: How and Why to Get Off', *Notes From
    the Underground*, vol. 3, pp.1–6, http://leda.lycaeum.org/?ID=8432.
Harrison, K. (2000), 'The Leaves of the Shepherdess', in C. Palmer and M.
    Horowitz (eds), *Sisters of the Extreme: Women Writing on the Drug
    Experience*, Park Street Press, Rochester, Vermont, pp.302–305.
Jacobi, J. (1959), *Complex/Archetype/Symbol in the psychology of C. G. Jung*,
    Princeton University Press, Princeton.
Jansen, K. L. R. (1989), 'The Near-Death Experience', *The British Journal of
    Psychiatry*, vol. 154, pp.883–884.
___(1997), 'The ketamine model of the near-death experience: a central role for
    the n-methyl-d-aspartate receptor', *Journal of near-death Studies*, vol. 16,
    no.1, pp.1–90.
Jenks, S. M. J. (1997), *The Phoenix has Risen from the Ashes: A Socio-Cultural
    Examination of the Neo-Psychedelic Movement*, Department of American
    Studies, Albuquerque, University of New Mexico.

Jung, C. G. (1960), *The structure and dynamics of the psyche. The collected works of C. G. Jung*, Sir Herbert Read, Michael Fordham and Gerhard Adler (eds), vol. 8, Routledge & Kegan Paul, London.

Jünger, E. (1970), *Annäherungen: Drogen und Rausc*, E. Klett Verlag, Stuttgart.

Kensinger, K. M. (1973) 'Banisteriopsis Usage Among the Peruvian Cashinahua', in M. J. Harner (ed.), *Hallucinogens and Shamanism*, Oxford University Press, London, pp.9–14.

Klüver, H. (1966), *Mescal and Mechanisms of Hallucination*, University of Chicago Press, Chicago.

Luhrmann, T. (1989), *Persuasion's of the Witch's Craft: Ritual magic in Contemporary England*, Blackwell, Oxford.

Luna, L. E. (1984), 'The Concept of Plants as Teachers Among Four Mestizo Shamans of Iquitos, Northeastern Peru', *Journal of Ethnopharmacology*, vol. 11, pp.135–156.

___(1986), *Vegetalismo: Shamanism among the Mestizo Population of the Peruvian Amazon*, Almqvist & Wiksell International, Stockholm, Sweden.

Luna, L. E. and P. Amaringo, (1991), *Ayahuasca Visions: The Religious Iconography of a Peruvian Shaman*, North Atlantic Books, Berkeley, California.

McKenna, D. J. and G. H. N. Towers (1984), 'Biochemistry and Pharmacology of Tryptamines and beta-Carbolines: A Mini-review', *Journal of Psychoactive Drugs*, vol. 16, no. 4, pp.347–358.

McKenna, T. K. (1992), 'Tryptamine hallucinogens and culture', *Yearbook for Ethnomedicine and the Study of Consciousness*, vol. 1, pp.149–174.

___(1993), *Food of the Gods: The Search for the Original Tree of Knowledge*, Bantam Books, New York.

Meyer, P. (1992), 'Apparent Communication with Discarnate Entities Induced By Dimethyltryptamine (DMT)', *Yearbook for Ethnomedicine and the Study of Consciousness*, C. Rätsch (ed.), Verlag für Wissenschaft und Bildun, Berlin, vol. 1, pp.149–174.

Ott, J. (1985), *The Cacahuatl Eater: Ruminations of an Unabashed Chocolate Addict*, Natural Products Comapny, Vashon, WA.

___(1994), *Ayahuasca Analogues: Pangæan Entheogens*, Kennewick, WA, Natural Products Co.

___(1996), 'Entheogens II: On Entheology and Entheobotany', *The Journal of Psychoactive Drugs*, vol. 28, no. 2, pp.205–209.

Pendell, D. (1995), *Pharmako/Poeia: Plant Powers, Poisons, and Herbcraft*, Mercury House, San Fransisco.

___(2002), *Pharmakodynamis: Stimulating plants, potions and herbcraft*, Mercury House, San Francisco.

Reichel-Dolmatoff, G. (1975), *The Shaman and The Jaguar: A Study of Narcotic Drugs Among the Indians of Colombia*, Temple University Press, Philadelphia.

Rogo, S. D. (1984), 'Ketamine and the near-death experience', *Anabiosis – The journal for near-death studies*, vol. 4, no.1 , pp.87–96.

Roob, A. (1997), *The Hermetic Museum, Alchemy and Mysticism,* Taschen, Köln.

Ruck, C. A. P., Bigwood, J., Staples, D., Ott, J. and Wasson, R. G. (1979), 'Entheogens', *Journal of Psychedelic Drugs*, vol. 11, nos. 1–2, pp.145–146.

Samuels, A. (1985), *Jung and the post-Jungians*, Routledge & Kegan Paul, London.

Strassman, R. (2001), 'Biomedical research with psychedelics: Current models and future prospects', *Entheogens and the Future of Religion*, R. Forte, Council on Spiritual Practices, San Fransisco, pp.153–163.

Trout, K. (1999), *Trout's Notes on Sacred Cacti: Botany, Chemistry, Cultivation, and Utilization*, Better Days Publishing.

Turner, E. (1993), 'The Reality of Spirits: A Tabooed or Permitted Field of Study?', *Anthropology of Consciousness*, vol 4, no. 1, p.10.

___(1994), 'A visible spirit form in Zambia', in D. E. Young. and. J.-G. Goulet (eds), *Being changed by cross-cultural encounters: The anthropology of extraordinary experience*, Ontario, Broadview Press, pp.71–91.

Valdés, L. J. I. (1994), 'Salvia divinorum and the Unique Diterpene Hallucinogen, Salvinorin (Divinorin) A.', *The Journal of Psychoactive Drugs,* vol. 26, no. 3, pp.277–283.

Valdés, L. J. I., Díaz, J. L. and Paul A. G. (1983), 'Ethnopharmacology of Ska María Pastora (Salvia divinorum, Epling and Játiva-M.)', *Journal of Ethnopharmacology*, vol. 7, pp.287–312.

von Franz, M.-L. (1980), *Projection and Re–collection in Jungian Psychology: Reflections of the Soul*, trans. William H. Kennedy, London, Open Court.

Wasson, R. G. (1963), 'A new Mexican psychotropic drug from the mint family', Botanical museum leaflets. *Harvard University*, vol. 20, no. 3, pp.77–84.

___(1974), *María Sabina and her Mazatec Mushroom Velada*, Harcourt Brace Jovanovich, New York.

White, W. E. (1997), The dextromethorphan FAQ: Answers to frequently asked questions about dextromethorphan (DXM). http://www.lycaeum.org/drugs/synthetics/dxm/faq/contents.html.

Chapter 9

Enchanting Women:
Priestessing in America

Wendy Griffin

In his examination of modern social theories of magic, Daniel O'Keefe (1982) argues that magic, like religion, is a process that creates belief and community. Magic occurs when we expropriate powerful cultural symbols and manipulate them enough to change the categories that sustain their frames of reference. This new meaning with which the symbols are imbued changes our understandings of the world.[1] Magic is a social act, O'Keefe concludes, and all new religions begin as magic. 'The difference between modern and primitive societies is not that they had magic and we do not. The difference is that they accepted the magic around them, whereas we deny it' (O'Keefe, 1982, p.xv). In a rational, secular world, magic may still exist. 'When a religion becomes too cognitive and its own magic dries up, either faith in the propositions of its worldview will weaken, or else magical challenges will appear at the periphery in the form of new sects using striking performatives to overthrow or renew the religion' (O'Keefe, 1982, p.55). Today, these magical challenges can be seen in Goddess Spirituality, in the enactment of innovative rituals that function to re-enchant women's bodies and sexuality, women's experiences, the bonds among women and women's connections to the natural world (Griffin, 1995). At the same time, a tension between the freshness and excitement of magical challenges and the need for structure and legitimation is present. Much of this tension revolves around issues of leadership: who may lead and how this may be done.

In part, this is because Goddess Spirituality can be understood as a cluster of beliefs and spiritual practices – not a uniform faith tradition, but one where different groups place emphasis in different places and have some unique characteristics. Yet, however different the groups are, they all honour nature, the female, the immanence of the Divine, and the creative and sacred potential of the erotic. In the United States, Goddess Spirituality includes feminist and women's spiritualities, as well as other contemporary polytheistic spiritualities that honour male deities as long as Goddess is given primacy, such as Druidism and most forms of Witchcraft. Scholars tend to group these spiritual traditions under the term Paganism, although not all practitioners would agree with the label. Profoundly influenced by feminism and its challenge to male authority, American groups all use female imagery to represent the Divine. While many groups use male images as well as female, none uses male alone. In some of these groups, both women and men serve in religious ministry; in others, only women fill this role. The focus of this chapter is on the latter, those American priestesses who serve groups primarily of women, who take the culture's powerful symbols of male Divinity and of the priest – the embodied link between the Divine and the human – and transform them into female myth and metaphor. Through the use of ritual performance for themselves and others, the priestesses facilitate what is believed to be a different experience of the Divine, and in changing the frames of reference, they magically re-enchant their world and, they believe, influence the larger world around them.

In women-only groups, Goddess spirituality posits that every woman can find the Divine within herself. It is a spirituality where, as psychologist of religion and popular Goddess scholar Naomi Goldenberg put it, 'Each is the priestess of her own religion' (Goldenberg, 1979, p.93). If this is the case, one might ask, what is the role of the priestess today? And how can there be a religious community? This chapter addresses these questions. It begins by exploring the material processes through which women become priestesses recognized by a community. These processes inspire significant debate and illustrate specific tensions that exist between the secular worldview and the magical one. The chapter then moves to interviews with priestesses about how they perceive their role as facilitators of enchantment. It concludes with an account of the ordination of a High Priestess where ritual magic, as O'Keefe describes it, flows.

Becoming a Priestess

In her examination of twelve women's' religions from around the world, anthropologist Susan Sered (1994) argues that, although there is no universal pattern, they tend not to have codified rules of moral behaviour, and that women typically do not choose a leadership role or undergo a formal, lengthy training. Instead, they become leaders through a slow process of self-recognition. Access to rank appears to be open to all, regardless of wealth or education. Sered concludes that the absence of formal training in women's religions is consistent with the aversion to canon and centralization.

However, in the United States, the process is somewhat different. Although access is open to all and rules are not codified, some formal training does exist, although it is very uneven. The United States is unusual in that religions and credentialed ministry can be legally recognized and offered certain privileges. For example, several Goddess groups have gained legal recognition as non-profit religious organizations; that means, among other things, they have the same tax status as a charity, without being responsible for doing charitable acts. This has advantages such as reduced postal expenses and potential eligibility for tax-deductible donations and certain federal funds under the 'charitable choice'

1   High Priestess Letecia Layson invokes Isis in a dawn ritual. Photo: Jeanne Leiter

2   Fortress Goolengook, 2001. Photo: Tony 'Quoll' Hastings

3   Lock-on in Goolengook Forest, 1997. Photo: Jeremy Little

provisions of the 1996 Welfare Reform. Some of these groups own lands that are protected by a collection of laws designed to maintain separation between religion and the State. Within these legally recognized religious organizations, the individuals who are recognized by their group as being clergy are also recognized by the government. To date, this simply means that they have the legal right to marry, bury, and counsel, but potentially it could also affect things like individual taxes, uses of private property, malpractice insurance, confidentiality of records, and licencing for psychological services. These actual and potential privileges for Goddess clergy result in an increased demand by the State and by some of the larger groups themselves for structure, record-keeping and other methods of formalization. This leads to tensions and often heated discussion concerning issues of regulation, gate keeping, and legitimation. Deciding who is 'legitimate' clergy and what training is necessary in order to obtain this status is an issue involving boundary maintenance and it therefore involves considerable power. This then leads to significant discussion about what it means to be a priestess or a priest. Women's groups tend to be more flexible in their boundaries and rules than more traditional Pagan groups.[2] Nevertheless, this discussion has been present in the women's Goddess community for at least a decade. At times, the debate has grown heated between those who argue for official training and ordination and those who support self-recognition and self-direction as an appropriate path to becoming a priestess.

'She had better be ordained, ordained by someone who has been ordained...' said Zsuzsanna Budapest, commonly known as the Mother of Dianic (feminist separatist) Witchcraft. She went on to point out that the Goddess community lacks a 'Goddess Vatican' to dispatch someone to start a ministry. 'There are self-taught women who totally I think are priestesses...But nobody who doesn't lead a circle gets to be ordained by me' (Budapest, 1992, p.7). Somewhat ironically, Budapest, as a founding member of Dianic or feminist separatist Witchcraft, was originally self-ordained.[3]

For Ruth Rhiannon Barrett, High Priestess and teacher of the Dianic craft, the word 'priestess' is both a noun and a verb. One may 'priestess', that is take on a leadership role at a particular ritual, without being a priestess. A woman who is carefully trained, has experience as a leader and has grown adept in disseminating her religious tradition or specialized knowledge, and who both serves a community and is accepted by it, qualifies as a priestess (Barrett, 2000). One of the most significant ways that priestesses participate in re-enchantment is by helping other women experience themselves as sacred. However, this may be done in various ways. Not all priestesses are trained for leadership in public ritual, where they are expected to facilitate the altered states of consciousness in which, it is believed, magic can occur.[4] Some priestesses specialize in areas like teaching, spiritual counselling, healing, or composing music or poetry. Rhiannon also points out the growing tendency among Goddess women in the United States to interchange the words 'Witch' and 'priestess' and she argues that this is because to many women the latter sounds less threatening. But she stresses that the words are not interchangeable. A Witch is a woman who is self-defined, whereas a priestess must be recognized by the community she serves (Barrett, 1992).

There are only a few paths to credentialed priestesshood in the United States. Three of these will serve as examples of what is available. The first, and least structured, is through the Fellowship of Isis (FOI), through the legally recognized Temple of Isis in California. Another path is through organizations such as Cella, the national program developed by the Women's Thealogical Institute.[5] Cella is affiliated with the Reformed Congregation of the Goddess (RCG), based in Madison, Wisconsin. The third common path is through membership and training in a Witches' coven that is part of the Covenant of the Goddess (CoG), a national umbrella organization for Witches. The first and last options also provide ministerial credentials to men.

The Fellowship of Isis

The Fellowship of Isis is an international organization dedicated to honouring the Goddess, although members may also belong to many different religions (Robertson, 2002). FOI requires neither vows nor commitments from its members, just a letter requesting membership. Titles such as priest/ess and arch-priest/ess are intended simply to describe the work that is done, and the organization's web site states that all members are equal. Ministerial credentials are fairly easy to obtain. Each individual religious centre, or Iseum, specifies the preparation that is needed, but the minimum time for training is supposed to be one year. In cases where there is no Iseum readily available, training may be done through a correspondence course. The ordination ceremony is a carefully scripted part of FOI liturgy, although creative licence is sometimes taken.

In 1996 an Iseum was established in Los Angeles and attracted some of the more visible and active Goddess women in the community. The founder had undertaken no structured training to be a priestess, nor had she any training in a specific magical tradition, though she was a voracious reader in the field and had been serving as a priestess in large public rituals of a generic Goddess group for about six years. In 1997, she and two other women affiliated with the Temple of Isis. The second of the three had some Dianic training, had been a founding member of the generic group, and had been serving as a priestess in the community for over 13 years. The third woman was a credentialed Dianic priestess and a priestess in a non-credentialed women's mystery school. Because of the flexibility inherent in the structure of the Iseums, the past work these women had done was acknowledged as their training. Without meeting additional training requirements, these women became priestesses with ministerial credentials in the Temple of Isis. Their spiritual beliefs are 'Goddess eclectic' and somewhat different from each other. Since that time, the founder of the Los Angeles Iseum has ordained 27 priestesses.

Cella

The Cella programme, through the legally recognized RCG, is a six-year programme that does not give credit for past experience or study. There are two options in Cella: participants may move to Wisconsin and serve an apprenticeship at the 'Mother House' at their own pace, or they may undertake the training through correspondence courses, which, in addition to individual work, includes three weekend trainings every year and an annual visit to Madison. There are eight Cella training centres in the country, and faculty fly to other cities to conduct weekend trainings for 10 or more people. Cella provides structure by setting broad parameters and assigning an adviser to each student who can assist her in her studies and give support and guidance as she progresses. The student may pick one or more areas of specialization. She sets her own pace, but her commitment and activities are expected to increase during the six years. Since 1984, Cella has ordained only 17 priestesses directly, but other groups affiliated with RCG set their own requirements for ordination, conduct training, and gain ministerial credentials through RCG's legal status.

The Covenant of the Goddess

The Covenant of the Goddess (CoG) is a non-profit religious confederation of covens and solitary practitioners of various Witchcraft traditions. It will grant ministerial credentials to anyone who has first been declared a priest/ess by her or his own coven, which must be a full member of CoG. Different Witchcraft traditions have different guidelines for how and when this is done, but CoG specifies that the person must have undergone at least a full year of active training for the ministry in her or his tradition. This is in addition to however long the coven requires for full membership, typically at least a year and a day. This usually results in a priestess having a minimum of two years' training in Witchcraft. The ministerial credentials remain valid only as long as the person remains an active member of the coven, which must itself remain an active member of CoG. Unlike the other groups that offer ministerial credentials, CoG requires that these be renewed every year.

The Priestesses

Interviews with 10 priestesses who are leaders in their own spiritual communities offered further insights about what it means to be a priestess. All of the women were middle-aged and had been involved in Goddess Spirituality from 10 to 35 years. Not surprisingly, since they all had ministerial credentials through one of the three organizational paths described above, all the women supported legal recognition of Pagan clergy, saying that legal recognition serves the community and gains potential access to hospitals and prisons, in addition to serving family needs in terms of marriage, funerals and other important rites of passage. Legal recognition was also seen as important as a political statement to others, as an affirmation that Goddess Spirituality is a valid religious tradition and should be respected as such. However, on the question whether there should be some kind of uniformity in the training a priestess receives for credentialing, their answers differed.

'Absolutely!' said one respondent. 'If a tradition is to be perpetuated, some uniformity is essential. Otherwise you have a woman practised in her own spirituality, but without a way to communicate and work with others easily.' 'No,' replied another. 'I would be very nervous about who would create the standard and what it would look like.' Another said no for a different reason. 'No. It should depend on the calling of the person. In my view, it should not be treated as involving special expertise, like a degree from a university.' Still another pointed out that, although it might be a good idea to have standard training in certain basic skills, it would be difficult to get the different traditions within Goddess Spirituality to agree on exactly what those skills were and how proficient the priestess should be in them. Interestingly, there was no significant difference in the answers given by those who had received fairly standardized training and those whose training had been more eclectic.

This question of legitimation is, however, increasingly problematic. Already there are priestesses in the country who are attempting to make a living through their ministry. Many Pagans believe this is a natural result of the growth in numbers of practitioners. Berger, Leach and Shaffer (2003, p.175) report that 51.5 per cent of 'Goddess Worshippers'[6] believe that full-time Pagan clergy should be financially supported, in spite of the reality that few agree on their qualifications or training. At the same time, answers from the priestess interviews suggest some are concerned that the kind of standardization that would offer legitimacy and acceptance might lead to homogenization of belief. O'Keefe (1982) would argue that this would threaten the innovation, spontaneity and creativity that lie at the heart of enchantment, of the radical reframing of a magical worldview.

Not all women who identify as priestesses see their role as ministering to others, whether individually or in groups. Although all the women interviewed for this chapter had taken leadership roles in public rituals, only three of them identified first and foremost as ritual priestesses. Other ways they identified their priestessing were as scholar, teacher, healer, writer, organizer, and role model, all of which may require very different training.[7] Most of them felt 'called' to be a priestess, and all took the role very seriously. Being a priestess meant working *on* the self and *for* the community. According to one priestess interviewed, being a priestess meant, 'To be able to embody the Goddess, to hold space for that energy and to find a variety of ways for women to discover Her within themselves.' In order to be effective, a priestess must have more than some basic skills; most respondents said words to the effect that she had to know herself, her strengths and weaknesses, and be honest with herself about what she had to offer the community.

'Becoming a priestess is a commitment to extra service, not extra authority of any kind. It is all to do with responsibility, not laurels and pedestals. It is not a reward; it does not confer power; it is not a symbol of special prestige. It is just answering a call from Goddess and making a significant commitment to that call,' said one priestess who has organized public rituals of several hundred participants.

The priestesses believe that re-enchantment lies in discovering the sacred within themselves and in helping other women to discover the Goddess within – in resacralizing women's bodies and experience. This is done through teaching, writing, and especially ritual. Ritual is particularly effective because ritual consciousness is an embodied, tacit knowledge (Grimes, 1992). It is not the message a ritual provides that is so important; it is the experience of the ritual itself that is significant. Thus, in an effective ritual and through the manipulation of symbols and the senses, priestesses take participants to a liminal place where magic is possible. When this happens, according to ritual theorist Victor Turner (1967), a powerful, albeit temporary, community emerges.

The Ordination

An example of ritual enchantment can be seen in the ordination of a community's High Priestess. Circle of Aradia (CoA) is a large Goddess group with a lineage that goes back to the early 1970s in southern California. When Budapest moved away in 1980, she ordained Rhiannon as High Priestess to carry on the Dianic tradition there. Although Rhiannon retained her title, the group evolved in a more democratic direction, with various 'circles' of responsibility, including the Business Circle, Spiritual Circle, and Ritual Facilitators' Circle. With this diffusion of responsibility, Rhiannon took on the role of High Priestess and Religious Director for CoA, a salaried position paid for by the classes she taught. Affiliating with RCG, and thus sharing its non-profit status and legal ministerial credentialing, CoA ordained thirteen priestesses, three high priestesses, and served several thousand women through its rituals, workshops and classes during Rhiannon's 21-year tenure.[8]

In 2000, Rhiannon relocated to the Midwest and chose Letecia Layson, who had been ordained as a Dianic priestess in CoA six years earlier, to take her place.[9] The ordination was marked by a large community ritual where magic and music were woven together in a sacred ceremony of blessing and transition. The setting was a community house in heavily wooded canyons. Approximately 150 women gathered in clusters in the large room inside. Letecia's mother and two sisters sat on chairs near the door and remained there throughout the ceremony. This was new to them and somewhat of a challenge, in particular for her mother, who was a devout Roman Catholic born in the Philippines. But she had always stressed the importance of family to her daughters, and they were there to support and celebrate Letecia, the first woman of colour to lead a large Goddess community.[10]

There were three parts to this ritual that I wish to detail, as they specifically address enchantment and what it means to be a priestess. The first occurred immediately after energy was raised, the circle cast, and the Goddess Diana invoked. Two women urged us to join hands and begin to walk, first into a circle and then into a spiral formation. This was not a spiral dance but the formation of a spiral path with our bodies. As we walked, we sang a song we had been taught just before the event began.

> Spinning out and spinning in
> So Zsuzsanna did begin
> As above, so below
> There did Ruth Rhiannon go
> By Diana's fearless stride
> So Leticia steps inside
> By water, fire, air and land
> Blessed by the place they stand
> (Richards, 2000)

When we had completed the spiral shape, the singing stopped and we sat on the floor. Letecia was brought into the room and an 'entrance' was cut into the air in the east for her to enter the space. She was dressed in the colours of the Goddess, a red satin gown and folds of black and white fabrics draped over each shoulder. They were caught at her waist by a long red cord, a symbol of the Dianic Craft reminding women of their link to the 'Mother'. Her dark hair, reaching down to the small of her back, glimmered with strands of silver in the candlelight, and it swayed gently as she walked through the lines of seated women whose bodies formed the spiral path. We were there to witness and offer support for her journey into the heart of the spiral. Women smiled up at her as she passed through their midst. Priestesses stepped out to greet her and offer their support and blessings: one from the Spiritual Circle, another representing a group of Crones or older women, and a high priestess from another women's community pledging sisterhood. Letecia reached the centre and Rhiannon entered the spiral walk. When she too reached the centre, they embraced, and the song began anew.

In this part of the ritual, the lineage of leadership for CoA was established and legitimated through the song sung by the community of women. Both the old and the new High Priestesses came to each other through the curving path created by women's bodies. The Goddess may have chosen these women, but it was the community that affirmed their leadership. The last line of the chant reinforced this: *Blessed **by** the place they stand* is not the same as *Blessed **be** the place they stand*. Their presence does not bless the place. The priestesses are blessed *by* the place – by the elements and by the earth they stand on that is the body of the Goddess. But the true place where they stand is in the centre of a spiral, in the heart of a community of women.

Later in the ritual, Rhiannon took the opportunity to ask women to work with the new High Priestess in partnership, to honour her gifts that were different from Rhiannon's own, and to bless this transition to a new place of growth for CoA. She gave Letecia several items, including part of a manuscript of her book on rituals and a wax scraper. In presenting the new priestess with something as mundane as a wax scraper, Rhiannon was reminding everyone that service means just that: service. The community house that CoA rents for many of its rituals is very strict about clean-up. Candles, always in abundance in indoor Goddess rituals, drip wax, and the High Priestess cannot be above getting down on her hands and knees and scraping the candle wax off the floor. In asking the women to honour Letecia's unique gifts, Rhiannon reminded both Letecia and the members that the organization would change, and that change is part of the life cycle and necessary for growth. The role of the High Priestess is to provide leadership that facilitates growth in others.

Finally, when the ritual was near its end, Letecia was given a ball of silver cord, and all the women stood. She wove between each person in the circle, linking them and making prolonged eye contact, and each woman reached out and grasped the cord in response. The group sang:

> Weave and spin, weave and spin
> This is how the work begins.
> Mend and heal, mend and heal
> Take the dream and make it real.

Some women sang a counter chant:

> Strand by strand, hand over hand
> Thread by thread, we weave the web.

And still others sang:

> She changes everything she touches and
> Everything she touches changes.[11]

There was no assigning of vocal parts; women simply joined in singing whichever chant struck them at the moment and then flowed effortlessly into another when they so desired. The music was so lovely and so all-embracing that many women danced as they sang, spinning slowly or swaying in its wake. Once Letecia had come full circle, joining every woman to the greater whole, she reversed her steps, weaving gracefully between women as she collected the cord and as the singing grew softer.

The significance of the third part of the ritual is fairly explicit. The weaving of melodies and words combined with the dance-like movements of women's bodies and the smell of incense and flowers. As the women sang, they invoked the kind of world they wished to live in, a changed world of healing and beauty and empowerment. They voluntarily reached out for the silver cord that bound them to Letecia and into a community. The effect was to create an enchanted sea of sacred sensuality within which an intimate relationship was affirmed between every woman there and the new High Priestess.[12]

The American Goddess Spirituality movement that began more than 30 years ago is becoming more structured than it was, as Weber (1964) suggested movements do, and as Berger (1995) demonstrated among mixed Pagan groups. At the same time, the desire for spontaneity, for enchantment and magic, is still present. Letecia's ordination demonstrates both dynamics. That priestess ordination exists, and is recognized by the State as legal, demonstrates the desire for structure and legitimation. *How* the ordination was done was magic – as O'Keefe articulates it. It was a profoundly sensual experience of a community of women, one that sees women's bodies and sensuality as sacred, and itself as participating in a sacred act. This was magic that expropriates and alters powerful symbols, opening up the women's world to new possibilities. That does not mean that the ritual itself was magic, but that it contained moments of magic, liminal moments when women experienced themselves as part of a sacred community that includes the immanent Divine.

As practitioners of enchantment, priestesses facilitate this kind of experience. As clergy, they also help shape the discourse on the Goddess, and thus the spiritual practice itself. The challenge for them will be to maintain the dynamic tension between the opposing needs of a growing spiritual practice: building structure and legitimation while, at the same time, keeping the magic flowing.

Notes

1   An example of this might be the symbol of the witch, reviled and feared by those who see it within a religious framework where the world is clearly separated into good and evil. The witch's power is believed to come from the Devil, and therefore it and she are evil. This symbol was reclaimed as positive by American feminists before the American Goddess Movement began (see Griffin, 2003). In Goddess Spirituality, the symbol of the witch is expropriated and revisioned to represent an individual who can draw upon the Divine energy in *all* things and manipulate it to achieve a desired end. Here the world is no longer understood to be divided into good and evil but is seen as interconnected through the flow of the immanent Divine.
2   This refers to those Pagan traditions that trace their roots back to Gerald Gardner in Britain (see Hutton 1999), rather than some of the more innovative forms of Witchcraft that have sprung up in the United States.
3   Rhiannon, who was ordained High Priestess by Budapest in 1980, confided to me that Budapest missed having an official ordination and asked Rhiannon to ordain her. This was done in 1999.

4   Here, to enchant is taken to mean both doing magic and facilitating magic for others, through techniques such as creating and leading performative rituals, drumming, meditation, and other forms of energy manipulation. Sometimes this is also referred to as 'weaving energy'.

5   Recently the Cherry Hill Seminary in Vermont has been gaining visibility in training for Pagan clergy, for both men and women. It does not specialize in training for leading women-only groups.

6   The authors define this category as distinguishing itself from other forms of Paganism by focusing on the Goddess exclusively.

7   One coven I studied demanded that a member get a degree in Chinese herbology for her priestess path, after she had experimented with brewing a 'trance tea' for ritual that made everyone urinate in colours.

8   Barrett has since founded a new six-year priestess training program in the Midwest that is affiliated with the Temple of Diana, where women may study and receive legal recognition as priestesses (http://www.womensriteswomensmysteries.com). Not to be left behind, Budapest created an online 'university' that originally proposed to grant degrees; however, the website was revised four months after it began in June 2003 and no longer mentions that possibility (http://www.zbudapest.com/du/).

9   Letecia was also one of the three priestesses of Isis who started the Los Angeles Iseum.

10   Letecia confided to me that, although her mother is proud that her daughter does work for the community and for women, she does not quite understand it, and occasionally has a priest say a mass for her.

11   All three chants are from the Reclaiming Collective, a well-known group that practises a tradition of feminist Witchcraft co-founded by Starhawk, noted Witch, author, and activist.

12   It should not be assumed that the enchantment experienced is necessarily permanent. It is not unusual to have tensions surrounding the ordination of a High Priestess; change is often difficult. In the aforementioned group, there have been a few serious challenges to the acceptance of Letecia in her new leadership position, but the great majority of the community and all the CoA circles support her leadership.

References

Barrett, R. (1992), 'The Priestess Path', *The Beltane Papers*, vol. 1, pp.8–11.

___(2000), 'The Ritual Priestess', *Of a Like Mind*, vol. XVII, no. 2, May.

___http://www.womensritesmwomensmysteries.com/ruth-book-excerpts.htm.

Berger, H. A. (1995), 'The Routinization of Spontaneity', *Sociology of Religion*, vol. 16, no.1, Spring, pp.49–61.

Berger, H. A., E. A. Leach, and L. S. Schaffer (2003), *Voices from the Pagan Census: A National Survey of Witches and Neo-Pagans in the United States*, University of South Carolina Press, Columbia, SC.

Budapest, Z. (1992), 'Speaking with the Grey She-Wolf', Transcript of an interview published in *The Beltane Papers*, vol. 1, pp.4–7, 22.

Goldenberg, N. (1979), *Changing of the Gods: Feminism and the End of Traditional Religions*, Beacon Press, Boston.

Griffin, W. (1995), 'The Embodied Goddess: Feminist Witchcraft and Female Divinity', *Sociology of Religion*, vol. 56, no. 1, pp.35–49.

___(2003), 'Goddess Spirituality and Wicca', in Arvind Sharma and Katherine Young (eds), *Her Voice, Her Faith: Women Speak on World Religions*, Westview Press, Boulder, CO, pp.243–281.

Grimes, R. (1992), 'Reinventing Ritual', *Soundings*, vol. 75, no. 1, pp.21–41.

Hill, A. (2003), 'Archetype, Paradox, and the Path of the Priestess', a paper presented at the *Women's Spirituality Conference*, New College of California, San Francisco, May, 2–4.

Hutton, R. (1999), *The Triumph of the Moon: A History of Modern Pagan Witchcraft*, Oxford University Press, Oxford.

O'Keefe, D. L. (1982), *Stolen Lightening: The Social Theory of Magic*, Continuum, New York.

Richards, L. (2000), No Title, Unpublished lyrics taken from the ritual outline for the ordination of Letecia Layson, High Priestess of Diana, Los Angeles.

Robertson, O. (2002), 'The Fellowship of Isis,' http://www.fellowshipofisis.com/intro.html.

Sered, S. S. (1994), *Priestess, Mother, Sacred Sister: Religions Dominated by Women*, Oxford University Press, London.

Turner, V. (1967), *The Forest of Symbols: Aspects of Ndembu Ritual*, Cornell University Press, Ithaca, New York.

Weber. M. (1964), *The Sociology of Religion*, Beacon Press, Boston.

Chapter 10

Becoming Radical Faerie:
Queering the Spirit of the Circle

Bill Rodgers

Five Elements – Five Correspondences – Five Confessions

Not many pagans realise that there are five elements, not four: earth, air, fire, water, and **POLYESTER**. *(Delilah, 1995)*

EARTH	*Grounding, beginning, source* – in 1995, I was an anthropologist of religion (and a Radical Faerie).
AIR	*Space, emptiness, vacuum* – in 1995, there were no major Radical Faerie Groups in Australia.
FIRE	*Ignition, impact, inspiration* – in 1995, I began an ethnographic journey into the queer spiritual frontier, to visit and document the Radical Faerie movement in the United States and Canada.
WATER	*Fluidity, change, flow* – in 1995, while doing fieldwork as a participant-observer on a Radical Faerie community in Tennessee, my ideas about *who* the Faeries are and *what* we are on about changed dramatically.
POLYESTER	*Synthesis, glamour, rebirth* – in 2004, I am a Radical Faerie (and an anthropologist of religion).

Looking Askance – Searching for Radical Faeries

Radical Faeries are elusive. Like our legendary namesakes – the faeries of the British Isles, the fees of France, the sprites and wood spirits of the Mediterranean – we are experts at camouflage and visual trickery. Delighting in inhabiting the borderlands of the mainstream worldview, we are the teasing images flickering in society's peripheral vision, which disappear (in a cloud of faerie dust to peals of bell-like laughter) when confronted with straight and four-square vision. We have to learn to look askance and use our peripheral vision to begin an investigation into the nature of the Radical Faeries. But how do you attempt to define a group of people whose favourite saying is: 'Ask four Faeries what a Radical Faerie is, and you'll get five different answers'? You simply don't.

In writing this piece, I am mindful that this is not an attempt at a definitive description of the Radical Faerie movement. It is merely one Faerie's perspective on the movement. (Quote what is written here as *gospel* to other Faeries, and you do so at your peril!)

Faeries have been described variously as a neo-pagan spiritual group (Adler, 1986, p.338), a gay tribe (Norman, 1991, p.281), a new religious/social movement or development (Hay in Thompson, 1995, p.83), a bunch of hippy-faggot-farmers and gender-fuck activists (Fey, 2000, p.732), and queer community anarchists (Thompson, 1987, p.268). Indeed, the number of definitions of Faerie is synergistically greater than the number of queer men and women who identify as part of the movement.

My evocation of the nature of Faerie has three focal points. Firstly, I explore Faerie origins. These are the people, the cultural institutions, and the theoretical paradigms that contributed to the establishment of the movement. Secondly, I look at what it means to be a Radical Faerie: that is, I examine any aspects of identity that Faeries have in common. Finally, I investigate any central core beliefs the Radical Faerie movement might have and the role that spontaneity plays (Berger, 1995) in the movement.

Origins – The Bones of Our Ancestors

> We are an old people
> We are a new people
> We are the same people
> Different from before
> (Conner, 1993, p.13)

This is a verse I heard chanted many times during my fieldwork with the Faeries. The first time I heard it, it seemed to me to be a series of statements in direct opposition to each other. Paradox and contradiction. As I joined in the chant with twenty or so Faeries in a circle, its meaning gradually shifted. Repetition building understanding. Harmony evoking memory. *We are an old people*: we have links to the past; we have a queer history across cultures far older than our own. *We are a new people*: we invent ourselves anew; we have a queer future. *We are the same people*: there is an indescribable link between who we are now, and who those queer ancestors were; we have affiliation of spirit. *Different from before*: nothing is static; reinvention is constant and necessary.

Sacred Drag and the Divine Androgyne

Frequently, figures of the 'other' in cultures of the past can be interpreted by us today as queer role models. Often they have the hallmarks of contemporary queerness – crossing gender boundaries in dress, behaviour and sexual preference. Some religious traditions, notably those that are nature-based or woman-centred, approach the category of Otherness from a unique perspective. In these traditions alterity is either positively reclaimed as a special transformative characteristic (Finley, 1991, p.358; Goldenberg, 1988, pp.139–140) or considered an inherent, natural and valuable part of the cultural pattern (Roscoe, 1987, p.77; Grahn, 1987, pp.4–6).

The relationship of the archetype of the androgyne to figures in myth and history has become a spiritual imperative for many Radical Faeries seeking a tradition to reclaim:

> The role of the fool, the trickster, the contrary one capable of turning a situation inside out, is one of the most enduring of all archetypes. Often cross-dressed or adorned with both masculine and feminine symbols, these merry pranksters chase through history, holding up a looking glass to human folly. Confidants to kings and commoners, tellers of truths, and cloaked in many disguises, these queer figures seem to spring from the shadow realm that lies between the worlds of above and below. (Thompson, 1987, p.52)

One source for the archetype of the androgyne in relation to gay spirituality can be located in the *berdache* tradition (Williams, 1986). These gender-variant men and women were found in tribal groups throughout North America, were well known for cross-dressing and participating in same-sex relationships, and often took on the mantle of shaman for the tribe (Lutes, 2000, p.114). However, unless the person using it for spiritual inspiration is a Native American, the *berdache* as a symbol of androgyny is somewhat remote. A figure whose symbolism hits closer to home for most gay men is, ironically enough, to be found in the urban nightclub. The image of the androgyne is a familiar one to contemporary gay men. Anyone who visits a gay nightclub is presented with myriad androgynous images, from the confronting stereotype of the brassy drag queen, to the lithe gender-neutral figures gyrating in sexless ambiguity on the dance floor.

The drag queen, the image of the glamorous cross-dressing male, is a modern embodiment of the androgyne figure – a figure firmly grounded in the realm of gender politics. Drag queens precipitated and led the Stonewall Rebellion in Greenwich Village on twenty eight of June 1969, a key event in the movement towards gay and lesbian liberation. The politics of 'drag' as a force for social change is self-evident: it has been the site of activism in part because it is activism in sight (Garber, 1992, p.159). By publicly confronting gay men, as well as society at large, with the image of the androgyne, drag queens take on the mantle of modern shamans – walkers between the worlds (Thompson, 1987, pp.59–60). If shamans from primal cultures mediate between the physical and the spiritual realms, drag queens mediate between the physical and political worlds. They make us think about gender variance by their very (obvious) presence. There is also often a sense of divinity about drag queens. The manner in which they bridge genders suggests communion with otherworldly, fantastic, spiritual realms. Their use of copious amounts of glitter and bold, brassy colours, coupled with their 'royal' sensibility, led drag queens to be considered divine and known as angels of light and children of paradise (Thompson, 1987, p.57).

The Radical Faerie movement brings the political and spiritual impetus of the androgynous drag queen and the *berdache* into the new millennium. In seeking to define a gay spirituality which allows the expression of what they perceive to be a 'gay window on the world', Radical Faeries recognize the power the androgyne archetype has to articulate gay spirituality. Much of this power relates to its constantly challenging accepted models of behaviour that are ingrained in mainstream society. The Faeries see that one of the important societal roles they have is to actualize that challenge:

> One of the powerful aspects of doing drag is that it jolts people out of the mindset of 'this is how people are supposed to be.' We as Radical Faeries have a lot to offer our society by jolting them in just that way. (Anonymous in Roques, 1992)

'Doing drag' is also seen by Radical Faeries as a means of personal transformation, a technique for liberating hidden parts of the self that, by being hidden, are impediments to spiritual wisdom:

> In putting on drag, you identify with it, becoming an actor, and you let out a part of yourself that you have been trying to hide. You become a shaman, identifying with that invisible world within you where the boundaries blur and flow together... (Polyandron, 1985, p.26)

From the Bottom of the Garden – The Birth of the Radical Faeries

I remember being told, when I was young, that faeries lived at the bottom of the garden. I would go out and sit among the flowers, hoping to catch a glimpse of tiny winged figures, or I would search the limbs of the camphor laurel for tricksy faces and playful sprites. I knew that faeries were shy and very good at hiding, so when I did not see them, I thought they were just avoiding the dragonflies and other fearsome, winged neighbours. Or what if that bumblebee was a faerie in disguise? Maybe if I sat very still and cultivated an air of quiet acceptance, they would come out to play. I like to think of the birth of the Radical Faeries along these lines: we have always been here, well camouflaged amongst our fellow inhabitants of the Garden.

Although the term 'Radical Faerie' appeared in print for the first time in the summer 1979 edition of the magazine *RFD: A Country Journal for Gay Men*

Everywhere, the movement toward the formation of a group seeking a locus for a distinctly queer spirituality had already been building for several years. The culmination of this search was a short article in *RFD* #20 entitled 'A Call to Gay Brothers: A Spiritual Conference for Radical Faeries' – the first ever notice for a Radical Faerie conference. In the article, Harry Hay and Don Kilhefner (1979, p.20) articulated the recently awakened search for gay enspiritment as follows:

> It's in the air. Heard everywhere. At the World Symposium on Humanity, the talk is about 'New Age Politics' – beyond Left and Right – a synthesis of the political and spiritual movements of the past two decades... Does all of this political/spiritual ferment have any relevance to gay men? Is there a gay vision of New Age society? Is a 'paradigm shift' also manifesting itself? The answer to all these questions is: YES!

The synthesis of these ideas of gay spirit and political ferment began in earnest in 1976. Simultaneously several people put forth their ideas in manifestos. Arthur Evans was conducting research into the relationship between pagan traditions, gay lifestyles and radical politics, and had started a 'faery circle' of gay men in San Francisco (Timmons, 1990, p.252). Harry Hay at the same time conceived of a fundamental concept of gay spirituality: 'subject-SUBJECT consciousness'. Mitch Walker, a psychologist in the neo-Jungian tradition, had contact with both Hay and Evans and was working on similar ideas of gay enspiritment: 'I work with the spirit and I'm a gay spirit worker and I'm a gay shaman and that's what I do' (Walker, in Timmons, 1990, p.259). But it was the publication of 'A Call to Gay Brothers' in *RFD* #20 that consolidated these different threads into a recognizable pattern. The resultant fabric could be given the name of Radical Faeries. The conference was held on the Labor Day weekend (31 August to 2 September) of 1979 at Desert Sanctuary, a gay-friendly retreat in the middle of the Arizona desert. Nearly 200 people made their way there from all over the United States. They discussed spirituality in circle groups, engaged in mud rituals, and built sweat lodges, to explore visions of what it means to be gay and spiritual. The agenda suggested by the four main organizers – Harry Hay, John Burnside, Don Kilhefner and Mitch Walker – focussed on a combination of politics and spirituality within the overriding context of gay perceptions and experiences. Already the pagan was being linked to the political.

Homo Faeriensis Radicalis – Who Are We?

What is a Radical Faerie? What are the defining parameters for inclusion under such a title, and who gets to decide them? These were questions I took into the field with me when in 1995 I went to Short Mountain Sanctuary, a Radical Faerie community in rural Tennessee. Naively, I arrived there thinking that I would be able to come back home with my field notes and interviews and go about the process of constructing a usable definition. Surely there must be a set of

characteristics which, when listed, could be used as a checklist for Radical
Faeriehood, such as:

- has neo-pagan beliefs
- wears drag
- is strictly vegetarian
- has activist ethos
- is queer community-oriented
- is proficient in the ritual use of polyester
- was Judy Garland in a past life.

I was dissuaded of my presuppositions, however, early on in the fieldwork
process. Almost everyone that I asked for a definition of Faeries baulked at the
question. 'You can't define Faeries,' they said. 'We just are! Don't even attempt it.
If you ask three people for a definition of what a Radical Faerie is, you'll end up
with five different answers'. I ended up with a lot of definitions...

How then to approach the subject of defining Radical Faeries? I will say here
at the outset: it is not possible. I do not believe that there is any way to give a hard
and fast definition of Radical Faeries. There are several reasons for this. First and
foremost is the fact that the definitions that I did receive were extremely varied and
often contradicted one another. Faeries, as Cohen (1991, pp.88–89) suggests of gay
groups generally, seem to have deliberately incorporated self-contradiction into the
processes of their political self-transformation and have consequently avoided the
pitfalls of fragmentation that occur when identity is 'fixed'.

Secondly, a significant number of the informants considered the process of
'labelling' offensive, unproductive, or even nonsensical. These people wanted to
talk, not about being 'Radical Faeries' (noun), but about becoming 'radical faerie-
ish' (adjective). They did not want to be pigeon-holed under a category called
'Radical Faerie' but saw themselves as having qualities of a Radical Faerie nature.
For them, nouns describe concrete entities, adjectives describe intentions and
possibility. The former is restrictive, the latter expansive. Here are three examples
of this idea, recorded from interviews conducted at Short Mountain Sanctuary:

> **Delilah**: nouns are really dangerous. Nouns, when you call something
> something, it stops being something that mirrors you and reflects you and
> which you have an intimate relationship with, and becomes something
> that's distant from you. (Delilah, 1995)

> **Khrysso**: there's a difference between a noun and an adjective and nouns
> label, adjectives describe and I am many things and I'm not limited by any
> of the things that describe them, whereas I might be limited by a label
> which is put on them. (Khrysso, 1995)

> **Robin**: I wouldn't call myself a Faerie.

Willow: that's what I was going to ask you. Like you said before that you don't consider yourself a Faerie, but you like the use of Faerie as an adjective.

Robin: yeah, there are ways in which I'm faerie-ish.

Willow: aha.

Robin: but I don't know what it means to be a Faerie. (Robin, 1995)

Frogskins and Faerie Princes – Early Conceptions of the Radical Faerie

Earlier we saw that the term Radical Faerie was reported to have been first coined by Harry Hay at the 1979 'Spiritual Conference for Radical Faeries' in Arizona. What was the attraction of using these two terms together? An examination of some of the meanings of 'radical' and 'faerie' can give an introductory understanding to the sense of identity that arises when the two terms are juxtaposed.

The use of 'radical' has two main implications. It suggests a state of being concerned with fundamental issues, indeed of things at the root level, but also of something or someone politically extreme. 'Faerie' also has a double-barrelled meaning: a nearly universal and powerful mythological figure, and a derogatory name applied to gay men by heterosexuals. It would seem that Harry Hay, in suggesting a conjunction of these two words, saw the identity of Faeries as an inextricable combination of revolutionary politics, magic, and, at its root, membership in a queer spiritual tribe (Timmons, 1990, pp.250–251). Hay, and his partner John Burnside, have both been integral to the development of the original concept of what they call Radical Faerie consciousness – the state of being a Faerie – and the worldview inherent in the assumption of this identity.

Another person who has contributed to the development of the concept of Faeries is Arthur Evans. A year before the first Faerie Gathering in Arizona, Evans had published his book *Witchcraft and the Gay Counterculture* (Evans, 1978) in which he put forward an alternative history of gay and lesbian spiritual traditions. In a strange synchronicity, he was working on the connections between gay men and the European faerie tradition at the same time as Hay and Burnside were developing their own, similar ideas about Faeries.

Early definitions of Faerie concentrated on delimiting the Faerie 'essence'. What are those characteristics that can draw us together as a community? What are the ties that bind? Hay, at the Arizona conference, talked of 'peeling off the ugly green frogskins of hetero-conformity to reveal the faerie prince underneath'. He was challenging us as a tribe to emerge into the light and take on our own identity, an identity that we as queer people are responsible for recognizing and developing according to our individual interpretations.

Contents of the Handbag – Faerie Core Expressions

While it is impossible to describe every belief and practice of the Radical Faeries that I encountered in my fieldwork, certain fundamental core expressions did become evident. The first is the concept of the Circle: faeries use a circular meeting as a way of interacting with each other. These Circles can be held at a regular time, such as the Dinner Circle when Faeries meet to share food; they can be held for a specific reason, such as a Planning Circle to plan a ritual; and they can be held as a way of identifying a particular group, such as The New York Faerie Circle. At Gatherings, Faeries send out a cry of 'YOOOO–HOOOO' and meet in Heart Circles which are a form of psychotherapy where Faeries listen to one another; a talisman is passed around the Circle and people have the opportunity to share their feelings, frustrations, dreams and desires.

Why are Circles so important to Faeries? I believe Faerie Circles have become a ritual form of unification and fellowship for a group that has diverse interests and agendas. As Cheal (1992, p.369) suggests, these ritual events validate the subjective and intersubjective meanings held by members of a group, and as such reinforce the group's solidarity.

Another core concept is that of Queer Community. In major cities, Circles of Faeries meet, usually monthly (at the full moon), either for Gatherettes (social teas) or at specific ritual times (Beltaine, Samhain, etc.) that are structurally similar to the Wiccan coven. In rural areas, Faerie Sanctuaries provide places for Faeries to live in community. There are over ten major Faerie Sanctuaries in the United States and Canada. Sanctuaries are usually open to anyone who wants to visit. Each is a haven, a safe queer space away from mainstream culture. A Sanctuary is usually owned by a body corporate or has a multiple-occupancy type structure. One Faerie Sanctuary, Wolf Creek in Oregon, applied for and was granted tax exemption on the grounds that 'Radical Faeries' was a religious organization. Residents of Sanctuaries host Gatherings, usually at solstices and equinoxes. Faeries speak of Gatherings as times when they recharge their Faerie batteries before going back to the city.

As O'Donovan (1999b, p.140) reports, Faeries have 'a paradoxically anarchist and communal utopian eschatology.' To convey a sense of this fearsome juxtaposition which characterizes Faerie community (or the cultural geography of Faerie), I include a page from my journal describing my first impressions of the Beltaine Gathering at Short Mountain Sanctuary in 1995:

> I wander in amazement through the woods. The Faeries have arrived and begun the process of transformation of place. The Faerie presence is widespread through the property. Some have opted for accessibility, being located right on the roadways that snake through the sanctuary. Already certain distinctions can be made regarding the 'feel' of certain areas. Almost like Faerie suburbs springing up, mushroom-like, after a heavy fall of glitter rain.

To begin with my own campsite. I am camped in the Yurt Yard, quite near James and Jombi's dwelling. My tent overlooks a beautiful creek gully. People are packing in here quite tightly. It is a prime site, being located very close to the fire pit, knoll and the pavilion. These are the main meeting places during the day. Not much decoration of tents – sort of like an upper-middle-class suburb. Building close to the shops for convenience.

Down the hill along a narrow path is 'Sodomy Acres'. This is where the self-designated 'bad Faeries' live. Last night there was a really loud party involving disco, drugs and lots of junk food. It is still close to 'Faerie Central', but far enough into the woods to be shady and uncrowded.

The back field is a third area. A few tents in amongst the flower beds. It is quiet and very beautiful. Popular with the banana-lounge set – a place for quiet repose.

Wandering along the road out to Chestnut Ridge, the campsites get more diverse and individualistic. Here is a young Faerie winding miles of organza ribbon around the trees surrounding his dome tent. Next door is someone seriously into ritual, setting up a vast collection of bones, images, piles of rocks, Nepalese prayer flags and some polythene tape which says 'Queer Safe Space' surrounding the site. Further along there are some large canvas tents – one that is being slept in, the other is a walk in wardrobe, containing racks of dresses and accessories.

Out along Halloween Ridge are some Faeries that I don't see much around the 'shops'. There is a firepit here and people are a long way from the centre of activity. I've heard that an alternate drumming circle happens each night around this fire.

The other major residential domain is 'The Brothel'. Situated on the top floor of the barn, this is where the Faeries who don't own tents sleep. Curtains surround mouldy old double-mattresses. Very hareem feel... I slept there a couple of nights. The place is aptly named – there is no privacy, and sounds of people having sex come thick and fast. It is hell to wake up to in the morning – hot and steamy (no insulation in the roof) and the fucking rooster is loud and totally without a sense of timing.

It is amazing to see what Faeries manage to trundle in for the duration of the gathering. The Rubber Maids work overtime – people pushing carts loaded high with clothes, ritual objects, drums, mattresses, statues of Eros, eskies of booze. And of course, there is Pinky's Winnebago with built in television, video, and spa bath, but that deserves a separate page...

A third core component of the Faerie Handbag is the concept of Queer Spirit. Writers such as Hay (1987, pp.285–291), Walker (1987, pp.222–225), and Burnside (1989, pp.15 20), suggest that the concept of subject-SUBJECT consciousness is a fundamental defining principle of queer spirituality. It has its basis in the notion that gay people experience and relate to the world in a fundamentally unique way. Hay proposes that subject-SUBJECT consciousness is:

> ...inherent to all gay people, arising from the egalitarian bond of love and sex between two similars... (and) pervade(s) all the relationships of a gay person – even the relationships with things not human, such as nature, craftsmanship, or ideals. 'Humanity must expand its experience of thinking of another not as object – to be used, to be manipulated, to be mastered, to be CONSUMED – but as subject – as another like him/her self, another self to be respected, to be appreciated, to be cherished'. (Timmons, 1990, p.255)

The Radical Faerie experience of spirituality, then, is intimately tied up with this subject–SUBJECT perception of the world. We, as shamans, pagans, and practitioners of Wiccan and Goddess traditions hold a reverence for the earth as a fundamental principle. The earth is perceived as being a part of each and every one of us, and the divine essence that is expressed as the Mother, Gaia, or the Goddess, is imbued in every individual. Only through respect for, and healing of, the earth can a sustainable future be envisaged. This is very much a queer version of the concept of immanence as expressed by many Neo-Pagans (O'Donovan, 1999a, pp.69–70; Starhawk, 1987, pp.16–17).

A final Faerie core concept is the practice of spontaneous ritual. As Berger (1995, p.49) notes, spontaneity and creativity are central to many expressions of religious behaviour among Neo-Pagans. The Radical Faeries are no exception. Faeries do not need an excuse to drop everything and co-create a ritual for a particular purpose. I witnessed and took part in many rituals that were mainly thought up and executed in a playfully serious frame of mind. At Amber Fox Sanctuary, a Radical Faerie Sanctuary in Ontario, Canada, we dressed in red, danced, and played music to bless the cherry grove – celebrating its beauty of blossom and fruitful bounty. At Short Mountain Sanctuary, a group of five of us, after fixing the community's damaged spring-fed water-collection system, spontaneously evoked guardian spirits to protect it in the future from marauding horse riders.

It is important to understand that Faerie Handbags – those mix-and-match holdalls of Faerie culture – are very personal objects. Every Faerie Handbag is unique. A fair measure of eclecticism goes into the choice of contents. For example, in mine (a very attractive organza quilted number with diamante beadwork), I have lots and lots of queer spirit concepts, numerous spontaneous ritual practices, a practical bundle of self-sufficiency and community-lifestyle ideas, and a thoughtful sprinkling of eco-politics. But for some Faeries, this handbag might be too heavy (one Faerie I know has a practical little hemp number that only contains queer community concepts) or too light ('Where, oh where are the pockets for the queer politics demonstrations, emergency drag outfits, Queer God Cologne, and the hardback copy of the Lonely Planet Guide to *Faerie Gatherings around the World*?').

Out into the World Anew – Always Becoming Faerie

The purpose of this piece was to introduce some aspects of Faerie. I have tried to do this in a way that precludes people from finishing this section and thinking to themselves, 'Oh, I know what Radical Faeries are now.' A description of identity based on definitions will never work for the Faeries. Rather, Faeries should be thought of as 'becoming', not 'being'. Let me finish with a perceptive musing on gay identity by Michel Foucault. It could very well serve as a summation of the process of *becoming* a Radical Faerie:

We must be aware of…the tendency to reduce being gay to the questions: 'Who am I?' 'What is the secret of my desire?' Might it not be better if we asked ourselves what sort of relationships we can set up, invent, multiply or modify through our homosexuality? The problem is not trying to find out the truth of one's sexuality within oneself, but rather, nowadays, trying to use our sexuality to achieve a variety of different types of relationships. And this is why homosexuality is probably not a form of desire, but something to be desired. We must therefore insist on becoming gay, rather than persisting in defining ourselves as such. (Foucault, 1984, p.385)

Now we have come full circle, albeit in queer and crooked manner. The circle was grounded with the *Earthy* origins of Faerie inspiration across past cultures. The *Airy* absences of Otherness and marginalization have provided a space for Faerie to expand into the vacuum. Faerie has been informed by the *Fiery* challenges of politicization and sparked into activism by community ideology. Beliefs, practices, and spiritual content wash though Faerie in *Watery* mutability. Binding these elements in a process of continuous reinvention is the synthesizing force of the fifth and crucial Faerie element, *Polyester*. The spirit of the circle is queered and the process of always becoming Faerie continues.

Note

1   This project would not have been possible without the help of many people. My thanks go out to: Lynne Hume for initial encouragement and criticism; all the Radical Faeries who shared their lives and homes with me during my fieldwork, especially the residents of Short Mountain Sanctuary and Amber Fox Sanctuary; CJ for the road trip of a life-time; Delilah for 're-membering' the Fifth Faerie Element; Jim Arachne for inspirational Faerie Path telephone confabs (requiring that protective Ginko tea!); and Simon Scholfield for wonderfully Dragonish critical editing and transformation of the text at the eleventh hour. Bright Blessings all.

References

Adler, M. (1986), *Drawing Down the Moon – Witches, Druids, Goddess-Worshippers, and Other Pagans in America Today*, Beacon Press, Boston.

Berger, H. (1995), 'The Routinization of Spontaneity', *Sociology of Religion*, vol. 56, no.1, pp.49–61.

Burnside, J. (1989), *Who are the Gay People?: and other essays*, Vortex Media, San Francisco.

Cheal, D. (1992), 'Ritual: Communication in Action', *Sociological Analysis*, vol. 53, no.4, pp.365–374.

Cohen, E. (1991), Who Are 'We'? Gay 'Identity' as Political (E)motion', in D. Fuss (ed.), *Inside/Out – Lesbian Theories, Gay Theories*, Routledge, New York, pp.71–91.

Conner, R. (1993), *Blossom of Bone – Reclaiming the Connections between Homoeroticism and the Sacred*, HarperSanFrancisco, San Francisco.

Delilah (1995), Open-ended interview recorded with author at Short Mountain Sanctuary.

Evans, A. (1978), *Witchcraft and the Gay Counterculture*, Fag Rag Books, Boston.

Fey, W. (2000), 'Radical Faeries', in G. E. Haggerty (ed.), *The Encyclopedia of Lesbian and Gay Histories and Cultures Volume II*, Garland Publishing, New York, p.732.

Finley, N.J. (1991), 'Political Activism and Feminist Spirituality', *Sociological Analysis*, vol. 52, no.4, pp.349–362.

Foucault, M. (1984), 'Polemics, Politics, and Problematizations: An Interview with Michel Foucault', in P. Rabinow (ed.), *The Foucault Reader*, Pantheon, New York, pp.381–390.

Garber, M. (1992), *Vested Interests: Cross Dressing and Cultural Anxiety*, Routledge, New York.

Gearhart, S. and Johnson, W. R. (eds.), (1974), *Loving Women/Loving Men: Gay Liberation and the Church*, Glide Publications, San Francisco.

Goldenberg, N. R. (1988), 'Stepping Out of the Circle: Overcoming Tribal Boundaries', in. L. J. Hammann, H. M. Buck and M. McTighe (eds), *Religious Traditions and the Limits of Tolerance*, Anima Books, Cahmbersberg, PA, pp.135–142.

Grahn, J. (1987), 'Flaming Without Burning: Some of the Roles of Gay People in Society', in M. Thompson (ed.), *Gay Spirit: Myth and Meaning*, St. Martin's Press, New York, pp.3–9.

Hay, H. (1987), 'A Separate People whose Time Has Come', in M. Thompson (ed.), *Gay Spirit: Myth and Meaning*, St. Martin's Press, New York, pp.279–291.

___(1995), 'Reinventing Ourselves', in M. Thompson (ed.), *Gay Soul: Finding the Heart of Gay Spirit and Nature*, HarperCollins, San Francisco, pp.79–96.

Hay, H., and J. Kilhefner (1979), 'A Call To Gay Brothers: A Spiritual Conference For Radical Faeries', *RFD*, vol. 20, p.20.

Khrysso, (1995), Open-ended interview recorded with author at Short Mountain Sanctuary.

Lutes, M. A. (2000), 'Berdache', in G. E. Haggerty (ed.), *The Encyclopedia of Lesbian and Gay Histories and Cultures, Volume I*, Garland Publishing, New York, p.114.

Norman, S. (1991), 'I am the leatherfaerie shaman', in M. Thompson (ed.), *Leatherfolk – Radical Sex, People, Politics, and Practice*, Alyson Publications, Boston, pp.276–283.

O'Donovan, C. (1999a), 'Ecce Homo: Ruminations on a Theory of my Queer Body', in C. Lake (ed.), *Recreations: Religion and Spirituality in the Lives of Queer People*, Queer Press, Toronto, pp.69–70.

___(1999b), 'My Journeys into Faerie and What I Found There', in C. Lake (ed.), *Recreations: Religion and Spirituality in the Lives of Queer People*, Queer Press, Toronto, pp.140–142.

Polyandron, H. (1985), 'Spirit in Drag', *RFD*, vol. 43, p.26.

Robin (1995), Open-ended interview recorded with author at Short Mountain Sanctuary.

Roscoe, W. (1987), 'Living the Tradition: Gay American Indians', in M. Thompson (ed.), *Gay Spirit: Myth and Meaning*, St. Martin's Press, New York. pp.69–77.

Roques, P. (director/editor), (1992), *Faerie Tales*, Video recording. Stanford University: Department of Communication.

Starhawk, (1987), *Truth or Dare: Encounters with Power, Authority and* Mystery, Harper and Row, San Francisco.

Thompson, M. (1987), 'Children of Paradise: A Brief History of Queens', in M. Thompson (ed.), *Gay Spirit: Myth and Meaning*, St. Martin's Press, New York, pp.49–68.

___(1995), *Gay Soul: Finding the Heart of Gay Spirit and Nature*, HarperCollins, San Francisco.

Timmons, S. (1990), *The Trouble With Harry Hay: Founder of the Modern Gay Movement*, Alyson Publications, Boston.

Walker, M. (1987), 'Visionary Love: The Magical Gay Spirit-Power', in M. Thompson (ed.), *Gay Spirit: Myth and Meaning*, St. Martin's Press, New York, pp.279–291.

Williams, W. L. (1986), *The Spirit and the Flesh: Sexual Diversity in American Indian Culture*, Beacon Press, Boston.

Chapter 11

Drumming and Re-enchantment: Creating Spiritual Community

Tanice G. Foltz

In a weekend frame drum workshop at a beautiful spiritual retreat in the Ozark Mountains, USA, Layne Redmond, master frame drummer, presents a guided visualization to a group of participants. She plays her frame drum as, rhythmically, she speaks:

> The walking and breathing meditation practice we are about to do
> Is a profound way of synchronizing mind and body
> By connecting to the energies of heaven and earth
> Our bodies are expressions of energetic fields of vibrations
> From the pulse of our hearts, to the rhythms of our breathing, to the patterns of our speech
> We are truly rhythmic beings
> We are conceived to the pulse of our mother's blood and born into a rhythmic world
> We are influenced continually by the cycles of the celestial bodies of the sun, the moon, and the stars
> And although we can never extricate ourselves from this web of rhythms,
> Many of us find that the rhythm of our modern lives is unconnected to the rhythms of nature and we feel a deep yearning to be in rhythm once again.
> ('Being in Rhythm', 1997)

During the course of the visualization she takes the group deeper. The content is meditative, trance inducing, and deeply spiritual. Her rhythmical chant continues, 'We begin by standing and walking in place. Walking on two legs is the basic pulse of being human. (pause) Step, step, step, step'. She encourages the group to step in time together as they breathe in and breathe out on the count of four. Participants synchronize their breathing and stepping for the duration, and at the end of the practice Redmond stresses the importance of rhythm in the creation of community. That night she presents a slide show of ancient goddesses and temple friezes of women holding frame drums. She explains that in prehistoric times, women were the spiritual mediators, the ones who communicated with the gods and who held a special status and power through their drumming. She integrates the spiritual history of drumming into every class she teaches and often includes slides she has made while researching the history of the frame drum and its relationship to the divine. She shares her view of the drum, 'Its voice inspires instant communion with everyone who hears it. I am convinced that the new drumming phenomenon answers a deep cultural need to re-establish our rhythmic links with nature and with one another' (Redmond, 1997, p.3).

Yet another type of spiritual drumming is happening on America's West Coast at a Catholic convent, where a group of people from California, Canada and the Midwest gather for Arthur Hull's weekend Drum Circle Facilitators' (DCF) Playshop™.[1] Hull is known worldwide as the 'father' of the drum circle movement. His focus is not on teaching people to play drums, but rather on guiding them to develop their rhythmic potential. Upon entering the Playshop one encounters a circle of people aged fourteen to sixty-five gleefully playing drums and percussion. What may not be so immediately apparent is that they are also learning to develop their awareness, spirituality and leadership skills through Hull's deft, charismatic facilitation and instruction. Drawing upon the philosophy of his recently deceased West African friend, world-renowned percussionist Babatunde Olatunji, Hull claims to be a 'rhythm evangelist' whose mission is to spread 'rhythmaculture' around the world. His business, Village Music Circles™, offers a variety of programs 'that use rhythm to explore and inspire community building while facilitating human potential'. His 2003 brochure begins:

> Now, more than ever, we find ourselves seeking ways to build community with an intention to serve, to inspire and to reach beyond what separates us. Playing music together puts us in touch with the creative force that directly connects with our humanity.

His training programs are directed towards those who intend to develop their facilitation skills in service to their communities (Hull, 1998, p.37). This orientation is evidenced by his own work: he facilitates team-building for corporations, offers programs for troubled adolescents, and is on the Board of Advisors for a violence-prevention programme. He mentors budding facilitators through weekend and week-long training programs in the United States, the United Kingdom, Germany and Sweden. His trainees work with a variety of groups such as autistic children, 'at-risk' teens, the elderly patients with Alzheimer's, and the mentally challenged.

The drum workshops of Redmond and Hull are just two of hundreds that are flowering throughout the United States alone. Drumming is reclaiming its time-honoured status as well as its function in traditional cultures as a community activity that creates a spiritual bond among its practitioners. Dating from the earliest recorded history, from Africa and the Middle East to Mongolia and pre-Columbian America, drumming has been used to mark life transitions (birth, sexual maturity, marriage and death), to serve as a consciousness-altering tool for healing and religious ceremonies, and to create solidarity in preparation for war

(McNeill, 1995). Rhythm-making continues to play a part in religious ceremonies today: the American Black Church features joyful tambourine-playing, Native American drummers hold the steady sound of a heartbeat, and contemporary Pagan drummers raise energy under the full moon while trance-dancers flow to their rhythms. Clearly, a spiritual community of drummers is developing around the world, and they are involved in the process of re-enchantment, whether they know it or not.

Modernity, Post-modernity and Re-enchantment

In the nineteenth century Max Weber feared that rationalization would result in the secularization of modern society, to the extent that religion would be so removed from modern culture that it would lead to a 'disenchantment of the world' (in Lyon, 2000, p.26). As recently as the late 1960s the secularization hypothesis was still influential, and Peter Berger suggested that it would extend to a 'secularization of consciousness' in which religion 'would not be a major instrument of self-knowing and decision making' (1967, p.107). This did not come to pass, however, as Robert Ellwood observes:

> By every rubric of secularist common sense, as science and affluence advanced, religion ought to have declined, yet it was quite evident that this was not happening as predicted and furthermore that . . . new and stranger forms of religion – for example, Timothy Leary's – were arising to take its place. . . . As I see it, Sixties secularization thought and its religious concomitants were actually the last phases of modernism. . . But the Sixties also saw the first great breakthrough of postmodern radical pluralism, in religion above all, as it ripped modernism's seamless robe apart from within. (1994, pp.123–4)

A radical pluralism indeed. The Sixties decade brought an anti-establishment and anti-Vietnam War focus, as well as a striving for racial justice, women's equality and students' free speech. Some churches practised social activism through 'liberation theology', and myriad 'new' Eastern religions were imported to the United States, with hippies and middle-class youth becoming their most avid followers. For many the emphasis on individualized religion and 'the spiritual growth of individuals' replaced institutionalized religion (Roof, 1999, p.64). Individuals were encouraged to find their own religious or spiritual authority through [personal] experience. Thus, instead of having encouraged secularization, Ellwood (1994, pp.19–20) views the Sixties as having brought the re-integration of religion into post-modern life:

> The Sixties did not so much secularize the sacred as *sacralized the secular*, turning its causes into crusades and its activism into liturgies, with their initiatory ordeals and their benedictions at the end . . . Of equal interest is the way in which even the secular wing of the Sixties placed the same virtually religious emphasis on symbol, gesture,

language, and community. The whole, in other words, amounted to a new spiritual awakening . . .

Other scholars agree. David Lyon (2000) addresses post-modernity and its relationship to religion and finds widespread attempts at religious and spiritual re-enchantment in the late twentieth century. He observes that 'subterranean theologies' have taken the form of 'unconventional practices, beliefs and spiritualities,' including astrology, the New Age and 'women-friendly religiosities such as Wicca' (2000, p.34). A multitude of spiritual and religious forms continue to flourish in the postmodern world, many of which emphasize a connection between mind, body and spirit as well as the empowerment of self and others.

I contend that the modern day drumming phenomenon can be viewed as a tool for spiritual re-enchantment as it evokes what Victor Turner calls *communitas:* 'a direct, immediate and total confrontation of human identities, a deep. . .style of personal interaction. It has something "magical" about it' (1982, pp.47–48). *Communitas* can be understood in relation to Turner's notions of 'structure' and 'anti-structure'. Whereas 'structure' includes the social relationships that people are expected to fulfill in everyday life, 'anti-structure' encompasses both 'liminality' and *communitas*. For Turner, 'Liminal entities are neither here nor there, they exist betwixt and between the positions assigned' (1982, p.95). When people step out of their normal social structures, statuses, roles and relationships and into liminality, it is 'a moment in time and out of time' (1969, p.96); they have entered into what he terms an 'instant of pure potentiality' (1982, p.44) that is transient and where anything is possible. This liminal state can give way to *communitas*, 'a spontaneously generated relationship between level and equal total and individuated human beings, stripped of structural attributes' (1974, p.202). *Communitas* can be felt as a bonding and sense of oneness among equals: 'when even two people believe that they experience unity, all people are felt by those two, even if only for a flash, to be one' (1982, p.47). Turner's concept of *communitas* can aptly be applied to what is experienced by those who drum. Drumming levels out differences, engenders altered states of consciousness,[2] and brings people together in abandoned play, where participants feel as though they are part of a single entity engaged in a unique creative experience that can never be repeated. Thus drumming is a form of spirituality wherein participants can heal the self, create community, and even transform society through their re-enchantment of the secular world.

The Call of the Drum: Research and Personal Interest

Although the drum has always been an essential part of jazz, swing, blues and rock, the 1950s and 1960s brought increased attention to drums when America's 'Beat' generation gathered in smoke-filled coffee houses to reflect upon poetry recited to the sharp accent of bongos. As a starving university student, I served coffee and cider in a coffee house such as this and revelled in the atmosphere. In the 1960s and 1970s, hippies and dropouts surrounded conga drummers who pounded out driving rhythms on college campuses and in parks while 'hippie chicks' like myself trance-danced to the beat. By the 1980s, shamanistic drumming became part of the New Age movement with the publication of Michael Harner's book, *The Way of the Shaman* (1980), which encouraged contemporary spiritual seekers to listen to methodical drumming to meet their 'spirit guides' and take away valuable insights (Foltz, 2000a). Although I found this attractive and tried it as part of my early research on holistic healing modalities, it only gave me a pounding headache. Since the 1960s, drum circles have taken on central significance as 'the heartbeat' at Pagan retreats and music festivals (Pike, 2002, p.183), which I explored as part of my research on Goddess spirituality in the early 1990s (see Foltz, 2000b). Traditionally, drumming in the United States has been male dominated, and Robert Bly showcased drumming as a way for men to get in touch with their masculinity and 'primal' selves (1992). However, in the last two decades, as evidenced by women's music festivals and drumming retreats, women have begun to teach and study drumming in greater numbers (Foltz, 2003, 2004; Hill, 2001; Childs-Helton, 2003). Social drumming is approaching a status that is no longer reserved for the deviant; in fact an article in *The Economist* titled 'Rhythm Goes Respectable' showcased a female drum circle facilitator and her 'orchestra' at Chicago's Rhythm club in May 2003.

My interest in studying drumming was kindled after attending Layne Redmond's weekend workshop and Ubaka Hill's drum intensive at a music festival, both during summer 1996. I took up drumming for fun and found it to be a valuable grieving resource when my parents died. I didn't consider studying drumming as a sociological phenomenon until December 1999, after having surgery that left me unable to walk for several months. Layne Redmond had sent an announcement for her six-month course in frame drumming called *Giving Birth to Ourselves* (GBTO). The flyer explained that the frame drum, hoop-shaped and with a head larger in diameter than the body, is often used for trance and ritual. The course would have a spiritual orientation, focusing on goddesses and drumming priestesses from ancient times. As the venue was only a three-hour drive away, I took the opportunity to conduct research and to seriously study drumming as a spiritual practice. I engaged in participant observation at Cybele's, a Midwestern spiritual drum retreat, during the summers of 2000 and 2001. Redmond taught the history of frame drums, as well as how to play the drum as a ceremonial instrument to induce trance. The program gave me access to over 30 students, many of whom I interviewed.

In summer 2001, I continued the participant observation research in a week-long drum intensive with Ubaka Hill, master djembe drummer, at Diana's Grove, a spiritual retreat in the Ozarks. There, during training that ran six hours a day, I learned to play the djembe, a large, heavy wooden goblet-shaped drum with a goatskin head. Playing this drum involved an entirely different 'stroke' system – a different language – and it had a qualitatively different 'feel.' Participants in the workshop completed my survey questionnaire or consented to in-depth interviews. In January 2002, I attended Arthur Hull's weekend Drum Circle Facilitators' (DCF) Playshop™[3] in California, and in summer 2003 his weeklong Hawaii DCF training; the latter attracted drum enthusiasts from eight countries, many of whom consented to interviews. In teaching their classes, all of these drum masters, Redmond, Hill and Hull, drew upon a deeply spiritual foundation that included drummers and ancestors who came long before them. This chapter highlights the themes of re-enchantment that surfaced in my interviews with drummers from each of these settings.

Connection, Community and Spirituality

In his research on the history of drill and dancing, William McNeill develops the argument that 'keeping in time together' (also the title of his book) creates a singularity of group purpose that has been instrumental in human evolution (1995, pp.12–35). He suggests that keeping in time through any rhythmic group activity contributes to social cohesion through what he calls 'muscular bonding': 'the euphoric fellow feeling that prolonged and rhythmic muscular movement arouses among nearly all participants in such exercises' (1995, p.3). This type of bonding increases solidarity among people, a solidarity that historically has been channelled into religious or healing ceremonies and war. McNeill reflects upon his own experience of marching to a drill as a young army recruit:

> Obviously, something visceral was at work; something, I later concluded, far older than language and critically important in human history, because the emotion it arouses constitutes an *indefinitely expansible basis for social cohesion* among any and every group that keeps together in time, moving big muscles together and chanting, singing, or shouting rhythmically. (McNeill, 1995, pp.2–3; my italics)

Drill is often accompanied by drumming as well as chanting, which assist recruits in keeping time. Both drumming and chanting can transport participants into a liminal phase that evolves into *communitas* due to the intense rhythmic focus. As Turner points out, 'individuals who interact with each other in the mode of spontaneous *communitas* become totally absorbed into a single synchronized fluid event' (1982, p.48).[4]   In my research, whether interviewees had played together in a one-hour drum circle, a weekend rhythm event, or had met regularly for years, the foremost theme they expressed was the sense of bonding and community they experienced through drumming. Teachers and students alike discussed the solidarity and cohesion that drumming together inspired. Barb Pitcher, co-owner of Cybele's spiritual drum retreat, describes her feelings about playing frame drums with others:

. . .there's the power of the drum and playing together . . .It's an ancient community feeling that comes through . . . there's a kind of spiritual 'wow' that comes with that group playing, when everybody's in the same groove and you see everybody just kind of tranced out. . . I don't know how to explain being part of a group, being part of the whole. Not being part of the 'I' but being part of the 'we.' . . . It's the bonding of passions. . . But there's something where the drum has spoken to your soul and to my soul and to her soul . . .so there's . . .that kind of community bonding that happens around this. (Barb, 6/22/01)

In discussing the trance state and the 'bonding of passions', Pitcher represents her sensory experiences using language that is spiritual. Her reference to being part of the 'we' rather than the 'I' brings to mind Buber's conceptualization (1958) of the '*I* and *Thou*', a relationship 'that arises in instant mutuality, when each person fully experiences the being of the other'; and the 'essential *We*', 'a highly potent mode of relationship between integral persons' (in Turner, 1969, pp.136–7). In another interview, a woman who is part of a djembe drum group talked about the effects of drumming, her words evoking the unique and transitory nature of *communitas*:

Yeah, it's a spiritual, emotional thing . . .it brings the energy together in a group of people . . . and I feel part of the whole, and it's a way to be bigger than I am, and be part of something and creating something . . .that is unique, that is only in that moment . . . it's magic, I guess that's what you'd call magic! (Night Owl,[5] 20/6/01)

This feeling is due to something drum teachers call *entrainment,* which, according to Health RHYTHMS™[6] music therapist Christine Stevens, 'happens when two people with separate rhythms can't help but join together in a common beat' (2003, p.14). Scholars have conducted physiological research on entrainment, but a discussion of their findings is beyond the scope of this chapter (see Mandell, 1980; Winkelman, 2000 and 2003 for further references). Redmond explains that drumming changes people's consciousness:

When a group of people play a rhythm for an extended period of time, their brain waves become entrained to the rhythm, and they have a shared brain wave state. The longer the drumming goes on, the more powerful the entrainment becomes. It's really the oldest holy communion. All of the oldest known religious rites used drumming as part of the shared religious experience'. (Quoted in Friedman, 2000, p.44)

The point is that drumming connects people in a profoundly powerful spiritual way.

Healing

Reconnection and Healing the Self

In addition to the strong sense of community, most participants discuss the personal spiritual experience that is engendered through the act of drumming. For instance, Medusa, a djembe teacher who has studied with a West African drum master, explains that drumming 'is the closest you can get spiritually to *the One or Essence of it all* . . . spiritually, it connects me to the core of things, it gives me perspective' (7/09/03). This theme is reiterated by other drummers such as Mickey Hart of the Grateful Dead. He suggests that people drum together in drum circles 'to share rhythm and get in tune with each other and themselves' (in Mattingly, 1995, p.16). The idea of 'getting in tune' implies that people in Western society are 'out of sync' or dissociated from the natural rhythms of their bodies and nature. This seems to be a common perception among drummers, many of whom see drumming as having a 'reconnecting' effect, both within the self and with the larger community. In fact Hart says that drumming is 'a form of practice like prayer, meditation or the martial arts' (in Mattingly, 1995, p.16). Indeed research shows that drumming produces 'enhanced theta and alpha wave entrainment', which, according to Winkelman, 'typifies general physiological affects of altered states of consciousness (ASC) and meditation' (2003, p.650). He adds that 'the physiological changes associated with altered states of consciousness assist not only in relaxation and healing, but also 'facilitate cognitive-emotional integration and social bonding and affiliation' (2003, p.650).

This theme of becoming reintegrated and whole through drumming was prominent in many interviews. Lipishau, an academic who named herself after the oldest known female historical figure who played a frame drum, reflects upon her personal experience:

> . . . one of the problems with being an academic is that it's very easy to stay in your head. . . drumming . . .on the frame drum . . . it's really helped heal that body-mind split.. . . I feel integrated now . . . I'm a whole person again, just like I was when I was a kid. (15/06/01)

An accomplished frame drum performer, Lipishau claims that drumming 'allows me to shut down the interior dialogue, which is very difficult for me. It's a form of body prayer. . . a celebration' (15/06/01).

Themes of 'letting go,' 'playing,' 'finding your inner child,' 'finding your voice,' and simply 'having fun' often appear in advertisements for adult drum workshops. In these settings, playing, forgetting about appearances, and *not* thinking are encouraged. In fact, students often hear 'don't think about it, just feel it!' from their drum instructors. Once a participant drops self-judgement and begins to experiment and get into a 'groove,' the door to healing possibilities opens.

Ubaka Hill, drum teacher, performer and founder of the DrumSong Institute,[7] discusses her view on the reconnecting, healing aspects of drumming:

> It awakens our ancestral lineage that brings us back to a time where we drummed as a way to communicate to our ancestors, to the earth spirits, to each other, and to help to heal each other and to awaken our bodies. In the Western hemisphere. . . we have shut down . . . So it reconnects the rest of the body to the head and it brings us into the body where we can feel, where we can move, where we can release, and where we can heal the old woundings of our ancestors. . . our parents . . . our culture. . . we're talking about healing the whole self (23/06/01).

Healing Others

In addition to promoting connection with self and others, recent studies have shown that drumming helps to resolve variety of physiological and psychological problems. Brain-wave research has led music therapists to integrate drumming into programmes for people with dementia, Alzheimer's or Autism, because it stimulates focus and interaction (Clair, Bernstein and Johnson, 1995). Heather McTavish, a drum facilitator who has Parkinson's disease, uses drumming to help herself and other special groups (Friedman, 2000); numerous addiction recovery programs incorporate shamanic drumming (Winkelman, 2003); and medical doctors have found 'composite drumming' to have a positive effect on strengthening the immune system of immuno-compromised patients (Bittman, et al, 2001). Other studies have shown drumming to be useful for reaching survivors of trauma, such as Vietnam veterans (Burt, 1995), as well as for anger management in survivors of abuse (Slotoroff, 1994). In the sense that drumming promotes an integration of and communication between the body, mind, and spirit, it has essential qualities that characterize holistic healing modalities.

Medusa is one drum teacher who has provided drumming programs for youth and adults, as well as for battered women and other trauma survivors, for over eight years. She feels that the drum is a powerful tool for communication and explains:

> For some (survivors), they are able to communicate with the drum in a way that they can't with the mouth . . . it pulls you into the present . . .and you don't think of anything else. Community. Being mindful. Having relationships with each other that they're not able to have in daily life. . . The power of healing in the drum feeds the own individual's needs – it's a unique instrument to channel those needs. (Medusa, 7/09/03)

She has found that drumming can be used to help people address identity issues, build self-esteem, and establish a sense of connection both within themselves and with others.

Social Change: Drumming for Peace

With the United States' bombing Afghanistan and in March 2003 initiating its war against Iraq, I intently followed the drumming e-lists. Voices from the U.S., Britain, the Middle East, Germany, Israel and Australia expressed their fears, hopes, and overwhelming desire to bring about peace, clarity and sanity through drumming. Although drumming has traditionally served to mobilize people to go to war, there were few requests to drum in support of U.S. troops in Afghanistan and Iraq in those early days. Rather, the conversations largely focused on drumming for peace as well as announcing peace concerts across the U.S. and globally, and some offered descriptions of personal drumming experiences at peace events. A drummer/singer from Israel, for instance, led a peace walk in Tel Aviv. A frame drum group met in Central Virginia for a 'weekend gathering of practising our rhythms and meditating upon peace' (March 2003). A San Francisco group was organizing 'Drummers for Peace.' Throughout the year, drum events were scheduled in the name of the peace effort. In April 2004, at the close of the Seattle World Percussion Festival, a young man publicized what he hoped would be the largest drum gathering ever for world peace, scheduled for September 2004 in northern California. At the same time, major drum gatherings were to be held in strategic locations around the globe. These growing drumming networks and communities are involved in spiritually-based social-change actions in which participants are thoroughly immersed in and connected to the whole of humanity. Their efforts correspond to Turner's idea that in *communitas* is 'the germ of future social developments of societal change in a way that the central tendencies of a social system can never quite succeed in being' (1982, p.45).

Discussion

Community service, increased self-awareness and social activism through drumming are striking themes in my research. Whether playing for a peace dinner, promoting team-building in the workplace, or teaching an ancient spiritual tradition, many drummers are pursuing their craft in the service of others. These people have been inspired by the power of the drum and are actively attempting to re-enchant the world through activities hat engender a sense of *communitas*.

Drumming is therapeutic in the deepest sense. It is a 'tool for unity' which can reconnect the self as well as unite groups and mobilize them for peace. It is used for celebration, healing, and religious and spiritual ritual. Some interviewees, as well as teachers Hill, Hull and Redmond, suggest that drumming is actually facilitating a 'paradigm shift' in Western society. This shift focuses on increasing self-awareness as well as an appreciation of others, strengthening personal efficacy, encouraging creativity, and developing cooperative ways of being. These characteristics flow into other facets of life and can be used to challenge the status quo. Drumming has 'arrived' in postmodern society as a potent force in personal transformation, in the creation of spiritual community, and in providing an impetus for positive social change. Even the American Association of Retired Persons' publication, *My Generation*, recognizes drumming circles to be 'among the country's fastest-growing holistic health trends' (2003).

Although drummers may not view themselves as practitioners of holistic healing, they do consider themselves agents of social change, and they *are* making a difference around the world. While Arabs and Israelis discuss their drum classes and peace gatherings on the Internet, Irish subscribers announce drumming for the Special Olympics, and a resident of Hawaii invites a drum e-list to join his group's Winter Solstice event. As evident not only in the number of such activities, but in their spiritual quality and community orientation, drummers are claiming their role as a compelling force of re-enchantment in the post-modern world.

Notes

1   This is the trademark for Arthur Hull's drum circle facilitation training programs that are offered through his business, Village Music Circles™. These trainings, which include Rhythm Alchemy Playshop™ and a Mentor's program in addition to drum circle facilitation training, are offered in weekend or weeklong forms and occur across the U.S.A. as well as in Europe and Japan.
2   See Mandell, 1980; Neher, 1962; Winkelman, 2000 among others.
3   In the DCF Playshops™ trainees learn how to guide drum circle participants to reach their full rhythmical potential; those who wish to continue may enroll in the Mentorship program if they are regularly running drum circles in their communities. Rhythmical Alchemy™ is not a DCF training, but rather a playshop of percussion games. See the Village Music Circles™ website for further information.
4   This is similar to Csikszentmihaly's (1990) concept of 'flow'.
5   NightOwl is a pseudonym, as is Medusa and Lipishau. Other interviewees asked me to retain their real names for the purposes of publication.
6   Remo Drums sponsors HealthRHYTHMS™, a group empowerment drumming program co-taught by Barry Bittman, M.D. and Christine Stevens, music therapist. The website offers articles, bibliographies and columns by doctors, scientists and music therapists who have conducted research on the healing effects of drumming.
7   The DrumSong Institute is an archive of women's drumming traditions in the U.S.A. Hill sponsors a women's drum event annually in the Catskill Mountains, NY, showcasing women drum teachers.

References

Berger, P. (1967), *The Sacred Canopy: Elements of a sociological theory of religion,* Anchor Books, New York.

Bittman, B. Berk, L. Felten, D. Westengard, J., Simonton, O., Pappas, J. and Ninehouser. M. (2001), 'Composite Effects of Group Drumming Music Therapy on Modulation of Neuroendocrine-immune Parameters in Normal Subjects', *Alternative Therapies*, vol. 7, no. 1 (January), pp.38–46.

Bly, R. (1992), *Iron John: A book about men*, Vintage Books, NY.

Buber, M. (1958), *I and Thou*, trans. R. G. Smith, Clark, Edinburgh.

Burt, J. (1995), 'Distant Thunder: Drumming with Vietnam Veterans,' *Music Therapy Perspectives*, 13, pp.110–112.

Childs-Helton, S. (2003), Personal communication at Women's Drum Weekend, Oakwood Retreat, October 18.

Clair, A.A., Bernstein, B. and Johnson, G. (1995), 'Rhythm Playing in Persons with Severe Dementia including those with Probable Alzheimer's Type', *Journal of Music Therapy*, vol. 32, no. 2, pp.113–131.

Csikszentmihaly, M. (1990), *Flow: The psychology of optimal experience*, HarperCollins, New York.

Ellwood, R. S. (1994), *The Sixties Spiritual Awakening: American religion moving from modern to postmodern*, Rutgers University Press, New Brunswick, NJ.

Foltz, T. (2000a), 'Spirit Guides', in W. Clark Roof (ed.), *Contemporary American Religion*, vol II, Macmillan Reference, pp.693–94.

___(2000b), 'Thriving Not Simply Surviving: Goddess spirituality and women's recovery from alcoholism', in W. Griffin (ed.), *Daughters of the Goddess*, AltaMira Press, Walnut Creek, CA, pp.119–135.

___(2003), 'Women, Drumming and Community: An Exploratory Study', *The Journal of the Indiana Academy of Social Sciences*, vol. 7, pp.100–109.

___(2004), 'Women's Drumming, Spirituality and Healing', unpublished paper presented at the annual meetings of the Association for the Sociology of Religion, August 14, San Francisco.

Friedman, R. L. (2000), *The Healing Power of the Drum*, Whitecliffs Media, Inc., Reno, NV.

Harner, M. (1980), *The Way of the Shaman*, Harper and Row, New York.

Hull, A. (1998), *Drum Circle Spirit: Facilitating human potential through rhythm.* White Cliffs Media, Reno, NV.

Hill, U. (2001), video interview at Diana's Grove, June 21.

Lipishau (2002), interview, Las Vegas, June 15.

Lyon, D. (2000), *Jesus in Disneyland: Religion in postmodern times*, Blackwell Publishers, Malden, MA.

Mandell, A. (1980), 'Toward a Psychobiology of Transcendence: God in the brain', in D. Davidson and R. Davidson (eds), *The Psychobiology of Consciousness*, Plenum Press, New York, pp.379–464.

Mattingly, R. (1995), 'Primal Pulse: The unifying power', *Percussive Notes*, (August) vol. 33, pp.8–20.

McNeill, W. H. (1995), *Keeping Together in Time*, Harvard University Press, Cambridge, MA.

Medusa, (2003), telephone interview, July 9.

Neher, A. (1962), 'A Physiological Explanation of Unusual Behavior in Ceremonies involving Drums', *Human Biology*, vol. 34, pp.151–60.

NightOwl (2001), interview at Diana's Grove.

Pike, S. M. (2001), *Earthly Bodies, Magical Selves*, University of California Press, Berkeley, CA.

Redmond, L. (1997), *When the Drummers were Women: A spiritual history of rhythm*, Three Rivers Press, New York.

Roof, W. C. (1999), *Spiritual Marketplace*, Princeton University Press, Princeton, NJ.

Slotoroff, C. (1994), 'Drumming Technique for Assertiveness and Anger Management in the Short-term Psychiatric Setting for Adult and Adolescent Survivors of Trauma', *Music Therapy Perspectives*, vol. 12, pp.111–116.

Stevens, C. (2003), *The Art and Heart of Drum Circles*, Hal Leonard Corporation, Milwaukee, WI.

The Economist. (2003), 'Rhythm Goes Respectable', May 29, www.drumallnight. com/economist.

Turner, V. (1969), *The Ritual Process: Structure and Anti-Structure*, Aldine, Chicago.

___(1974), *Dramas, Fields, and Metaphor*, Cornell University Press, Ithaca, New York.

___(1982), *From Ritual to Theater*, Performing Arts Journal Publications, New York.

Weber, M. (1964), *The Sociology of Religion*, Beacon Press, Boston.

Winkelman, M. (2000), *Shamanism: The neural ecology of consciousness and healing*, Bergin & Garvy, Westport, Conn.

___(2003), 'Complementary Therapy for Addiction: "Drumming out Drugs"', *American Journal of Public Health*, vol. 93, no. 4 (April), pp.647–651.

PART 3

Disrupting the Rational:
Enchantment as Political Response

Chapter 12

Believing in Post-modernity: Technologies of Enchantment in Contemporary Marian Devotion

Kathleen McPhillips

In 1994, at Yankalilla, a small town just south of Adelaide in South Australia, an extraordinary image appeared on the wall behind the altar in the local Anglican Church. On closer inspection by several parishioners it was revealed to be a figure, raised out of the plaster wall, of the Virgin Mary holding the baby Jesus. Over a period of years following the discovery of this image, the tiny church became a site of pilgrimage for thousands of spiritual tourists from all over the world and is now popularly known as the Shrine of our Lady of Yankalilla. The Shrine is also closely connected to an important site associated with Australia's first saint, Mary MacKillop: in 1867, MacKillop opened one of her first schools for poor Catholic children in a small cottage that stands near the church.

What is interesting about this site is its polyvalency: while it appears in the first instance to be a traditional site of Marian pilgrimage, it is also invested with claims that would sit more comfortably within New Age narratives. For example, one parishioner claims to channel the voice of the Virgin Mary (www.shrine. yankalilla.granite.net.au), while other parishioners claim that the church stands on an Aboriginal corroboree site where massacres may have occurred (Kahl, 1999, p.34). In addition, the church in which the image appears is the local Anglican (Episcopalian) church, which caused some consternation with the local Catholic Church – the customary site for such phenomena.

The image of Mary and baby at Yankalilla precedes two other Marian events: an apparition of Mary at the seaside suburb of Coogee in Sydney during the summer of 2003; and a weeping statue of Mary in Rockingham, a northern suburb of Perth in Western Australia in 2002/3. The three sites have received significant media attention and continue to be a source of public speculation. While these events are recent and seemingly unrelated to each other, the roots of such experiences can be traced back to nineteenth- and twentieth-century European Catholicism and its cultures of saints and pilgrimage (Cusack, 2003, p.116; Turner and Turner, 1978, 1982). Yet the contemporary expressions are dramatically post-modern in character, evoking a multiplicity of spiritual responses from the public, New Age philosophers, the Church and the State. Their appearance at this particular time invites careful investigation and analysis as to what they might say about post-modern, and indeed post-Christian, culture.[1]

In this chapter I will argue that the shrine at Yankalilla, the apparition at Coogee and the weeping statue of Rockingham are spectacles of contemporary enchantment that blend traditional elements of pilgrimage and devotion, with spiritual practices characteristic of the New Age. In other words, a site which may initially appear traditional and religious has the potential to develop with pace into a post-modern, post-Christian source of enchantment and tourist-style spiritual pilgrimage. The analysis is situated within and between two uses of the concept 'post-modernism': on the one hand a condition that emerges from a temporal relationship to modernity and pre-modernity, and on the other an interpretive framework of textual reading processes. By adopting both uses, I aim to develop a strategic understanding of the emergence and evolution of Marian devotion in order to explain why such phenomena arise at particular times and places, and what functions Marian pilgrimage might have for both the local community and the wider culture.

The Virgin Mother at Yankalilla: Reconciling Opposites

The first question we need to ask is 'Why the Virgin Mother?' – particularly given her decline in status in late modern times. Marina Warner (1976) presents a compelling argument about the decline in symbolic power of the Virgin Mary as an iconic and powerful religious figure in recent Western modernity. Where once the Virgin had relevance and affective power for millions of believing Catholics, she has now receded into the realms of legend and political irrelevance where her traditional role in a modern church is no longer functional or helpful to contemporary women and their search for identity (see also Joy, 1994 and McPhillips, 1997). This is despite the fact that the clerical male hierarchy of the Catholic Church continues to uphold her as the archetypal and desired image of womanhood. Warner argues that in pre-modern and early modern times Mary's paradoxical identity (both Virgin and Mother) had the important function of marrying divinity with femininity. Mary's potential – her claim to power – was that she alone represented a great reconciliation of opposites: the sign of her divinity, having given birth to an incarnate God, was virgin motherhood (Warner, 1976, p.336). Yet Warner argues that the myth of the Virgin Mother 'is translated into moral exhortation. Mary establishes the child as the destiny of woman, but escapes the sexual intercourse necessary for all women to fulfill this destiny.' (1976, p.336). Women searching for meaning and fulfillment have in general rejected motherhood as the highest form of feminine identity. Indeed, Mary has become largely irrelevant to women searching for authentic expressions of sexuality and self.

According to Warner, in pre-modern and early modern Catholic cultures the Virgin Mother was a significant force of enchantment with particular powers to reconcile and heal. However, her shift from goddess to heroic female figure does not necessarily mean that the efficacy of her power is lost completely. Indeed it might be that she has become what Featherstone refers to as a 'floating sign' (1995, p.75, and developed in relation to religion in Lyon, 2000, p. 43). Such signs develop from the disintegration of the sacred canopy that once stretched across the religious world, separating out secular and sacred society in very specific and functional ways (Berger, 1967). According to David Lyon, as the sacred canopy recedes in post-modern culture we witness a phenomenon of 'cultural cross overs' where religious beliefs and practices 'that once were sealed within an institutional form now flow freely over formerly policed boundaries. New possibilities for enchantment emerge creating liturgical smorgasbords, doctrinal potlucks' (Lyon, 2000, p.43). This recession of the sacred canopy, then, witnesses the multiplication of floating signs 'where the problem becomes less how do I conform and more how do I choose?' (Lyon, 2000, p.43). For example, the images of Mary and child might initially be quite clearly associated with Western Christian traditions of Marian devotion and pilgrimage. However, there is evidence that post-Christian communities appropriate these sites and rites which in effect release Mary into new realms of enchantment.

At Yankalilla, the Virgin Mother and baby becomes a sign for narratives of Reconciliation in the sense that the emergence of the image can be seen as a symbolic response to events that were deeply affecting the community. The image first appeared in 1994 at the height of the national debate about Reconciliation and the Stolen Generations.[2] The local community were aware that Yankalilla is the local Aboriginal term for 'place of refreshment', yet it is also the site of corroborrees[3] and a possible massacre; and the face of the Virgin is darker than the rest of the image, raising speculation about her message and origin (www.shrine.yankalilla.granite.net.au). There is also a connection to Mary MacKillop. She was canonized as Australia's first saint in 1995, a year after the image appeared, and this too could be read in terms of reconciling the colonial past with the post-colonial present. The image appeared not in the Catholic but in the Anglican Church, which the local community again understood in terms of reconciliation: as a sign of interfaith dialogue and possibly re-unification towards one Church. Hence, the Virgin Mother appears in her formidable role as the sign of a reconciliation of opposites, but not a reconciliation of femininity and divinity; rather she has floated into public discourse for the purpose of other reconciliations. This can be read as an indication of the depth of desire for racial, ethnic and religious reconciliation in Australian communities, and despite its clumsiness, as an authentic sign of hope. Interestingly, the Yankalilla parishioner who is 'channelling' the voice of Mary has said that Mary has been sending her messages about Princess Diana whom she calls the Princess of Light and who has done great works of compassion throughout the world (Kahl, 1999, p.36). Given that Diana has been called 'the people's saint' and has been linked to the Roman goddess

Diana, such a connection might enable women to access the Yankallila Virgin through a variety of narratives, side-stepping the more traditional version with its repressed sexuality (McPhillips, 1997).

Indeed, the cult of the saints has some obvious parallels with the contemporary cult of celebrities. Dyer (1994) and Marshall (1997) both argue that the efficacy of celebrity is premised on expressions of charisma where an individual star can act as a symbol reconciling contradiction, and that 'specific instabilities, ambiguities and contradictions in the culture ... account for the rise of certain charismatic figures and forms' (Dyer, 1994, p.35). Dyer contends 'that charismatic appeal is effective especially when the social order is uncertain, unstable and ambiguous and when the charismatic figure or group offers a value, order or stability to counterpoise this' (ibid.). Hence the cult of celebrity also functions to reconcile contradiction. But what happens to the efficacy of floating signs when multiple contradictions and national anxieties confront individuals and communities, especially post September 11? Signs, according to Lyon (2000, p.39), have the potential to be polyvalent.

The Coogee Virgin and the Sea of Polyvalency

'[L]ife is increasingly experienced as pastiche, polyvalence, and of course, uncertainty'. (Lyon, 2000, p.39)

On 22 January 2003, a local newspaper in the Sydney seaside suburb of Coogee published an interview with a local resident who reported that an apparition of the Virgin had appeared two months earlier on a fence-post jutting out towards the headland. The apparition was visible between 3.15pm and 4.30pm every day, and it coincided with a decision by the local council to rename the headland 'Dolphins' Point'[4] in memory of 18 Eastern Suburbs residents who had perished in the Bali bombings in September 2002 (Cusack, 2003, p.121). Local and state newspapers then took up the story, followed by TV and radio, and reported that the apparition was almost certainly a result of an optical illusion. Hundreds of people converged on the site, some as sightseers wanting to be part of a larger phenomenon and some as pilgrims to pray. Much of the crowd's behaviour and the site's management were conventional: religious souvenirs such as medals and rosary beads were for sale, offerings were left by the fence-post where the shadow of the Virgin fell, and the local parish priest visited and subsequently declared the apparition an optical illusion (Cusack, 2003, p.122). In typical Sydney style, local residents complained to the press about horrendous parking problems around the area, visitors blocking sea views and inhibiting walks across the headland, and general disruption to their daily lives. Disruption, however, is more than just inconvenience. It points to the potential 'otherness' of an ordinary place, not in a transcendent sense but as Foucault would argue in a heterotopic sense, where sacred space continues to exist alongside everyday space, contesting and confirming it in a strange dialectic

(Foucault, 1998). This causes a series of uncomfortable contradictions: the consumption of religious relics and paraphernalia sits alongside the gift of a miracle vision; the believer stands next to the disbeliever. Heterotopic spaces such as these disable the closed and certain spaces of modernity, giving way to expressions of 'otherness' and difference. Also, time becomes heterochronic, allowing a radically different sense of time to connect with normal time. The apparition appears in the afternoon disrupts and destabilizes the everyday sense of time, yet according to those who see it, the vision lasts for exactly 45 minutes. Time and space in this situation is precarious.

In early February 2003 the press reported that the fence-post had been vandalized: a toilet bowl had been chained to the fence and paint had been splattered around (Cusack, 2003, p.123). This vandalism caused great distress in the local community, both because it was felt to be an offence against those who had died in Bali and because it was interpreted by believing Catholics as an attack on faith. It also signalled the demise of the apparition: after this, no further public sightings were recorded. Interestingly, the vandalism of the headland where Mary appeared can be read as an act of desecration: the toilet chained to the fence-post unequivocally marked it out as a sacred space, drawing a clear boundary between purity and pollution, which, as Douglas argues, symbolically represents the line of social cohesion/chaos (Douglas, 1984).

The apparitions of the Coogee Virgin can be understood as a polyvalent: they are not reducible to any one particular meaning. Clearly they were a lament to a collective religious experience long gone (Warner, 1976), but also a reaction to recent traumatic national events (Cusack, 2003). It is possible they could also be seen as a celebration of summer seaside culture, revelling in excess and shimmering heat by the beach. The apparitions of Mary might signal what Bauman terms 'life in fragments', where floating polyvalent signs merge and mix without any single overarching meaning (in Lyon, 2000, pp.42–43); hence a series of collective national and local anxieties are attached to a site capable of extra-discursiveness. Could we then expect that such post-rational phenomena might increase as global and national uncertainty increase and as signs slip between discourses?

Possibly, the Coogee apparition of Mary worked partly because it echoed quite closely the great apparitions and visions witnessed mostly by Catholic peasant children and religious women in nineteenth- and twentieth-century Europe (Turner and Turner, 1978), even down to a specific time each day when the apparition was visible. For some people, then, the Coogee apparition was a traditional expression of Marian efficacy. The fact that the Catholic Church refused to legitimate it did not necessarily reduce its potency, although an official blessing may have lengthened its life. Carole Cusack (2003) argues that this Marian apparition is significantly different from more traditional modern expressions of apparition culture. There was no designated visionary or individual who was specially called, and there was no one message (Cusack, 2003, p.122). The woman who first sighted the apparition, local resident Christine Cherry, said that while she was not a

Christian, she was spiritual; and it was she who indicated when the apparition was visible and who linked it to the Bali Bombings (Cusack, 2003, pp.122–3). Cherry was also seen selling religious medals and candles (Cusack, 2003, p.122). Claims were made by other residents and visitors too: one woman said that the Virgin touched her shoulder; another that she heard the Virgin speak (Cusack, 2003, p.122).

It is certainly paradoxical when traditional devotional interpretations sit side-by-side with national anxieties and New Age consumerism. But as a floating sign, paradox does not necessarily constitute a problem, particularly where the sign's function is to unite opposites and where its polyvalency makes the Virgin accessible to the broader population rather than only to a traditional cohort of believers. The other possibility is that Marian apparitions such as these provide non-rational, even non-linguistic expressions. That is, the traditional ground of enchantment might be located in the non-rational, and although constantly translated to the rational, is not reducible to it. When one resident declares, 'I see a fence-post. And I have seen that same fence-post for many years. If all these people want to come to Coogee then that's wonderful, but the parking has become horrendous' (in Cusack, 2003, p.122), it is a recognition both that a mystery is at the heart of the phenomenon and that such events radically disrupt the everyday. Warner (1976, p.336) argues that at the core of metaphysical mysteries is a refutation of reason and it is this that establishes an event's sacredness. Of course, the reasoned responses of the media and the Church were certainly influential but not necessarily dominant. This brings us to the final point, that technologies of enchantment such as these apparitions give individuals tools for negotiating and developing identity and ethics within shifting discursive frameworks. Indeed all three Marian sites described here constitute potential moments for negotiation, which raises interesting questions about the dynamic relationship between rationality and belief.

The Rockingham Virgin: the Intersection of Science and Faith

In March 2002, Patty Powell, a local parishioner in the northern suburb of Rockingham in Perth, noticed that a small statue of Mary she had bought in Bangkok eight years before had begun weeping a rose-scented oil-like substance (www.visionsofjesuschrist.com/weeping43.htm). The statue was taken to the local Catholic Church where the parish priest put it on display for the entire congregation. The statue appeared to weep only on auspicious religious days – saints' feast days and Easter. Following significant media interest the church quickly became a site of pilgrimage. Pilgrims interviewed at the church indicated that their interest was fairly traditional: they were hoping for miraculous intervention for various problems including alcoholism, cancer and drug addiction (ibid). However, unlike the Coogee Virgin, the Rockingham statue was a material object that could be tested using scientific methods. Late in 2002 the statue was taken to a local university. A number of scientists tested it but were unable to find any leakage that could explain the weeping. Although they were unable to explain the phenomenon, they insisted that there must be a rational explanation, which most likely involved some form of trickery. The local parish priest, meanwhile, predicted that if the statue were found to be an act of God, then the church would immediately become a shrine (ibid).

Following the scientists' tests, the Archbishop of Perth instigated a formal investigation by the Church; this included an array of scientific tests, interviews with parishioners and the statue's owners, and lengthy consideration by a committee of professionals. The three-member team, which included a scientist, examined the statue closely using magnification, X-ray and a CT scan. The tests revealed no explanation for the weeping. From 14 August 2002 – the feast of the Assumption of Our Lady – the statue wept continually. It only stopped when it was in the hands of the investigation team and when the Church's investigation was to produce its report. The Archbishop stated, cautiously, that one could not conclude that the statue was of divine origin. He was, however, reluctant to say that it was a hoax, and he returned the statue to its owner, forbidding it to be put on public display. "'We believe in miracles,'' Archbishop Hickey said yesterday. "But we can't say this was definitely one of them"' (ibid). On 28 April 2003 – Good Friday – the statue began crying again. Pilgrims from around the world are still flocking to see the weeping statue; it now resides permanently at Patty Powell's home, which she has renamed The Holy Family House of Prayer (ibid).

Science, Rationality and Technologies of Enchantment

> We can think of a culture as enchanted when it customarily traffics in the odd and unexplained… (Schneider, 1993, p.5)

It has been consistently argued (Weber, 1978, Giddens, 1991 and Foucault, 1998) that the success of the rationalization of social and cultural life in modernity is only ever partial, and that in late or post-modernity, rationalization as a mode of knowledge is under increasing threat. This was stated most famously by Max Weber, who argued that although instrumental forms of rationality would dominate the organization of social life, the fields of irrationality would also simultaneously expand (Weber, 1978, pp.1111–1157); disenchantment might lead to a loss of meaning and a sense of collective imprisonment, but this would be contrary to the growth of non-rational phenomena contributing to state and other legitimating processes. Indeed, Weber chronicled the role of the irrational in the legitimating processes of institutional life (1978, Chs 12 and 13). Likewise, Victor and Edith Turner (1978, 1982) identified the revival of Marian apparitions and pilgrimage in nineteenth- and twentieth-century Europe as a response to modernity, in which the increasing rationalization of social life – through the emergent nation state and capitalized, industrialized economies – impacted directly on the everyday life of rural Catholic peasants. Apparitions of the Virgin generally heralded apocalyptic messages (Cusack, 2003, p.116) of devastation and war: redemption depended on the population at large performing mass penance. On the one hand this is an expression of religious regulation, on the other an act of resistance to Church centrism – both responses to the immense changes brought about by modernity.

Foucault argues (1984) that in modernity, while the discourse of rationality dominates institutional forms and social behaviour, its hegemony is never stable: it is under constant challenge. Thus the Marian apparitions could be understood as part of a broader phenomenon of technologies of enchantment, which emerge from the discourses of rationality but is irrational in character. For Foucault, the term 'technology' had a dual function; it signified mechanisms of social regulation as well as techniques for the development of the self (see Danaher et al., 2000, p.xv). Foucault argued that while the self is largely scripted through discourses, institutions and relations of power, the subject also actively crafts or negotiates his or her own identity. In order to do so, the self makes use of technologies or mechanisms that are themselves produced by regulatory institutions and discourses. By appropriating various technologies, one finds a way to live tactically and even ethically (Danaher et al, 2000, p.131). Marian devotion is therefore a regulatory practice aimed at the Catholic proletariat with the purpose of maintaining the mystery of divinity through the regulation of the soul and the body via unexplained phenomenon, and at the same time an opportunity for subject-formation that includes a tactical response to life in the modern world. Likewise, says Lyon (2000, p.51), 'Religious actors tend to choose to construct religious identity in an ongoing, dynamic way, from the different offerings of religious groups'. For those who feel specially chosen to witness the apparitions of the Virgin, we can understand this as an active process of self-construction, 'wishing to be the sole connecting line with God' (Bauman, 1996, p.21) and bypassing the regulatory forces of the Church. When Patty Powell took the weeping statue of Mary home and set up a shrine in The Holy Family House of Prayer, she was rejecting the official Church response yet maintaining a direct line to divine revelation. The fact that the bishop was unwilling to denounce the phenomenon as trickery is testament to the function and power of miracle discourses in the life of Catholic believers. Were he to have accepted it, he would have been legitimating an irrational phenomenon and putting the Church at odds with science and rationality, the pre-eminent discourses of modernity. Were he to have denounced it entirely, he might have been suggesting that miracles have no place in Catholic belief systems – a dangerous statement because Catholicism in particular has encouraged the belief that the realms of mystery are at the heart of the religious experience (Turner and Turner, 1982).

This is not to suggest that religious institutions have not exerted an enormous regulatory force on the community of believers, shaping not just the moral dimensions of the self, but also bodily and affective expressions. However, as Foucault points out, if the success of disciplinary and regulatory forces tends to be partial rather than complete, then there is potential for other ways of seeing and speaking. While religious traditions might be organized around discursive boundaries, the flexibility of such boundaries becomes clear when we look closely at the phenomenon of Marian devotion. It might also be the case that if *the order of things* in the modern episteme situates rationality and secularism as dominant discourses, then the dynamic of post-modernity might involve the destabilization of these discourses – expressed as excessive behaviour or even extra-discursive meaning. Given that an episteme works to exclude all other ways of speaking, might a 'post' location create tears in the veil, where to hear the 'other' is possible in new ways?

The Function of Enchantment in Place and Identity

Prior to modernity, the cult of the saint was associated with specific socio-geographical areas, where a local saint's shrine marked off boundaries between villages and between cultivated and uncultivated lands. In contemporary times we can see that the cult of the Virgin Mother has the capacity to 'mark critical points in the ecosystem – contact points with other worlds' (Turner and Turner, 1978, p.146) at sites that are predominantly local but also quickly accessible through mass media, forming global access to points of pilgrimage. Some deities and saints, such as the Virgin Mother and child, become 'nationalized' and function to hold in tension unreconciled opposites.

For the local communities, I would argue that the intermeshing of place and identity – both national and personal – is critical in determining the potency of an apparition. The Coogee Virgin appeared at the seaside when national anxieties about terrorism in Bali were at their height. The Virgin at Yankallila coincided with public lamentation over the Stolen Generations and over the Reconciliation movement. The weeping statue in Rockingham appeared soon after the traumatic events of September 11. All three sites destabilize dominant arrangements of space and time, promising the possibility of other ways of seeing and being. They are also important moments in collective understandings of spirituality of place and the re-enchantment of Earth.

If post-modernity is understood as a development or authorization of the irrational or inexplicable, then one could expect not only an increase in moments of enchantment (public and private) but also an increase in the floating symbols that enable this. In general the function of these symbols might be to provide anchor points between post-modern/traditional and secular/sacred experiences, creating cohesive moments in which one can mark out identity. Indeed, as Hodge notes in this volume, the tourist can be understood as a spiritual pilgrim, in the sense that the tourist visits other places to re-enchant everyday life. This view upsets the normal distinctions we draw between those who visit such places as tourists and those who visit them as religious pilgrims, and it opens up the possibility that tourists and pilgrims alike are all spiritual tourists in search of meaning and understanding. Indeed, Zygmunt Bauman (1996) argues that post-modernity itself is similar in style to pilgrim culture, for in each case a journey replaces tradition as the instrument of cohesion. Pilgrimage has become necessary if we are to avoid getting lost in the fragmentary landscapes of post-modernity because it implies a journey and a destination, 'where one is walking to a place, leaving tracks, creating a history, cementing identity' (Bauman, 1996, p.22). One can reflect on the road past, see the way forward, and understand this as progress. Time can be understood spatially as a time 'ahead' and a time 'behind'. 'Destination, the set purpose of life's pilgrimage, gives form to the formless, makes a whole out of the fragmentary, lends continuity to the episodic' (Bauman, 1996, pp.21–22). Religious/spiritual pilgrimage also involves a basic connection to the supernatural, linking the pilgrim to the realms of divinity (Turner and Tuner 1978, p.146), the body acting as a contact point for communication with the supernatural 'other' through visions, apparitions and miracles.

Finally, these sites of Marian devotion and apparitions are profoundly contradictory: they are simultaneously signs of hope and moments of re-inscription. They re-inscribe normative expressions of body, identity and place, yet they point to other, extra-discursive ways of being. The power of these expressions of re-enchantment may lie precisely in their contradictory, unstable nature, and we might expect an amplification of such post-rational phenomena as national and global uncertainty increases.

Notes

1 The term 'post-Christian' signifies a destabilization of what could be considered a stable meta-discourse (Christianity) through a series of interjections: feminist, post-colonial, and so on. Post-Christian points towards a condition of the unravelled nature of Christianity; of the breakdown of duality as the principle organizing force of knowledge particularly through disruption to the relationship between believer and institution. (see McPhillips, 1999).

2 The movement for Reconciliation reached its height in the late 1980s to the late 1990s, when public discourse on the discussion of race relations in Australia was prominent and productive. In 1997 a national report into Aboriginal people who were taken from their families by governments of the day became known as the Stolen Generations Report (Bringing Them Home, 1997) and caused serious public trauma to Aboriginal and non-Aboriginal alike. It was one of the first moments in Australian public life when past racial violence was collectively and consciously acknowledged.

3 A corroboree is a gathering of peoples for celebration involving traditional dance and song.

4 Named after a local football club: some players and members were killed and injured in the bomb blasts in Bali.

References

Berger, P. (1967), *The Sacred Canopy*, Anchor-Doubleday, New York.

Bauman, Z. (1996), 'From Pilgrim to Tourist – or a Short History of Identity' in S. Hall and P. Du Gay (eds), *Questions of Identity*, Sage Publications, London, pp.18–36.

Bringing Them Home. National Inquiry into the Separation of Aboriginal and Torres Strait Islander Children from their Parents (1997), Human Rights and Equal Employment Opportunity Commission, Sydney, April.

Carrette, J. (2000), *Foucault and Religion*, Routledge, London.

Cusack, C. (2003), 'The Virgin Mary at Coogee: A Preliminary Investigation', *Australian Religion Studies Review*, vol. 16, no.1, pp.116–129.

Danaher, G. Shirato, T. and Webb, J. (eds), (2000), *Understanding Foucault*, Allen & Unwin, Sydney.

Derrida, J. (2002), 'Hospitality', in Gil Anidjar (ed.), *Acts of Religion*, Routledge, London, pp.356–420.

Douglas, M. (1984), *Purity and Danger*, ARK Paperbacks, London.

Dyer, R. (1994), Stars, BFI Publishing, London.

Featherstone, M. (1995), *Undoing Culture*, Sage, London.

Foucault, M. (1998) 'Of Other Spaces', in N. Mirzoeff (ed.), *The Visual Culture Reader*, Routledge, New York, pp.237–244.

___(1984), *The Care of the Self, History of Sexuality*, vol. 3, Penguin, London.

Giddens, A. (1991), *Modernity and Self-Identity*, Polity Press, Cambridge.

Jantzen, G. (1998), *Becoming Divine: Towards a Feminist Philosophy of Religion*, Manchester University Press, Manchester.

Johnston, J. (2002), 'The "Theosophic Glance": Fluid Ontologies, Subtle Bodies and Intuitive Vision', *Australian Religion Studies Review*, vol. 15, no. 2, pp.101–117.

Joy, M. (1994) 'Sainthood or Heresy: Contemporary Options for Women', in M. Joy and P. Magee (eds), *Claiming our Rites: Studies in Religion by Australian Women Scholars*, AASR, Adelaide, pp.117–134.

Kahl, J. (1999), 'Miracle image of Mary at Yankalilla, South Australia', *Australian Religion Studies Review*, vol. 12, no. 1, pp.32–39.

Lyon, D. (2000), *Jesus in Disneyland: Religion in Postmodern Times*, Polity Press, Cambridge.

McPhillips, K. (1997), 'Postmodern Canonisation', in Re:Public (ed.), *Planet Diana: Cultural Studies and Global Mourning*, UWS Nepean: Research Centre in Intercommunal Studies, Sydney, pp.87–92.

___ (2002), 'Re-figuring the Sacred: Re-enchantment and the Postmodern World' in V. Walkerdine (ed.), *Challenging Subjects: Critical Psychology for a new Millennium*, Palgrave, London, pp.177–190.

Marshall, D. (1997), *Celebrity and Power: Fame in Contemporary Culture*, University of Minnesota Press, Minneapolis.

Martin, L. Gutman, H. and Hutton, P. (eds), (1988), *Technologies of the Self: A Seminar with Michel Foucault*, Tavistock, London.

Rabinow, P. (ed.) 1984, *The Foucault Reader*, Penguin, London.

Schechner, R. (1993), *The Future of Ritual. Writings on Culture and Performance*, Routledge, London.

Schneider, M. (1993) *Culture and Enchantment*, The University of Chicago Press, Chicago.

Sutcliffe, S. and Bowman, M. (eds) (2000), *Beyond New Age. Exploring Alternative Spirituality*, Edinburgh University Press, Edinburgh.

The Shrine of Our Lady at Yankalilla – *http://www.shrine.yankalilla.granite. net.au/*

The Weeping Statue at Rockingham – *http://www.visionsofjesuschrist.com/ weeping43.htm*

Turner, V. and Turner, E. (1978), *Image and Pilgrimage in Christian Culture*, Columbia University Press, New York.

___(1982), 'Postindustrial Marian Pilgrimage', in J. Preston (ed.), *Mother Worship: Themes and Variations,* The University of North Carolina Press, Chapel Hill, pp.145–173.

Warner, M. (1976), *Alone of all Her Sex: the Myth and Cult of the Virgin Mary*, Vintage Press, London.

Weber, M. (1978), *Economy and Society*, vol. 2, G. Roth and C. Wittich (eds), Berkeley, University of California Press.

___(1993), *The Sociology of Religion*, Beacon Press, Boston.

Wyschogrod, E. (1990), *Saints and Postmodernism: Revisioning Moral Philosophy*, University of Chicago Press, Chicago.

Chapter 13

Practising New Age Soteriologies in the Rational Order

Steven J. Sutcliffe

This chapter examines a variety of New Age soteriologies which aim to disrupt the dominant epistemological order of instrumental rationality in post-Christian societies. I provide brief, contextualized samples of three practices – guidance, meditation and healing – which are rooted in what I call a *soteriological epistemology*. I set out their claims and assess their achievements with reference to Max Weber's concept of 'rationality' and Pierre Bourdieu's concept of *habitus*. I also examine the political alignment of these practices in the context of a wider argument to re-think the heterogenous contents of New Age (Sutcliffe, 2003a) as popular, rather than alternative, religion.

Three concepts are central to this chapter: epistemology, soteriology, and instrumental rationality. Epistemology means *discourse on knowledge* (from the Greek words *logos* and *episteme*, respectively): in other words, an analysis of what we mean by *knowledge* in any particular instance. Soteriology means *discourse on salvation* (Greek *soteria*, 'salvation'). I use it here as a tool for comparative analysis, based on discussions in Gombrich (1988) and Fitzgerald (2000) which seek to disaggregate the reifying construct religion into more tangible behavioural strands. For Gombrich (1988, p.25), soteriology 'concerns the individual, his [*sic*] highest goals and his [*sic*] fate after death. It provides an answer to the question, "What must I do to be saved?"'. For Fitzgerald (2000, p.121), soteriology promises 'a release from this world into a transcendent reality or consciousness'.

The three practices sketched later in this chapter promise an answer to Gombrich's question. But *how* they do this raises questions about the relationship of soteriological epistemology to instrumental rationality. The latter is famously defined by the German sociologist Max Weber (1970, p.293) as 'the methodical attainment of a definitely given and practical end by means of an increasingly precise calculation of adequate means'. In Giddens' (1994, p.152) convenient summary, this instrumental type of rationality involves rational assessment of 'the probable results of a given act in terms of the calculation of means to an end'; that is, the individual 'weights the relative effectiveness of each of the possible means of attaining the end, and the consequences of securing it for other goals which [s/he] holds' (ibid).

Weber calls this type of rationality *zweckrational*. In his scheme, the *zweckrational* belongs to a four-fold typology, alongside value-oriented (*wertrational*), emotional and traditional types of rational action. This chapter concentrates on the impact of an instrumental rational (*zweckrational*) disposition – which I treat as a basic, pervasive modality of thinking and acting in post-Christian societies – on soteriological practices. I also examine evidence of value-oriented (*wertrational*) action in the practices of meditation and healing. But despite the 'softening' of instrumentality in *wertrational* action, in which ideal values become ends in themselves, I will argue that both types of action – the instrumental (*zweckrational*) and the value-oriented (*wertrational*) – inevitably entail 'the calculation of means to an end' (Giddens, 1994, p.152).

Focusing on the widespread dissemination of these soteriologies also helps us question common characterizations of New Age as alternative or countercultural religion.[1] The empirical evidence suggests rather that the emblem or label covers a spectrum of diffuse practices, implicit in the prodigious assimilation and listing of heterogeneous phenomena in the secondary literature (Wood, 2003, pp.162–165). This scattering of beliefs and practices across traditional lines of demarcation has the effect of blurring boundaries between alternative and popular expressions of religion, an effect concomitant with wider destabilizations of order, taste and canon that some see as characteristic of post-modernizing forces (e.g. Lyon, 2000). The easy accessibility – the user friendliness – of practices like guidance, meditation and healing has encouraged a drift in use since the 1970s, broadly-speaking from alternative to popular sectors. Furthermore, questions of how to act and what to believe tend to be decided on an *ad hoc* basis by local collectives and individual practitioners, rather than settled systematically by an overarching organization or ideology. So, both the location and the mode of action serve to blur the boundaries of the more-or-less discrete New Age movement typically portrayed in the secondary literature.[2] And increasingly the term New Age is being replaced in both popular and academic accounts by cognate terms such as *mind body spirit* and *holistic* (e.g. the *holistic milieu*, in Heelas and Woodhead, 2004). Significantly, these new terms do not carry the earlier apocalyptic and millenialist associations of New Age, which, between the 1930s and 1960s, aligned practitioners with alternative social identities (Sutcliffe, 2003a, pp.45–103). Hence I argue that the practices discussed here, and others like them, are better represented as popular rather than alternative religions.

There is a complex and subtle interplay between the subjectivities of New Age practitioners on the one hand, and socio-structural conditioning on the other. This is a contemporary variation on the classic tension between agency and constraint in the practice of religion. The fact that there is no organized New Age Movement does not mean there are no norms of thinking and behaving to be negotiated, or that there is no discernible demographic base:[3] It just means these are less immediately obvious and must be observed in local, particular contexts. Indeed, since instrumental rationality retains such a strong grip on the social and symbolic orders through which practitioners represent themselves, I argue that the epistemological disruptions of the rational order that are actually achieved through the practices in question, and hence the durability of the release or salvation attained by practitioners, are only local, contingent and temporary. This stands in contrast to the rhetoric that New Age practices are re-enchanting (Berman, 1981) and reimagining (Spangler and Thompson, 1991) the world. Insofar as New Age soteriology depends upon the promise of achieving release through utilizing accessible practices in everyday life settings, it makes strategic use of the logic of instrumental rationality in pursuing a practical, given end – and strategic action is certainly an important level of analysis in relation to popular practices. However, in doing this, it cannot also automatically claim to be *transcending* instrumental rationality; that is, popular soteriological practice cannot both have its cake and eat it. It is my contention, therefore, that practitioners may even reinscribe elements of the rational order into the very form and content of their guidance, meditation and healing. Hence it may ultimately be better to represent the effect of their practices as *managing* the dominant epistemic order, rather than *transcending* or *overthrowing* it: *managing* it, that is, in the dual sense of *adjusting* (accommodating to its logic) but also *subverting* (turning its instrumentality to practitioners' immediate advantage). This means that the social and behavioural impact of guidance, meditation and healing must be considerably more nuanced and contingent than the totalizing, utopian rhetoric suggests.

The Relationship between New Age Soteriologies and Instrumental Rationality

Having established a context and an argument, let us return to the central theoretical issue: the relationship between soteriological practices and instrumental rationality. As noted, epistemology deals with the scope and status of knowledge claims: that is, 'what constitutes justification or warrant for holding a belief and thereby deeming that belief to be "knowledge"'(Edgar and Sedgwick, 1999, p.127). Now, it is not epistemology as formal philosophical analysis that interests me here, but people's *use* of popular epistemological practices in order to construct and validate practical soteriologies. So the issue is not the validity (or otherwise) of soteriological knowledge, but *how* it is produced and justified; that is, the social processes through which practitioners come to value and defend some kinds of knowledge over others. Making knowledge-claims the product of social fields inevitably raises questions about the relative status and power of New Age practitioners. Although the field is largely free of organizational hegemonies, analysis of the internal histories of particular collectives *within* the field – for example, the Findhorn colony in Scotland[4] – and of the negotiation and contestation of insider discourses, for example on the precise meaning of the emblem New Age[5] – reveals a subtle but nonetheless real struggle, amongst rival factions and alternative discourses, to authorize practices and regulate meanings.

The practices considered here – guidance, meditation and healing – are a case in point. Each is the outcome of a history of negotiation over proper execution and interpretation, although lack of space precludes reconstructing their specific histories here; each also continues to be subject to reform and innovation. Negotiation and dispute, however muted or camouflaged, necessarily arise by nature of the powerful claims made for these practices by practitioners and teachers: in effect, that guidance, meditation and healing can save, in Fitzgerald's (2000, p.121) sense of conferring knowledge of a transcendent reality. How they accomplish this is explained and validated by practitioners on the basis of an epistemological distinction between an inferior knowledge *about* the desired state or goal, commonly available in the rational order, and a superior, participative knowledge *of* it (on this distinction, see Donovan, 2000, pp.376–381). New Age soteriologies differ from the more mundane order of instrumental rationality, it is claimed, by virtue of their special experiential quality: only in experience, represented as a holistic and embodied state of participation and identification (in contrast to the 'merely' cognitive status of knowledge offered in the dominant order), can they be realized or fulfilled.[6] This claim must in turn be understood within a wider turn to the epistemic, indeed existential, value of 'experience(s)' in contemporary religion.[7] In New Age culture, the distinction between knowledge *of* and knowledge *about* has produced a hierarchy of knowledge claims, with the former attained and verified through personal experience(s) – becoming superior to the latter, and hence more highly prized.

It follows that these practices of obtaining and verifying soteriological knowledge become subject to negotiation within the field, with criteria being created to sort and validate those who have had the requisite experience from those who have not. The former thereby acquire a status that attracts fellow seekers (Sutcliffe, 2003a, pp.200–213), pursuing the same goal. But the picture is complicated by a further interpretative layer, since the practices are set, I argue, within a wider epistemological order in which instrumental rationality is both ubiquitous and normative. As discussed, instrumental rationality is a product of 'rules that determine the most efficient means for achieving any given end' (Edgar and Sedgwick, 1999, p.326). Its ubiquity in modern societies disposes people to think and act in certain ways. The French sociologist Pierre Bourdieu's concept of *habitus* is helpful here. By *habitus* Bourdieu means 'a system of lasting, transposable dispositions' informing everyday human behaviour, functioning as 'a matrix of perceptions, appreciations and actions' (Bourdieu, 1977, pp.82–83). *Habitus* is not a set of skills or behaviours that is consciously mastered: it is how we think and act without reflection, with a concomitant blurring of easy distinctions between thinking and acting. That is, *habitus* is how we express ourselves when we are on 'automatic pilot': that is, when we have assimilated, and duly reproduce, social norms. The resultant *habitus* is an instrumental rationalist (*zweckrational*) disposition that inscribes the epistemology of the dominant order in our everyday intentions and acts.

The claims of New Age soteriologies inevitably find themselves in tension, if not outright conflict, with the dominant order at precisely this point. This is because the everyday *habitus*, in Bourdieu's sense, constitutes *in itself* the system and matrix within which accounts of the power of New Age soteriologies must be formulated in the first place. In other words, instrumental rationality as a mode of everyday thinking and acting is learned and absorbed by people from birth, as a determinant of their subjectivities, in and through the enduring social institutions of family, education and work. Consequently, soteriological practices like guidance, meditation and healing can only be conceived within these institutions powerful epistemic matrix. And because this matrix works by calculating the relative effectiveness of different means (the practices) to achieve a particular end (the promised experience of release or salvation), the claim that the practices provide 'release from this world' (Fitzgerald, 2000, p.121) is actually constructed in terms of the same means-to-end logic of instrumental rationality which the practices ostensibly seek to disrupt. While this does not necessarily deny that a state or experience of release or salvation is achievable, it does mean that it cannot be easily represented, simply because the practices themselves – their form and content – are already infected by the same *zweckrational* logic they oppose.

If this is so, then questions must arise as to how much these practices can actually thwart the epistemic order, as well as to their political implications in terms of either reinforcing or contesting instrumental rationality as a function of late capitalism. I argue that the uncertain politics of New Age religion that can be deduced from the secondary literature[8] reflect its popular practice base. In a well-known essay, Raymond Williams (1976, p.199) found that, by the late twentieth century, popular practices had come to signify 'culture actually made by people for themselves'. Complications arise from the fact that, as I noted in connection with Findhorn's history and with the meaning of the emblem New Age, culture or religion is not something fixed and immutable. We must take account of dispute and change in popular formations in particular, since what is widely favoured and well-liked – Williams' (ibid., p.198) terms – is especially prone to negotiation and revision in the absence of fixed canons and hegemonic institutions. So we must acknowledge that the preferences of, and differences between, particular groups and networks *within* New Age constituencies are a central factor in producing the field's widely-remarked but inadequately-explained structural indeterminacy. To put this in terms of a more dynamic exposition of popular practices, what is at stake in representations of New Age (or indeed any religious tradition) 'is *not* the intrinsic or historically fixed objects of culture, but the state of play in cultural relations' (Hall, 1994, p.462). This state of play is doubly manifest in New Age religion: internally, through the processes of negotiation and contestation amongst New Age practitioners; externally, in the unresolved political relationship of this particular religious field to the dominant culture.

The soteriological epistemology underpinning guidance, meditation and healing encapsulates these indeterminacies. The following case studies represent popular sites of struggle with the practical implications of a dichotomy between a constrained and constraining knowledge *that*, inscribed in instrumental rationality and embodied as *habitus*, and a liberating, soteriological 'knowledge *of*', tantalizingly promised by New Age soteriologies.

Guidance, Meditation, Healing: New Age Soteriologies in Practice

The practice of guidance is seminal in New Age. For example, the founders of the Findhorn community were taught how to discern guidance in everyday life by Sheena Govan (1912–1967). Govan was the daughter of a family that founded a Scottish Evangelical Protestant movement, the Faith Mission, in 1886. In the late 1940s, she was serving as an independent spiritual director to a small circle of seekers in London. Peter Caddy (1917–1996), then her husband and a future Findhorn leader, describes her method:

> Sheena believed that at this time many people were going through an initiatory experience of self-realization .... She was like a midwife helping them to go through that process ... She was not a spiritual teacher in the traditional sense ... but would help people to see God in their lives. (P. Caddy, 1996, p.74)

Caddy calls himself Govan's scribe, recording messages that she 'received in her meditations' (P. Caddy, 1996, p.74), including practical advice on relationships and work, as well as instruction on prayer and meditation, and prophecy on the post-war world. He also practised paying attention to everyday tasks, in line with Govan's teaching that 'when everything is done with love ... it raises the "vibrations" – the quality of the atmosphere of a place and its conduciveness for spiritual work' (ibid, p.78). Govan's circle included another future Findhorn leader, Eileen Combe (b.1917; later Eileen Caddy), who was raised as an Anglican but had leanings to Christian Science and also to a popular evangelical movement, Moral Re-Armament (Caddy, 1988). Its characteristic practice was the quiet time, in which it taught that guidance could be received in meditation and then followed through in daily life. Through Moral Re-Armament she met Peter Caddy and moved to London, where she began meditation under Sheena Govan's direction, recording messages from the inner God (ibid, p.31*ff*). This epistemology of getting guidance in everyday life was to become central to the practice of religion at Findhorn, as shown by Eileen Caddy's first book of messages received there in the 1960s, called, simply, *God Spoke to Me* (Caddy, 1992 [1971]). Guidance remains a core practice at Findhorn (Sutcliffe, 2003a, chapter 7) and, more widely, continues to provide content in a range of New Age texts, from Alice Bailey's instructions on New Age discipleship (Bailey, 1981[1944]) to *A Course in Miracles* (Anonymous, 1985[1975]) and the recent series, *Conversations with God* (Walsch, 1997).

Sheena Govan's role in Findhorn's formation demonstrates affinities between Evangelical and New Age practices that deserve further exploration. The example of guidance is a case in point: it crosses New Age and Evangelical boundaries, forming a continuum of practice that is obscured by clumsy typologies of alternative versus mainstream, or occult versus Christian.[9] Govan's methods of inner listening, discernment and prayer recapitulate – in a post-Christian context – the evangelical piety of her father, the Victorian patriarch John Govan, who in the 1880s would instruct Faith Mission audiences to 'get into this position of entire surrender to God ... He will show you when to wait upon Him, and how long to wait ... and He will visit you and bless you' (Govan, 1978, p.29). Likewise Sheena Govan's notion of the God within, which would become formative at Findhorn through Eileen Caddy's teaching, is foreshadowed by her father's commitment to the 'work of God to be done in my soul' (ibid., p.24). In brief, Sheena Govan put a soteriological method of Victorian evangelicalism to popular religious ends in post-war Britain. The practice was open to all, irrespective of religion (or irreligion), and could be put to work in the thick of everyday life, providing detailed instruction on everything from group relationships to a New Age of divine intervention: that is, from the mundane to the apocalyptic.

My second example of a New Age soteriology is free-style meditation, a popular and hybrid style of meditating that does not belong to any particular religious tradition or lineage. In 1995 I attended a weekly meditation session in Edinburgh called Prayer for Peace. This was held on Friday lunchtimes at the Salisbury Centre, a self-styled 'alternative education centre' set up in 1973 in a suburban villa with organic garden. The session had run sporadically for at least ten years. At its height, up to thirty people gathered weekly, although only a handful was present when I attended: English, Americans and Scots in their 20s and 30s, mostly men. We meditated barefoot in a plain room, sitting in a circle on cushions and small stools. The common goal of the session, I was told by the *de facto* leader, was to 'let the transcendental in'. Composite systems and postures were evident: I followed the movement of my breathing; my neighbour told me he chanted inwardly; another said he began with a prayer then tried to still his mind. Although most of us sat in a loose circle, facing in, one meditator sat facing the wall, Zen-style. The 40-minute session concluded with three strikes of a small Tibetan bell, some leisurely yoga stretches, and a shared vegetarian lunch.

A typical explanation for participating in Prayer for Peace came from an Englishman, who had dropped out of a university course in Religious Studies because, he said, 'it didn't make sense *writing* about Buddhism'. Here, by contrast, he felt comfortable, practising meditation in his own way in a sympathetic environment. The implication was that the academic model of rational enquiry was intrinsically self-defeating. Just doing it – meditating – was the point. This popular approach was also evident at a Findhorn gathering on Celtic spirituality the same year, when I overheard audience members describe several of the presentations disapprovingly as 'too heady' (i.e., conceptual or intellectual). When I suggested to the conference organizer that a debate between practitioners and scholars might be stimulating, he disagreed on the grounds that academic debate was interesting but inherently polarizing and hence, by implication, destructive – a red herring from the knowledge promised by direct, unmediated experience (whether in divine guidance or meditation practice). The objective of practitioners – whether Salisbury Centre meditator or Findhorn audience member – is to substitute an enriched knowledge of 'for a stale knowledge *that*'.

My third and final example of a New Age soteriology is Reiki healing (Melton, 2001), which develops the more somatic and embodied approach to soteriology characteristic of free-style meditation In popular discourse, to be healed is not to be cured of disease, but to find release or to be saved: as Coward (1989, p.12) puts it, 'a *health* movement has become the repository of any number of aspirations about individuals achieving a new state of spiritual awareness' (ibid.).[10] This approach was evident at a Reiki demonstration I attended in Glasgow. The Reiki Master outlined the soteriological premiss of Reiki while treating local women in their 30s and 40s on stage, placing one hand on top of the head and the other on the upper back. She stressed the universality of the practice, claiming that, since the Japanese word meant literally universal (*rei*) life force energy (*ki*), Reiki was a universal spiritual path in which the opening of healing channels between healer and healed gave direct, unmediated access to divine energy or power. This picture was now supported by science, she said, which saw the universe as a vibrant energy field in which all bodies were wholes, with different levels of atomic vibration. Reiki healing was therefore simply a matter of 'restoring the appropriate vibrationary level' to the body. To do this, the healer draws energy from the divine source into her own body, and then transmits this energy, through her hands, into the body requiring healing (as she demonstrated on the platform). A flyer advertising her services linked this simple technique to an impressive soteriology:

> As Reiki begins to move in and heal our whole system, it begins to move us into the next step in our evolution. It starts to work on and break through our limiting beliefs and attitudes, thus increasing our ability to take responsibility for our lives and well-being.

In other words, Reiki promises that 'release from this world' that Fitzgerald (2000, p.121) sees as the hallmark of a soteriology. But in contrast to 'guidance', which emphasizes the discursive content of messages (with directions on what to do and not to do), the epistemologies of meditation and healing are less cognitive and directive. Rather, they emphasize bodily presence and awareness, thereby seeking to place individuals within what Csikszentmihalyi has called the 'flow' of experience:

> Flow denotes the holistic sensation present when we act with total involvement ... It is the kind of state in which action follows upon action according to an internal logic which seems to need no conscious intervention on our part. We experience it as a unified flowing from one moment to the next. (Csikszentmihalyi, 1975, cited in Hedges and Beckford, 2000, pp.182–3)

The experience of flow can be directed towards particular ends, such as practising meditation as a *prayer for peace*, or the more abstract goal of *letting the transcendental in*. Or entering the flow might mean *just doing it* – that is, meditating for the sake of it. In Reiki discourse, entering a flow state might translate as simply being open to receive life force energy into the body. To the extent that experiencing flow, rather than aiming for a specific goal, becomes paramount in practice, we move – in Weber's terms – from a *zweckrational* or instrumental disposition to a *vertrational* or value-oriented one. But although the quality of the experience may be different for practitioners, becoming less discursive and more somatic as it shifts from instrumental strategy to value-oriented flow, its overall status as rational action remains constant: that is, it is still behaviour which is directed towards 'the methodical attainment of a definitely given and practical end' (Weber, 1970, p.293). In other words, due to the constraints of *habitus*, its soteriology remains couched in terms of the rational order.

Conclusion: New Age Soteriologies, Instrumental Rationality and the Politics of Popular Religion

Although much qualitative research remains to be done in the area of post-Christian popular religion, I would argue on the basis of my own fieldwork in the UK, and of scattered Anglo-American ethnographies,[11] that casual conversations in everyday settings can turn quickly to popular soteriologies when questions about religion are introduced. For example, a university tutor who had recently returned from an ashram in India showed me a double-ended crystal one afternoon in my home city of Stirling. He asked me to put it against my third eye and monitor the effects. 'It may be quite subtle', he said, 'just see what happens'. He told me he was setting up an *electronic buddhafield* in cyberspace to link up different spiritual centres. A Salisbury Centre resident told me he organized his spiritual quest along similar lines to this *see what happens* approach, practising *whatever feels right* and trusting in that choice, in the moment. This *laissez-faire* epistemology of *hunch, instinct* and *feeling* can punctuate everyday encounters. Travelling by train to a conference in 1996, I spoke with a middle-aged woman. She showed me a pack of crystal healing cards which she used in spiritual healing: aluminium rectangles in bright colours, impregnated with crushed crystals. She was studying *The Celestine Prophecy* (Redfield, 1994), a popular text whose principal teaching – that there are no coincidences in life – she used to explain the esoteric significance of our own encounter that day on the train. Several other practitioners I met during my fieldwork also told me quietly that I was *meant* to be studying New Age religion and that at some future date I would understand, retrospectively, the deeper meaning of my research.

But notwithstanding practitioners' claims that guidance, meditation and healing are epistemological acts of resistance against instrumental rationality, the outcomes of popular practice, in both soteriological and political terms, are rather less certain. Re-thinking New Age practices as popular rather than as alternative religion will increasingly allow us to expect, and understand, this indeterminacy. I have discussed some of the epistemological problems associated with examining the release promised by these soteriologies. Now I will briefly address political indeterminacies.

The history of Findhorn is once again a case in point. A decade before co-founding the colony, Peter Caddy published an essay in the *RAF Quarterly* (1952) entitled *Leadership and Morale*, in which, in a brisk, popular style, he affirmed Jesus Christ as an example of a model leader and urged a return to the Christianity of the man in the street as a post-war antidote to the 'distorted half-truths of Communist ideology'. The essay ended with a rousing call for 'spiritual as well as military rearmament of the nation (Caddy, 1996, p. 449*ff*). The deeply conservative politics of this essay (written when Caddy was involved in Sheena Govan's group) contrast sharply with the counter-cultural disposition of the hippies, who, less than a generation later, would provide much-needed personnel at Findhorn (Sutcliffe, 2003a, p. 118*ff*).

This tension between the conservative, even authoritarian, leadership of the earlier generation and the liberal-libertarian *do your own thing* lifestyle of the counterculture[12] has left its mark on Findhorn's political economy. On the one hand it retains an oligarchic structure, with overall policy being formulated by a core group of elders, based on guidance received in free-style meditation. This places the exercise of authority in the colony in a conservative tradition, since membership of core group comes only after lengthy apprenticeship and peer approval. A further conservative tendency stems from the colony's need to survive financially: it is largely dependent upon income from its residential courses in holistic education and spirituality, which must be marketed in the private sector like any other commercial product.[13] On the other hand, Findhorn values consensus and group processes in day-to-day decision-making; similarly, it has attained the status of educational consultant to the United Nations, the standard-bearer of liberal internationalism. From yet another angle, it has been widely identified with environmentalism and green politics, from the early days of giant vegetables in the magical Findhorn garden (Findhorn Community, 1988[1975]) to the colony's reinvention in the 1990s as an eco-village with wind-turbine power and natural sewage treatment (Walker, 1994, pp.112–119). In contrast to conservative models of leadership, these aspects of colony life, together with its broad tolerance of religious pluralism, align Findhorn with classic liberal values of equality of opportunity, liberty, individuality and, significantly, rationality (Bellamy, 1999, p.24).

The politics of New Age healing are similarly indeterminate. At a simple level this is evident in the progress of its qualifying descriptor between the 1960s and the present: from fringe through alternative to complementary (Wicks, 1982, p.4), the most recent tag in the UK being Complementary and Alternative Medicine, or CAM.[14] Ambiguities continue at the level of practice: on the one hand, emphasis on personal choice in healthcare, including informed, critical use of mainstream health services (an information network called *What Doctors Don't Tell You* was prominent in the UK in the 1990s), aligns the field with classic liberal values. On the other hand, the growth of the field as a profession over the last 30 years has proceeded (until quite recently) almost entirely in and through the free market. Bowman (1999, p. 186), for example, sees alternative healing as 'very much in the "small business" ethos of the [Margaret] Thatcher era'.[15] The entrepreneurship and self-reliance characteristic of CAM fit quite neatly with the de-regulated markets, multiple suppliers and consumer choice favoured by conservatives and neo-liberals alike. The case of Reiki encapsulates the issue: crudely put, is it an empowering epistemology of grassroots healthcare for a hitherto marginalized, subaltern female constituency; or the entrepreneurial franchising of a new brand of spiritual healing for a bull market?

In conclusion, the implications of New Age epistemology, political as well as soteriological, are unpredictable and cut all ways. Re-thinking New Age as popular rather than countercultural religion clarifies this indeterminacy and incompleteness and opens the way for fresh analyses. My argument here has been that the epistemologies which structure and validate New Age practices are constituted by the same instrumental rationality they ostensibly critique and transcend. By this I mean that guidance, meditation and healing are set within a wider order of rationality, either instrumental (*zweckrational*) or value-oriented (*vertrational*), which assesses the relative efficiency of the technique in question for achieving the desired soteriological goal. Practitioners necessarily are guided, healed or meditate under the conditions of a prevailing order – rational calculation – that is already inscribed in their collective *habitus*. Hence these and similar practices are better interpreted as attempts to manage rather than to overcome the rational order: as strategic practices, rather than expressions of revolt.

Notes

I would like to thank the volume editors, Tim Haydon, and an anonymous reviewer for their critical feedback on earlier versions of this chapter.

1   See Sebald (1984), and Melton (1988, p.36), who writes: 'The New Age Movement [*sic*] can best be dated from around 1971' in the figure of Baba Ram Dass, a transformed refugee from the psychedelic age'. Similarly Hanegraaff (1996, p.10) finds the 'movement' (*sic*) to be 'commonly, and rightly, regarded as rooted in the so-called counterculture of the 1960s'; and York (1995, p.37) calls 'New Age' a 'generic term' for 'the exploding re-interest in the 1960s counterculture concerns of ... all things alternative'.

2   For example, Steyn (1994), York (1995), Heelas (1996) and Hanegraaff (1996). For a detailed critique, see Sutcliffe (2003a, Chps 1, 5, 9), summarized in Sutcliffe (2003b, pp.8–14).

3   Despite the lack of institutionalization, there is a broadly replicable demography for New Age, at least in the USA, UK, Western Europe and Australasia: largely white, middle-class, middle-aged (30–50 year olds), superiorly-educated, made up of professional, managerial, IT, arts and

entrepreneurial occupations, and well-represented by women, typically 2:1 over men. For UK demographic data as an example, see York, 1995, Chapter 5; Rose, 1998, 2001; Heelas and Seel 2003. These demographic trends suggest that New Age is more accurately described as the post-Christian (especially post-Protestant) popular religion of the white middle classes. For UK demographic data as an example, see ... Heelas and Seel 2003; Heelas and Woodhead 2004.

4   See Sutcliffe (2003a, Chp 7) for an ethnography of Findhorn, described by Bloom (1991, p.2) as 'the most important New Age centre on the planet', and Sutcliffe (2003a, Chps 3 and 4) for a history of the founding and early period of the colony in the context of UK and international New Age culture.

5   See Sutcliffe (2003a, pp.25–29, 95–102, 122–130).

6   Experience in the common sense of 'practical acquaintance with any matter gained by trial' (Chambers English Dictionary, p.502).

7   Indicative post-war sources (roughly paralleling New Age) include Laski (1961) and Hardy (1979). See Sharf (1998) for analysis of the rhetorical function of 'experience' in both legitimations and explanations of religion.

8   Portrayals in the secondary literature range from 'countercultural' to 'establishmentarian' and beyond, or Left-Liberal to Libertarian Right in the political spectrum. Sebald (1984) and Riches (2003) favour countercultural representations, as do most historiographies (see note 1). Heelas (1996, p.138) tries to accommodate two divergent 'wings', one made up of 'people who have lost faith in the ... capitalistic mainstream' and who seek an alternative, the other consisting in people 'pursuing the utopian vision provided by the capitalistic system itself'. York (1995, p.330) initially aligned New Age with neo-Pagan counterculturalism, but subsequently argued that it promotes spiritual commercialization in which spiritual traditions are 'bought and sold ... according to basic free-market principles' (York, 2001, p.361). Several studies (e.g. Rupert, 1992; Salamon, 2001) find an elective affinity between New Age values and Anglo-American corporate business ideology. The argument by Lau (2000, p.7*ff*) that an 'ideology of the alternative' is at work offers an instructive retrospective of these various portrayals. At the furthest end of the spectrum, Kalman and Murray (1995) and Sjoo (1992), in rather different ways (as journalists and polemicist respectively), claim that New Age harbours extreme right wing, even fascist, currents.

9   The method and epistemology of guidance is also similar to Spiritualist mediumship (Hazelgrove, 2000) and American channeling (Brown, 1997).

10   Further on popular epistemologies of healing, see Albanese (1992), McGuire (1993), Bowman (1999) and Sutcliffe (2003a, pp.174–180).

11   For example, Bloch's (1998) analysis of interviews with New Age and Pagan practitioners in the USA; Heelas and Seel (2003) on popular spiritualities in the rural English town of Kendal.

12   'A guy just wants to practise his religion, just wants to do his thing, man': from the oral biography of 'Otis Cook – A Hippie Odyssey' in Neville (1971, pp.191–203).

13   On Findhorn economy, see Brierley and Walker (1995); on internal management, see Chapter 10, 'Decision-Making Structures', in Walker (1994, pp.339–390).

14 See *New Scientist* (London) 26 May 2001, 'Hype, Hope and Healing', pp.28–53. The acculturation and increasing legitimation of healing as a consumer item in popular culture can be seen by comparing the titles of 2 reports in the UK magazine *Which?*: 'Magic or Medicine?' (October 1986) and 'Healthy Choice' (November 1995).
15 Conservative Prime Minister in the UK between 1979–1990. Famously, M. H. Thatcher (b.1925) was the daughter of a provincial grocer.

References

Albanese, C. (1992), 'The Magical Staff: Quantum Healing in the New Age', in J. Lewis and J.G. Melton (eds), *Perspectives on the New Age*, SUNY Press, New York , pp.68–84.
Anonymous (1985 [1975]), *A Course in Miracles*, Arkana, London.
Bailey, A. (1981[1944]), *Discipleship in the New Age Volume I*, Lucis Publishing Co, New York.
Bellamy, R. (1999), 'Liberalism', in R. Eatwell and A. Wright (eds), *Contemporary Political Ideologies*, Continuum, London, pp.23–50.
Berman, M. (1981), *The Re-enchantment of the World*, Cornell University Press, New York.
Bloch, J. (1998), *New Spirituality, Self and Belonging: How New Agers and Neo-Pagans Talk about Themselves*, Praeger, Westport, CT.
Bloom, W. (ed.) (1991), *The New Age: An Anthology of Essential Writings*, Channel 4/Rider, London.
Bourdieu, P. (1977), *Outline of a Theory of Practice*, Cambridge University Press, Cambridge.
Bowman, M. (1999), 'Healing in the Spiritual Marketplace: Consumers, Courses and Credentialism', *Social Compass* vol. 46, no. 2, pp.181–189.
Brierley, J. and Walker, A. (1995), 'Financing a Sustainable Dream', *One Earth* [Findhorn Foundation magazine], vol. 18, pp.32–34
Brown, M.F. (1997), *The Channeling Zone: American Spirituality in an Anxious Age*, Harvard University Press, Harvard.
Caddy, E. (1988), *Flight into Freedom*, Element, Shaftesbury.
___(1992 [1971]), *God Spoke to Me*, Findhorn Press, Forres.
Caddy, P. (1996), *In Perfect Timing: Memoirs of a Man for the New Millenium*, Findhorn Press, Forres.
Chambers English Dictionary, (1991) Edinburgh, p.501.
Coward, R. (1989), *The Whole Truth: The Myth of Alternative Health*, Faber and Faber, London.
Donovan, P. (2000), 'Can We Know God by Experience?', in B. Davies (ed.), *Philosophy of Religion: A Guide and Anthology*, Oxford University Press, Oxford, pp.370–381.

Edgar, A. and Sedgwick, P. (eds), (1999), 'Epistemology', in *Key Concepts in Cultural Theory*, Routledge, London, pp.127–131.

Findhorn Community (1988[1975]), *The Findhorn Garden*, Findhorn Press, Forres.

Fitzgerald, T. (2000), *The Ideology of Religious Studies*, Oxford University Press, New York.

Giddens, A. (1994[1971]), *Capitalism and Social Theory: An Analysis of the Writings of Marx, Durkheim and Max Weber*, Cambridge University Press, Cambridge.

Gombrich, R. (1988), *Thervada Buddhism: A Social History from Ancient Benares to Modern Colombo*, Routledge, London.

Govan, I. (1978 [1938]), *Spirit of Revival: the Story of J.G. Govan and the Faith Mission*, the Faith Mission, Edinburgh.

Hall, S. (1994 [1981]), 'Notes on Deconstructing "the Popular" , in J. Storey (ed.), *Cultural Theory and Popular Culture: A Reader*, Harvester Wheatsheaf, New York and London, pp.455–466.

Hanegraaff, W. (1996), *New Age Religion and Western Culture*, Leiden, Brill.

Hardy, A. (1979) *The Spiritual Nature of Man: A Study of Contemporary Religious Experience*, Clarendon Press, Oxford.

Hazelgrove, J. (2000), *Spiritualism and British Society between the Wars*, Manchester University Press, Manchester.

Hedges, E. and Beckford, J. (2000), 'Holism, Healing and the New Age', in S. Sutcliffe and M. Bowman (eds), *Beyond New Age: Exploring Alternative Spirituality*, Edinburgh University Press, Edinburgh, pp.169–187.

Heelas, P. (1996), *The New Age Movement: the Celebration of the Self and the Sacralization of Modernity*, Blackwell, Oxford.

Heelas, P. and Seel, B. (2003), 'An ageing New Age?', in G. Davie, P. Heelas, and L. Woodhead (eds), *Predicting Religion: Christian, Secular and Alternative Futures*, Ashgate, Aldershot, pp.229–47.

Heelas, P. and Woodhead, L. (2004), *The Spiritual Revolution: Why Religion is Giving Way to Spirituality*, Blackwell, Oxford.

Kalman, M. and Murray, J. (1995), 'New-Age Nazism', *New Statesman and Society* (London), vol. 23 June, pp.18*ff.*

Laski, M. (1961), *Ecstasy: A Study of Some Secular and Religious Experiences*, The Cresset Press, London.

Lau, K. (2000), *New Age Capitalism: Making Money East of Eden*, University of Pennsylvania Press, Philadelphia.

Lyon, D. (2000), *Jesus in Disneyland: Religion in Postmodern Times*, Polity, Cambridge.

Maclean, D. (1980), *To Hear the Angels Sing*, Findhorn Press, Forres.

McGuire, M. (1993), 'Health and Spirituality as Contemporary Concerns', *Annals of the American Academy of Political and Social Sciences,* vol. 527, pp.144–154.

Melton, J. G. (1988), 'A History of the New Age Movement', in R. Basil (ed.), *Not Necessarily the New Age*, Prometheus Books, Buffalo, New York, pp.35–53.

___(2001), 'Reiki: the International Spread of a New Age Healing Movement', in M. Rothstein (ed.), *New Age Religion and Globalization*, Aarhus University Press, Aarhus, Denmark, pp.73–93.

Neville, R. (1971[1970]), *Playpower*, Paladin/Granada, St. Albans.

Possamai, A. (2000), 'A Profile of New Agers: Social and Spiritual Aspects', *Journal of Sociology*, vol. 36, no.3, pp.364–377.

Redfield, J. (1994), *The Celestine Prophecy*, Bantam, New York.

Riches, D. (2003), 'Counter-Cultural Egalitarianism: a comparative analysis of New Age and other "alternative" communities', *Culture and Religion*, vol. 4, no. 1, pp.119–139.

Rose, S. (1998), 'An Examination of the New Age Movement: Who is Involved and What Constitutes its Spirituality', *Journal of Contemporary Religion*, vol. 13, no. 1, pp.5–22.

___(2001), 'New Age Women: Spearheading the Movement?', *Women's Studies*, vol. 30, no. 3, pp.329–50.

Rupert, G. (1992), 'Employing the New Age: Training Seminars', in J. Lewis and J. G. Melton (eds), *Perspectives on the New Age*, SUNY Press, New York, pp.127–135.

Salamon, K. (2001), '"Going Global from the Inside Out": Spiritual Globalism in the Workplace', in M. Rothstein (ed.), *New Age Religion and Globalization*, Aarhus University Press, Aarhus, pp.150–172.

Sebald, H. (1984) 'New-Age Romanticism: the Quest for an Alternative Lifestyle as a Force of Social Change', *Humboldt Journal of Social Relations,* vol. 11, no. 2, pp.106–127.

Sharf, R. (1998), 'Experience', in M. Taylor (ed.), *Critical Terms for Religious Studies*, Chicago University Press, Chicago, pp.94–116.

Sjoo, M. (1992), *New Age and Armageddon: the Goddess or the Gurus? Towards a Feminist Vision of the Future*, The Women's Press, London.

Spangler, D. and Thompson, W.I. (1991), *Reimagination of the World: A Critique of the New Age, Science and Popular Culture*, Bear and Co, Santa Fe, New Mexico.

Steyn, C. (1994), *Worldviews in Transition: An Investigation into the New Age Movement in South Africa*, University of South Africa Press, Pretoria.

Sutcliffe, S. 2003(a), *Children of the New Age: A History of Spiritual Practices*, Routledge, London.

___2003(b), 'Category Formation and the History of "New Age"', *Culture and Religion*, vol. 4, no. 1, May, pp.5–29.

Walker, A. (ed) (1994), *The Kingdom Within: A Guide to the Spiritual Work of the Findhorn Community*, Findhorn Press, Forres.

Walsch, N. D. (1997[1995]), *Conversations with God, Book 1*, Hodder and Stoughton, London.

Weber, M. (970[1948]), 'The Social Psychology of the World's Religions', in H. H. Gerth and C. Wright Mills, (trans. and ed.), *From Max Weber: Essays in Sociology*, Routledge and Kegan Paul, London, pp.267–301.

Wicks, H. (1982), 'Introduction: Health and Healing', in R. Adams (ed.), *The New Times Network: Groups and Centres for Personal Growth*, Routledge and Kegan Paul, London, pp.3–5.

Williams, R. (1976), *Keywords: A Vocabulary of Culture and Society*, Fontana, Glasgow.

Wood, M. (2003), 'Capital Possession: a Comparative Approach to "New Age" and Control of the Means of Possession', *Culture and Religion*, vol. 4, no.1, pp.159–182.

York, M. (1995), *The Emerging Network: A Sociology of the New Age and neo-Pagan Movements*, Rowman and Littlefield, Lanham, MY.

___(2001), 'New Age Commodification and Appropriation of Spirituality', *Journal of Contemporary Religion*, vol. 16, no. 3, pp.361–372.

Chapter 14

'There's Bulldozers in the Fairy Garden': Re-enchantment Narratives within British Eco-Paganism

Andy Letcher

Mr Pok:	Hello Mr Longshanks.
Mr Longshanks:	Hello there Mr Pok. How's your fairy garden?
Mr Pok:	Terrible, terrible news from the garden.
Mr Longshanks:	Oh dear, what's wrong then?
	Some kind of infestation?
	Greenfly, bugs and aphids?
Mr Pok:	No, no, much worse.
Mr Longshanks:	Worse? What could possibly be wrong?
Mr Pok:	There's BULLDOZERS!
Mr Longshanks:	Bulldozers?
Mr Pok:	Bulldozers in the fairy garden! It just won't do.
Together:	Well let's get together and DO something!

(From Space Goats, 1999)

One of the defining features of the 1990s in Britain was large-scale popular campaigning against the construction of new roads. In the late 1980s the then Conservative government, siding with the roads lobby in the 'great transport debate', announced a massive £23 billion programme of new road building across the length of the country. The resulting protest movement was without parallel in British post-war history, both in terms of the scale of public opposition, and the primacy placed upon the use of non-violent direct action. Starting with two protesters at Twyford Down near Winchester in 1992, the movement grew until by the time of the A30 campaign in 1997 at Fairmile in Devon, many thousands of people were involved. Whilst protesters entertained the possibility that their actions might prevent a particular road being built, their primary aim was to add so much extra cost to construction (through policing and security), that future projects would be rendered economically unviable. Through sheer weight of numbers they were able to use the profit-motive as the leverage point with which to disrupt, and eventually overturn, government policy. Following the Fairmile evictions the government quietly kicked road-building into touch, reducing the budget to £6 billion, where it has remained until quite recently when the Labour government announced a package of new roads as a part solution to Britain's ever worsening traffic congestion problems.

Protesters, variously motivated but united by the belief that road-building would create more traffic congestion not less and that the swathes of countryside lost therefore to development would be sacrificed in vain, placed themselves bodily in the way of construction. Combining the idea of the protest camp from the earlier anti-nuclear demonstrations at Greenham Common, with direct-action tactics from American Earth First!, they built camps, tree-houses, tunnels, towers, tripods and various other ingenious 'locking-on' points[1] along the proposed routes of new roads, thereby requiring an expensive operation to remove them safely before construction might commence.

Much has been written about the protests and this utilization of direct action as a tactic of resistance. Protests have been interpreted variously as being the latest expression of a counter-cultural tendency with its roots in the 1960s (McKay, 1996); as representing a new development in environmental campaigning (Seel et. al., 2000); as being part of the continued Marxist and Anarchist struggle against the forces of global capitalism (Aufheben, 1998); as the legitimate exercise of democracy by people disenfranchized by the political process (Monbiot, 1998, 2000); as a form of societal performance in which the tensions, contradictions and power relations within modern society are articulated and negotiated (Szerszynski, 1999); and as an expression of a detraditionalized, yet neo-tribal, identity (Hetherington, 1998; Letcher, 2001a,b).

However, much less attention has been given to protester spiritualities, worldviews and narratives. Many protesters adhered to a form of Eco-Paganism[2] in which nature was regarded, not in instrumental terms for its economic worth, but in emotional terms (Milton, 2002) as sacred, enchanted, and crying out for protection from further human amelioration (Letcher, 2001a; Letcher, 2003). The warning that there were 'bulldozers in the fairy garden' should not be seen as metaphorical: for Eco-Pagan protesters it was a statement of literal belief (Letcher, 2001b). The aim of this chapter is therefore to turn attention away from the more obvious and dramatic aspects of protesting and direct action, to a consideration of underlying Eco-Pagan spiritualities and belief-narratives and how they re-enchant the world. Examples are given throughout, drawn from my own experiences as a protester during the Newbury Bypass campaign (1995–6), from interviews conducted for this research and from other published first-hand accounts. I begin by presenting a brief overview of Eco-Paganism.

Eco-Paganism – an Overview

The diverse and detraditionalized nature of protest-movement spiritualities resists their easy categorization into a single label, but nevertheless certain themes predominate suggesting two broad types of Eco-Paganism. On the one hand the term refers to pre-existing initiates of Pagan spiritualities (for instance, Wiccans, Druids and Heathens – see Harvey, 1997) who, as a consequence of their beliefs and practices, choose to become involved in protesting and, crucially, direct action. For these practitioners environmentalism is the means by which the commonly articulated Pagan belief that 'all the earth is sacred' is put into practice. The exemplar of this kind of Eco-Paganism is the Dragon Environmental Network, a group founded by London-based 'progressive' Wiccans (see Jennings, 2002), influenced particularly by the writings of Starhawk (for example Starhawk, 1982), and committed to blending direct and magical action through techniques of 'eco-magick' (see Letcher, in press). Dragon members were active in many of the road campaigns, and regarded the reprieve of London's Oxleas Woods as proof of the efficacy of their endeavours.

On the other hand the term refers to the diverse spiritualities found amongst protesters living more permanently at protest camps who exhibit Pagan tendencies but are not initiates of any particular tradition. These spiritualities, in keeping with the times, are detraditionalized (Heelas et al., 1996), elective and affectual, and combine elements from diverse sources in a 'pick and mix' fashion (Sutcliffe and Bowman, 2000). That is, spiritualities are assembled according to the needs of the self in an ad hoc, individualized manner, from a diverse range of sources including Buddhism, Hinduism, 1960s psychedelia, practices from the New Age and Human Potential movements, shamanism, British folklore, feminism and Goddess Spirituality. Practitioners may be reluctant to identify themselves with any particular spirituality, but nevertheless there remains a core Pagan doxa. One protester typifies this when he states 'I'm not exactly a raging pagan myself, I'm more of a…Free-Floating [Earth] Mother Lover, but if any religious perspective is represented on site, it's pagans' (Merrick, 1997, p.73). Thus, for example, the eight principle Pagan festivals are marked, but unlike more 'orthodox' Pagan rituals, and in keeping with the pronounced sense of alterity, there is an emphasis on spontaneity, improvisation and celebration (see Letcher, 2001a).

This chapter focuses on the second type of Eco-Paganism, that found within the protest camps; but there are a couple of points that must be stressed. Firstly whilst the focus of this chapter is the second type of Eco-Paganism, that found within the protest camps, it must be noted that the two types are not mutually exclusive: members of various Druid orders regularly reside at protest camps, as do Wiccan initiates (see Roberts and Motherwort, 1997; Pendragon and Stone, 2003). Secondly, while by no means all protesters exhibit 'spiritual' inclinations – indeed some are antagonistic towards those that do (Letcher, 2001b) – Eco-Pagan narratives remain extremely widespread throughout and suffuse the movement as a whole. Thus it has become common parlance to refer to 'eco-sabotage' as 'pixieing', even amongst non-religious protesters (Letcher, 2001b).

Protest Camps, Liminal Lifestyles

The decision to build a new road creates, in effect, the space in which alternative lifestyles and spiritualities can flourish, albeit temporarily. For example, the government decision to build the Newbury bypass, and the consequent acquisition of land, created a nine-mile corridor along the proposed route upon which protesters would otherwise have had no reason, or opportunity, to live. Unlike other large-scale contemporary protest movements, such as those opposing globalization or genetically-modified food, road-protesting requires practitioners to be physically present at such locations for considerable periods of time, in some cases years not months. This 'embedding' in a liminal space enables the development of a distinct protest lifestyle, the formation of neo-tribal identities (Hetherington, 1998; Letcher 2001,a,b), the establishment of relationship to place, and the emergence of Eco-Pagan practices and belief-narratives.

Drawing upon various commensurable theoretical positions, protest camps spaces may be regarded as liminal sites of *communitas* (Turner, 1969), as heterotopic (Foucault, 1998), as carnivalesque (Bakhtin, 1984), or as temporary autonomous zones (Bey, 1991). Each of these perspectives, whilst differing in the details, theorize spaces in which societal norms, rules and conventions are juxtaposed with their antitheses and thereby tested, inverted, challenged or ridiculed. Protest camps, by definition sites of contestation, are just such places, and here I describe how the transformation of space, of time, of identity, and of consensual reality cause the break with ordinary *societas* (Turner, 1969) that allows alternative narratives to flourish.

Space is transformed, initially, by the decision to construct a new road, whereby a new organizing narrative is imposed upon conceptually unrelated pieces of land. In the case of the Newbury bypass, arable land, woodland, nature reserves, stretches of river basin and canal, houses and gardens and brownfield sites, physically apart and unlinked by ordinary lines of communication, were given a new conceptual coherence by the prospect of development. Whilst the process of acquiring the land and obtaining permission to develop it is occurring (a lengthy legal procedure), its ownership status remains uncertain: a corridor of land is therefore rendered marginal, and it is into this uncertain space that protesters move. The transformation continues with the construction of camps such that a piece of woodland becomes a habitation, a tree becomes a dwelling, the space between trees becomes connected by a series of aerial walkways that preclude the need to come down to earth. 'I came down one morning after a week long stint in the trees' (Hindle, n.d., p.11).

In addition to entering a transformed space, protesters slip through the grip of the quotidian into a different sense of time, what might elsewhere be called 'festival time' (Bakhtin, 1984; Schechner, 1993). No longer bound by the conventions of nine to five – or the working week – protesters break into a different rhythm, what Foucault calls heterochronia (Foucault, 1998, p.182). The single most important moment is the point of closure that will come with the inevitable eviction. On the one hand this notion of 'ragnarok' produces a permanent air of insecurity and instability,[3] such that, daily, defences are constructed in preparation for the 'big event'. On the other, the sense that this point of closure lies in the unspecified future creates a sense of an ever-unfolding present, of living outside of time. Life, in this way, becomes a succession of moments, with little thought for the future beyond that of the eviction.

For example, the protester Jim Hindle, in a moving account of his battles against both roads and illness, describes how with a small group he decided to walk from Newbury to a reunion gathering of protesters at Solsbury Hill near Bath, a journey of some 50 miles (Hindle, n.d., pp.17–21). The spur-of-the-moment decision to go was accompanied by very little planning or forethought about how long it would take, how far they would walk each day, or where they would sleep or eat. The group simply arose at dawn and left, sleeping in opportunistically acquired barns or on the towpath, and 'scrumping' food from supermarket skips. What mattered was 'the moment', and thus for Jim it was simply 'a bimble to Solsbury Hill' (Hindle, n.d., p.17). 'Bimbling', the act of directed but unhurried walking (an anti-urban form of flaneurism, or drive, perhaps), was commonplace: 'pretty soon I was entirely at home in the Valley [Stanworth Valley, Lancashire] bimbling round the pathways and the steps playing my whistle as I went' (Hindle, n.d., p.24). Another protester, Josh, one of the Dongas Tribe at Twyford Down, wrote the following song lyrics that typify the sense of timelessness whilst 'bimbling':

Walking along the ancient ridgeways of Wessex, with my friends
We watch the sun rise, we watch the sunset, we watch it rising again.
(Josh, 1996)

Certainly this feeling of being outside time, bimbling or otherwise, can lead to indolence or inactivity – 'half a dozen people were round the fire doing a whole lot of nothing' (Hindle, n.d., p.53) – but just as equally it can create a sense of personal autonomy, a sense that many protesters seek. As 'Jason' put it:

'It's romantic when you're risking your life and digging down holes and you're just like kids again, you're allowed to get on with it, no one's telling you to shut up, you can stay up all night, you know, you can share the same bottle, and share the same bed partners.'
('Jason', interview conducted 21/1/2000)

This identity of alterity and freedom is something that protest culture invests considerable effort in establishing. The typical juxtaposition of, say, ex-army boots and dreadlocks stylistically inverts and contests societal norms, and together with a 'resistance through dirt' (Hetherington, 1998) marks the wearer as outsider. In addition, protesters reify indigenous cultures as exemplars of alterity through a conspicuous 'tribalism' (see Bowman, 1995; Letcher, 2001a,b, 2003; Butler, 2003). Many protesters refer to themselves as tribes, most famously the Dongas at

Twyford Down, their shared aesthetic as 'tribedelic'. Gypsies are especially romanticized and emulated, the Dongas for example regarding themselves as the indigenous travelling people of the British Isles: 'the magical peoples – the Dongas and the Dragons; tribes who came from nowhere and whose place was with nature' (Crow cited in Butler, 2003, p.399).

The frequent usage of psychoactive substances at protest camps, a transgressive act in itself, is also justified through recourse to tribalism, for consumption of entheogens[4] is 'what tribal peoples do' and therefore something to be emulated. Additionally the experiences engendered by the regular use of cannabis, and the frequent consumption of LSD and indigenous psilocybin-containing mushrooms, serves to highlight the break with *societas* by challenging ordinary, consensual, 'paramount' reality (Schutz, 1967).

In these ways protest camps may be seen as liminal spaces, marginalized by, and on the margins of, mainstream society. In addition to their function of obstructing construction work, they are places where norms and conventions can be inverted and contested. Thus at Claremont Road, a 'squatted' street blocking the M11 expansion in London, protesters 'chose to describe and to commemorate their experiences as a "festival of resistance"' (Butler, 2003, p.377). 'Claremont Road was also a place of transformation – of misrule – of the carnivalesque, like the fair that comes and goes, sprinkling chaos and misrule in its place' (ibid., p.376). It is within these liminal spaces that Eco-Pagan beliefs flourish, and it is to a description of these and the way in which they re-enchant the landscape that I now turn.

Trees, Fairies, Mushrooms – Eco-Pagan Narratives of Enchantment

Protest camps, the protest lifestyle, are then both heterotopic (disruptive of space) and heterochronic (disruptive of time) (Foucault, 1998). As stated above, by no means all protesters have spiritual inclinations; but Eco-Pagan enchantment narratives are widespread and serve to 'fill' these liminal spaces. This is particularly evident in the naming of people and things. Any human grouping will tend to develop its own identity, expressed linguistically through a vocabulary of slang, narrated events, jokes and so on (Hetherington, 1998). Protest culture is unexceptional in this regard, except that the narratives it espouses tend to describe or delineate an enchanted world; the events it relates take on an epic, almost mythic quality.

The 27 camps along the route of the Newbury Bypass were each named: Gotan, The Pixie Village, Skyward, Fluff Central, Camelot, Rickety Bridge, and so on. Likewise several of the larger treehouses at Newbury – the Mothership at Kennet Camp, and the Good Ship Venus at Skyward – whilst the wood burner in the communal bender[5] at Granny Ash camp was known as 'Puff the magic burner' (Hindle, n.d., p.54). Trees in general were venerated , but the naming of certain individual trees marked them as being of particular significance – Granny and Grandfather Ash, Middle Oak, Hern, Melea. This overall renaming of places, things, and artefacts served to create an enchanted cartography, linking the disparate camps, the objects and features within them, into a coherent and meaningful whole. As one Druid told me, 'It's kind of like re-enchanting the land…[a] hill will always be the same, but if it's got a myth around it, it makes it much more magical to the people who live around it' (Dave, interview conducted 28/7/99).

The mythological sources upon which Eco-Pagans draw are often literary, and the writings of J. R. R. Tolkien are hugely influential here (Letcher, 2001b). Patrick Curry has noted that amongst protesters at Newbury he found 'only one person out of dozens who hadn't just read *The Lord of the Rings*, but knew it, so to speak, inside out' (Curry, 1998, p. 54). Not only did protesters relate to the narrative of the little people standing up to the corrupt forces of Mordor (Letcher, 2001b), they embraced Tolkien's enchanted world of tree-dwelling elves: 'I had to move around [in the treetops], like the elves of Lothlorien' (Hindle, n.d., p.9). Other popular sources included C. S. Lewis's Narnia stories, the legends of King Arthur and Robin Hood (see Merrick, 1997, frontispiece[6]), and even Enid Blyton's *Enchanted Forest*.

However vivid the imagination, when reading a novel the reader is always outside of the narrative, a spectator looking in. By contrast Eco-Pagans and protesters took on nicknames which placed them *into* this enchanted land and, most importantly, made them *actors* within its epic and unfolding narrative. Potty Phil, Jip the Jacksy, Badger, Brave Sir Robin, Angle the Bard (my own), Nutty Brown and Balin were just a few of these enchanted identities. 'You just saw people step into their own archetype and live it,' recounts Ann, a protester at Fort Trollheim, adding that 'every day was a story' (Ann, interview conducted 21/1/2000). Hindle recalls:

> Kit looked not unlike a dreaded version [i.e. with dreadlocks] of Genghis Khan, Caleigh was slender with long red hair with long boots and a red cape, she looked like something out of a fantasy novel. Other folks would come and go such as Nuala, a girl named after a figure from Irish legend, she played the harp… (Hindle, n.d., p.15)

For Eco-Pagans this enchanted world of which they are a part is not delusory, escapist or infantile, but a neglected, forgotten, and *truer* [aspect of] reality. It is this reality, this secret and enchanted nature, that 'ancient tribal peoples' are surmised to have had access to, and that Eco-Pagans, as re-created tribes, are remembering to experience. This belief is certainly used to form an identity of alterity from mainstream culture (Letcher, 2003), but it is given credence by phenomenological encounters with enchanted nature. Here I illustrate this with reference to the spiritual significance of trees and fairies and to the use of indigenous entheogenic mushrooms.

The naming of trees was not simply to give them a symbolic force, such that, say, the cutting of 'Middle Oak' would reveal the gross insensitivity of the road-builders[7]; they were named because they were 'other-than-human-persons'

(Harvey, 2003, pp.9–11) with whom their defenders developed relationships. At Skyward Camp, the ash tree 'Melea' was so named because that is how she 'introduced' herself to Nick, the protester defending her. For Jim, his spiritual connection with trees was of paramount importance:

> When we came down off the hillfort we stopped by a tree shedding its leaves. Badger and Moonflower approached it and put their hands on it with an air of reverence…I'd never seen people treat trees with such respect before….I preferred living in the trees, there was a sense of security up there and a feeling of being in the arms of an older, [more] powerful being….The trees themselves would give off this fantastic sensation at night… (Hindle, n.d., pp.8, 11, 12).

Jim adds, 'I did…have the most amazing dreams up that tree' (ibid., p.9). The tree's name, he surmised, was Hern, and to his surprise he found that another protester had quite independently reached the same conclusion. 'Trees can speak volumes if you listen to them, that one had obviously spoken to the both of us' (Hindle, n.d., p.11).

Trees then are other-than-human-persons and it is as natural to honour them, defend them, and to lament their passing as with any meaningful personal relationship. When Skyward camp was cleared, protesters returned the following day to take stock of the previous days' evictions, to salvage possessions and to inspect the damage. Finding the trunk of Melea amongst the carnage of broken branches and mud it was decided to burn her in a funeral pyre (see Letcher, 2002). While this was an attempt to deny anyone profit from her timber, a final act of defiance and an attempt to claw back some sense of victory, it was at heart a funeral to mark the passing of a treasured friend. For all present, it was a deeply moving occasion.

Trees are not the only beings with whom Eco-Pagans regard themselves as sharing the world: the landscape is peopled with a whole variety of elves, pixies, gnomes and other denizens of the fairy garden (whom I will collectively refer to here as 'fairies'). I have written about the nature and significance of fairies to protest culture in detail elsewhere, so will not repeat my findings here (Letcher, 2001b). However, it is worth briefly mentioning that for Eco-Pagans, fairies are regarded literally not metaphorically, and their appearance is proof that protesters, by dint of their actions, have accessed nature's hidden, secret realms. Nature is, in other words, on their side. Visual manifestations, or just the sounds of fairies, were frequently reported. At Stanworth Valley the sound of strange music, or an unlocateable penny whistle, was often heard (Hindle, n.d., *passim*); and Ann at Trollheim recalls, 'I'd go for a shit in the morning and there was a fairy watching me' (Ann, interview conducted 21/1/2000). For Jason the increase in non-ordinary phenomena was a sign that nature was aware of the impending destruction, rather like the supposed prescience of animals and insects before an earthquake:

I don't know if it came [sightings of fairies etc] because we were actually there, or whether because the place is going to get trashed…when some of these places are going to get trashed the energy is altered…there was definitely something going on [and] we were just little players really. (Jason, interview conducted 21/1/2000)

Some, but by no means all, of these encounters occurred whilst under the influence of entheogenic mushrooms. Since the rediscovery in the late 1960s that ingesting the fruiting bodies of *Psilocybe semilanceata* produces certain psychophysical effects, and since the concomitant adoption of an interpretive framework by which those effects came to be regarded as both desirable and 'spiritual', the religious and recreational usage of 'magic mushrooms'[8] has become extremely common in Britain (Letcher, forthcoming).

For Eco-Pagans the ingestion of mushrooms is of spiritual significance and the practice appeals for a number of reasons. For one thing mushrooms are, for a movement with little spending power, freely available. Growing in the autumn months in enormous quantities mushrooms are regarded not only as a 'natural', and therefore a more preferable psychoactive to pharmaceutical alternatives (see Letcher, 2003), but as a gift from the spirits of enchanted nature. The long-standing association of fairies with mushrooms and toadstools, not to mention the resemblance of the magic mushroom to the archetypal goblin's cap, places them directly into the Eco-Pagan 'enchanted' worldview. Most significantly, however, the ingestion of mushrooms has a tendency to produce an *experience* of nature as alive, aware and enchanted (see Letcher, 2004), which confirms the Eco-Pagan worldview. Thus Julian Vayne writes that 'the practice of harvesting them fresh and eating "on the hoof" can be a rewarding way to enjoy the great outdoors' (Vayne, 2001, p.88), whilst another informant refers to mushrooms as 'a Babel fish to the vegetable kingdom'. Jim Hindle took his first mushrooms at Newbury: 'Beccy…told me it was a shame I was taking my first mushrooms in a house, "You need to be out in the woods where the 'shrooms can talk to you"' (Hindle, n.d., p.5).

A full critical examination of the use of these mushrooms and the experiences they engender is beyond the scope of this chapter. However dominant discourses pertaining to psychoactive substances tend to criminalize, pathologize or label as infantile or deranged those who consume them, and it is noteworthy that Eco-Pagan discourse resists all of these categorizations. Eco-Pagans would concur with Vayne's assertion that '[t]aking drugs for "magical purposes" is a rational desire' (Vayne, 2001, p.7). Not only is the taking of psychoactives in protest culture a transgressive act in itself, but the experiences produced question consensus or paramount reality. These experiences reinforce the belief that nature is enchanted and grateful for protesters' actions and self-sacrifice, and that mainstream society is ignorantly unaware of the true nature of the world. Consequently they reinforce Eco-Pagan identities and worldviews.

Conclusion

The nature of road-protesting creates liminal spaces in which Eco-Paganism flourishes. Cultural norms, and categories of space and time, are challenged and transgressed, and the resultant cultural space is filled with Eco-Pagan belief-narratives. These present an enchanted world in which practitioners are engaged in a mythological struggle against a corrupt modernity, and they are reinforced through phenomenological encounters with the non-human world.

Since the road protests of the 1990s, the focus of the counter-cultural agenda has moved to genetically modified foods, to globalization in general, and to the war in Iraq. None of these offers commensurable spaces in which Eco-Paganism has been able to flourish in quite the same way. However, the present government's plans to return to road building as a transport solution will undoubtedly create a second wave of protests, and with the felt need to remove bulldozers from the fairy garden a resurgence of Eco-Pagan narratives of enchantment seems inevitable. We await developments.

Notes

1   A 'locking-on point' consists of iron bars set in concrete, to which protesters padlock themselves. To be removed, the authorities must drill through the concrete and cut the padlock; a timely and costly business.
2   'Paganism' (UK) and 'neo-paganism'(US) refer to the same phenomenon of contemporary spirituality. I use the British terminology throughout.
3   This feeling of impending doom is akin to 'ragnarok' in Norse mythology. 'Ragnarok' was the predicted final battle between the Norse gods and the Ice Giants, culminating in the 'twilight of the Gods'.
4   Most terms to describe psilocybin mushrooms and other psychoactive substances are regarded as pejorative by those who find spiritual value within the experiences they occasion. For example the term 'drug' implies criminality, whilst 'hallucinogen' inaccurately defines the substance as something which distorts reality by inducing hallucinations. Many practitioners prefer the neologism 'entheogen' – producing the experience of God within – to describe mushrooms but this too contains its own discursive assumptions. For the origins and a critique of the term, see Letcher 2004.
5   A bender is a temporary dwelling, constructed from a framework of hazel poles, 'bent' to form a low dome, which can be covered with tarpaulins. Communal benders were built as temporary dormitories.
6   The poster reproduced in Merrick 1997 was written by myself in a conscious attempt to alter the public's perception of protesters, by equating them with the legend of Robin Hood.
7   In the end, the road was re-routed slightly in order to save Middle Oak, to avoid just such a media representation. By the late stages of clearance Middle Oak had become symbolic of the entire campaign.
8   Henceforth I simply refer to these as 'mushrooms'.

References

Aufheben (1998), 'The Politics of Anti-Road Struggle and the Struggles of Anti-Road Politics: the Case of the No M11 Link Road Campaign', in G. McKay (ed.), *DIY Culture. Party and Protest in Nineties Britain*, Verso, London, pp.100–128.

Bakhtin, M. (1984), *Rabelais and His World*, Indiana University Press, Bloomington.

Bey, H. (1991), *T.A.Z. The Temporary Autonomous Zone, Ontological Anarchy, Poetic Terrorism*, Autonomedia, New York.

Bowman, M. (1995), 'The Noble Savage and the Global Village: Cultural Evolution in New Age and Neo-Pagan Thought', *Journal of Contemporary Religion*, vol. 10, no.2, pp.139-49.

Butler, B. (2003), 'The Tree, the Tower and the Shaman: The Material Culture of Resistance of the No M11 Link Roads Protests of Wanstead and Leytonstone, London', in G. Harvey (ed.), *Shamanism. A Reader*, London, Routledge, pp.375–401.

Curry, P. (1998), *Defending Middle Earth. Tolkien, Myth and Modernity*, London, Harper Collins.

Foucault, M. (1998), 'Different Spaces', in J. Faubion (ed.), *Aesthetics, Method and Epistemology*, Harmondsworth, Allen Lane, pp.175–185.

Harvey, G. (1997), *Listening People, Speaking Earth. Contemporary Paganism*. London, Hurst and Co.

___ (2003), (ed.), *Shamanism. A Reader*. London, Routledge.

Heelas, P. Lash, S. and Morris, P. (eds), (1996), *Detraditionalization*, Blackwell, Oxford.

Hetherington, K. (1998), *Expressions of Identity. Space, Performance, Politics*, London, Sage.

Hindle, J. (n.d.), *The Apple Tree. A Protester's Tale*, Unpublished manuscript.

Jennings, P. (2002), *Pagan Paths. A Guide to Wicca, Druidry, Asatru, Shamanism and Other Pagan Practices*, London, Rider.

Josh (1996), 'Walking Song', from the album *Tribal Voices*, cassette only release.

Letcher, A.J. (2001a), *The Role of the Bard in Contemporary Pagan Movements*, unpublished PhD thesis, King Alfred's College, Winchester.

___ (2001b), 'The Scouring of the Shire: Fairies, Trolls and Pixies in Eco-Protest Culture', *Folklore*, vol. 112, pp.147–161.

___ (2002), '"If You Go Down to the Woods Today...": Spirituality and the Eco-Protest Lifestyle', *Ecotheology*, vol. 7, pp.81–87.

___ (2003), '"Gaia told me to do it": Resistance and the idea of nature within contemporary British Eco-Paganism', *Ecotheology*, vol. 8, pp.61–84.

___ (2004), 'Mad Thoughts on Mushrooms: Discourse and Power in the Study of Psychedelic Consciousness', paper presented at the 'Exploring Consciousness' Conference, Bath Spa University, June 2004.

___ (2004), 'Raising the Dragon: Folklore and the Development of Contemporary British Eco-Paganism', *The Pomegranate*, vol. 6, no. 2, pp.175–198.

___ (forthcoming), *Shroom. A Cultural History of the Magic Mushroom*, Faber & Faber, London.

McKay, G. (1996), *Senseless Acts of Beauty. Cultures of Resistance Since the Sixties*, Verso, London.

Merrick (1997), *Battle for the Trees. Three Months of Responsible Ancestry*, Godhaven Ink, Leeds.

Milton, K. (2002), *Loving Nature. Towards an Ecology of Emotion*, Routledge, London.

Monbiot, G. (1998), 'Introduction' in K. Evans, *Copse. The Cartoon Book of Tree Protesting*. Orange Dog Productions, Chippenham, p.8.

___ (2000), *Captive State. The Corporate Takeover of Britain*, Macmillan, London.

Pendragon, A. and Stone, C.J. (2003), *The Trials of Arthur. The Life and Times of a Modern-Day King*, Thorsons, London.

Roberts, J. and Motherwort (1997), 'Lyminge and the Pagan Heart', *Pagan Dawn*, vol. 125, pp.24–27.

Schutz, A. (1967), *Collected Papers 1. The Problem of Social Reality*, Martinus Nijhoff, The Hague.

Schechner, R. (1993), *The Future of Ritual. Writings on Culture and Performance*. Routledge, London.

Seel, B., Paterson, M. and Doherty, B. (eds), (2000), *Direct Action in British Environmentalism*, Routledge, London.

Space Goats (1999), 'Pixie People', from the album *Tribadelica*, Mandala SG23.

Starhawk (1982), *Dreaming the Dark. Magic, Sex and Politics*, Beacon Press, Boston.

Sutcliffe, S. and Bowman, M. (eds), (2000), *Beyond New Age. Exploring Alternative Spirituality*, Edinburgh University Press, Edinburgh.

Szerszynski, B. (1999), 'Performing Politics: the Dramatics of Environmental Protest', in L. Ray and A. Sayer (eds), *Culture and Economy After the Cultural Turn*, Sage Publications, London, pp.211-228.

Turner, V. (1969), *The Ritual Process,* Aldine, Chicago.

Vayne, J. (2001), *Pharmakon. Drugs and the Imagination*, El Cheapo Books, London.

Chapter 15

Reclaiming the Future at Goolengook: Going Feral and Becoming Native in Australia

Graham St John

The darkest horror lurking in the imaginings of nineteenth century Australians was that this wild continent might somehow claim them, or their children, to itself. As the currency lads and lasses grew up, tall, barefooted and at ease in the bush, those dark fears increased, for their parents saw degeneration in every deviation from standard European practice. The continent, they feared, somehow forced all of its inhabitants … into a base and primitive form … Today that dark, lurking fear – that this wide brown land might somehow claim us as its own – is, I suspect, our best hope for a sustainable, long-term future.

In his Australia Day Address in 2002 [quoted above], Tim Flannery, palaeontologist and public commentator, stated that the strength of Australian nationhood lay in surrender to country rather than in the colonialists' struggle against a hostile and forbidding landscape. Such a capitulation would, in Flannery's mind, enable settler-descendents to become natives and, thereby, 'true' Australians. The statement reminds me of the commitments made by many settler-descendents over recent decades to protect and preserve a threatened ecology and 'heritage' dependent upon an ecological sensibility and identification with place. I am reminded of those whose actions represent redemption from the malpractice of settler forebears – particularly those young Australians who strive to protect the forests, wetlands, coastlines and species, symbols of which have become vital to 'nationhood'.

Growing awareness of modernity's environmental despoliation and the planetary momentum towards an 'unsustainable future' has triggered the raising of a global ecological consciousness. Inscribed in that which Andrew Dobson (1995) calls 'ecologism' is an ethical commitment to balance and diversity, sustainable levels of production and consumption, and non-exploitative practices apparent in green populisms from environmental movement organizations like The Wilderness Society to toxic waste activism. Taking various philosophical and pragmatic forms, ecologism is predicated upon the realization that humans possess kinship with the natural world – a relationship often evoked as *sacred*. This ecologism recognizes place as both significant and the source of wholeness, vitality and strength. Responses to nature under siege, to the imperilment of place (especially that deemed to possess 'high conservation' or 'heritage' values), are as spiritual as they are political. The ecological imperative consists in a concerted commitment by individuals to counteract the causes of imbalance and to restore contact with nature (the sacred). This implies a pre-existing state of disenchantment, and its resolution may be found in the performance of special 'works', commitments and sacrificial behaviours.[1]

New 'works' are afoot in Australia. In an investigation of 'ecologically defined nationalism', Nick Smith, for instance, has documented the redemptive character of Australian 'naturework' (2000). As settler-Australians have grown to identify with country – an identification implicit in attempted reconciliation with Australia's indigenous inhabitants – a post-colonial spirituality is manifested in nationalist discourse. Recognition of a shameful intercultural history and deplorable environmental record informs contemporary efforts at settler belonging (see Read, 2000). These days it is increasingly acknowledged that Australia was (and remains) a landscape *imprinted* by those recognized as the country's First People, who in many places continue an 'ecological poetics of connection' (Rose, 1996) despite the history of dispossession. Expressing what has become an increasingly popular sentiment, on Australia Day 1988 the Chairman of the Northern Land Council, Galarrwuy Yunupingu, announced that 'Australia's too old to celebrate birthdays' (Morton, 1996, p.123). As recognition of the antiquity of the continent and its original inhabitants percolates through the national consciousness; as the Aboriginal sacred breaks out 'all over the place' (Gelder and Jacobs, 1998, p.25); and as antipodean legitimacy seems predicated upon the belief that '[t]he wounds we have inflicted on the land and on its first peoples have also wounded us' (Judith Wright, in Brady, 1998, p.6), 'country' becomes a significant and unpredictable stimulus for a broad spectrum of the non-indigenous population.

Some of the most assiduous legitimacy-seeking initiatives are performed outside formal politics and religion. With the evolution of ecological conservationism and the emergence of a 'sorry' movement,[2] independent youth formations demonstrate an inspired commitment to 'naturework'. While such formations constitute an activism that is simultaneously indigenizing (local) and cosmopolitan (global), here I am concerned with the former tendency. In campaigning for ecological and indigenous issues, nascent 'DiY communities' (McKay, 1998), which possess the fragile, ephemeral and paroxysmal characteristics of 'neotribes' (Maffesoli, 1996) but are also heavily motivated by political and spiritual commitments based upon anarchistic principles and an ecological consciousness, perform a substantial role in the sacralization of place.

Forming eco-tribes whose principal, though not exclusive, agenda became that of saving remnant 'old growth' forests at various remote regions around the continent, those who were designated or who identified themselves as 'ferals'[3] became the driving edge of a broadly reclamational youth 'tribalism'. Downstream from the confluence of hippy and punk, cross-fertilized by deep ecology and direct activism, commonly – though not exclusively – middle class and tertiary educated, ferals embody an inspired culture of opposition not dissimilar to that of Earth First!, with whom they share eco-radical post-settler kinship (see St John, 2000; for Earth First! see Taylor, 1994). Out of this milieu of identifying with threatened country and species and of subscribing to various ecosophical, pantheistic and anarchical principles, a diverse ecological neotribalism has flourished.[4] Contemporary events such as the Earthdream nomadic carnival (St John, 2001b) or Kevin Buzzacott's 'Coming the Right Way' ceremony[5] represent experimental rituals of legitimization enacted by new generations of settler descendents in collaboration with or under the authority of traditional custodians. When the stories of all these individual formations are compiled, what emerges is a meta-narrative of enchantment – strategic, youthful and independent. In this chapter, I discuss the ongoing defence of East Gippsland's Goolengook Forest (in Victoria) by members and affiliates of the Goongerah Environment Centre (Geco). First it is necessary to background the emergence of the feral character at the heart of such eco-strategies.

Terra-ism: Pursuing Excellence

For the Australian 'ecological pioneers' (Mulligan and Hill, 2001) who are disenchanted with the exploitative disposition of settler society, new mateships[6] and sacrifices form around environmental sensibilities. Established to 'care for country', such associations include radical youth cohorts whose interventions during the 1980s and 1990s earned them the title of 'bush punk' or 'feral'. Bricoleurs of confrontationalism and new spirituality, ferals might illustrate what David Tacey, in his *Re-Enchantment: A New Australian Spirituality*, calls a 'politically astute settler spirituality' (2000, p.146). The celebration and defence of threatened nature embodied in feral practice presents a possible 'postcolonial enchantment' (Tacey 2000, p.99, 250). While critics of the 'new feralism' accuse ferals of plundering indigenous culture for its perceived authenticity (Cuthbert and Grossman, 1996, pp.23–26), I would argue that this depiction relies upon a conception of 'feral' as exclusively predatorial, a conception which fails to recognize the counter-colonial character of this youth milieu.

The feral milieu possesses a curiously enigmatic and ambivalent status in the national imagination. *The Macquarie Dictionary* defines 'feral' as 'gross; disgusting' *or* 'excellent; admirable' (see St John, 1999). The contrary definitions hold intimations of excess, defilement and iniquity on the one hand; discipline, purity and virtuosity on the other. Thus 'feral' becomes a highly contested social category: while resource developers and practitioners of cultural studies alike often use the term pejoratively to discredit people, those who appropriate or reclaim the term wear it as a badge of honour.

The deprecatory definition of 'feral' corresponds with the colonial perception of the bush as having a degenerative influence', while the laudatory definition seems consistent with the post-colonialist sensibility that Flannery claims is essential for a sustainable environmental future. The first correlates with the characterization of young activists as 'deviant' boundary-violators lurking in development-frontier regions where their operations threaten propriety, property and patriarchy[7] – a characterization that insinuates an intrusive, menacing presence, even a 'terrorist' threat. The second definition demonstrates sympathy with those youth whose spectacular confrontations with state bodies and corporate interests on development-frontiers are shaped largely by a shared grievance for heritage lost and by a commitment to preserve what remains. As such, in a body of custodial practices that we might call *terra-ism*, we can identify nascent rites of belonging and new strategies of becoming native.

Geco and Goolengook

Based in the mountain forest hinterlands of Victoria's East Gippsland, Geco is one node in a national and international network of forest activism. It attracts many activists who are variously referred to and/or self-identify as 'feral' (or 'fezza' in the local idiom), and it represents the last line of defence of Victoria's remaining high-conservation-value forest. Geco evolved out of blockades mounted in 1993 and 1994 and is dedicated to non-violent direct action. Its screen-printed dictum, 'old growth – fucken oath' has become familiar. Geco is a *terra-ist* collective which networks with other environment groups and the land's traditional owners, liaises with police and forestry workers, surveys endangered species, monitors logging operations and forest management, and advocates the development of a diversified regional economy for East Gippsland that would include nature-based eco-tourism. The collective also holds public awareness campaigns, workshops, fundraising events and festivals (see website: www.geco.org.au). Geco activists combine spectacular obstructions, banner dropping and eco-political performances to attract the attention of major media and to increase the operating costs of an unsustainable, environmentally-destructive forestry industry. Geco's ethos is far from the bureaucratic environmentalism characteristic of Greenpeace and Friends of the Earth and much closer to the 'sectarian ecological piety' of other eco-anarchist formations like Earth First! in the US and the Dongas Tribe in the UK (Szerszynski, 1997).

In December 1996, Geco united with other environmental groups to form a community of resistance at Goolengook, part of the last remaining five per cent of Australia's original old growth forest. The rare cool and warm temperate rainforest includes Goolengook River, listed as a heritage water catchment. Since the early 1970s, over 150,000 hectares of native forest have been clear-felled in the region. Hundreds of rare and endangered animal species are found here and in the surrounding rainforest, including the Spot-Tailed Quoll, the Powerful and Sooty Owls, the Longfooted Potoroo, Baw Baw Frog and Long-Nosed Bandicoot, and tree species such as the Slender Tree Fern and the Southern Sassafras. With the signing of the Regional Forest Agreement in 1997, and against the recommendations of botanists and prominent scientists from the Department of Natural Resources and Environment (DNRE), Goolengook became exposed to clear-fell logging and slash burning. Seventy-five percent of the region's logged trees are destined for the government-subsidized export woodchipping mill at Eden in southeast New South Wales, which is owned by the Japanese company Daishowa. These logged trees are replaced with single-species tree farms that are often sprayed with 1080 poison to prevent (kill) native wildlife from interfering with the crop.

Goolengook became the longest running blockade – referred to by The Wilderness Society as a 'forest rescue camp' – in history. The original base camp was broken up by police on the eve of World Environment Day, 4 June 1997, and this was followed over the next 18 months by hundreds of arrests (including that of Australian Greens' Senator, Bob Brown) and the eventual re-establishment of the blockade. After protesters were brutally attacked at their camp by loggers in February 2000, they erected a medieval-style fort – equipped with a drawbridge, eight-foot walls, and a multi-poled structure enabling above-ground mobility – to protect activists and the forest. 'Fortress Goolengook' was subsequently besieged several times by DNRE officers and police and was finally overrun on 5 March 2002 after which ninety hectares of old growth forest were logged.[8]

When occupying this landscape under threat, Geco acknowledged that the forests had previously been inhabited by the Bidawal and the Krauatungalung peoples. This recognition of Aboriginal occupants – perhaps more compelling in the case of the North East Forest Alliance's (NEFA) association with the Bundjalung Nation (Ricketts, 2003, p.129) – challenges the idea of an untouched 'wilderness', a misperception which persists amongst environmentalists and developers alike, and which, like the doctrine of *terra nullius*, tends to deny the presence and authority of indigenes and thereby lends legitimacy to occupation and dispossession. While occupation by settler-Australians often relies upon an essentialist and primitivist notion of Aboriginality not dissimilar to that endorsed by New Age spokespersons (see Mulcock, 2001), the 'fezza' regularly acknowledges the suffering of land and people, an acknowledgement indicative of new ways of belonging to place.

Ecological Rites of Passage and the Enchanted Forest

Trees are the most pervasive and powerful symbols of nature, often standing for nature in Western eco-discourse. Where nature possesses intrinsic value, trees often symbolize anti-modern values – that is anti-urban, anti-consumerist and anti-industrial values (Rival, 1998, p.16). Thus a tree is not just a tree, nor a river only a river. In the following passage from James McQueen's *The Franklin: Not Just a River* (cited in Lohrey, 2002, p.24), we can observe how Tasmania's south-west river, scheduled to be dammed by the state's Hydro Electricity Commission in the early 1980s, came to hold a complex significance:

> It seems to me now that the river – the River – is not just the Franklin, not just a river. For those of us who have been drawn, often despite ourselves, to its defence, it has become far more than the sum of its parts. For me it is the epitome of all the lost forests, all the submerged lakes, all the tamed rivers, all the extinguished species. It is threatened by the same mindless beast that has eaten our past, is eating our present, and threatens to eat our future: that civil beast of mean ambitions and broken promises and hedged bets and tawdry profits.

As rivers, or trees and forests for that matter, come to stand for nature, for country, the struggle for their preservation becomes a symbolic struggle for the preservation of country, for the defence of that which is held sacred. An old growth forest may then become a contested site, as antagonists who ascribe different values to it and apply contested meanings to its inhabitants wage a conflict that is as much symbolic as it is literal.

Blockades at Goolengook and other locations are intended to defend threatened high-conservation-value ecosystems. They are also expressions of the individual and collective will to 'blockade', or at least forestall, the rapacious spread of industrialism. Thus strategies for halting road building operations and immobilizing logging machinery are at the same time profound expressions of the activist's desire to impede the advance of modernity. Tripods,[9] tree-sits,[10] 'lock-ons'[11] and 'black wallabies'[12] are tactical devices designed to prevent or delay logging. These tactics require activists to intentionally place their bodies (and lives) at risk, which puts the onus on police to undertake what are often delicate extraction procedures without causing harm; they are also powerful personal symbolic devices, which signify an objection to the rampant despoliation of the sacred. The Goolengook road fortification was itself a powerful symbol of resistance against the crushing advance of modernity.

These 'arboreal melodramas' (Lohrey, 2002, p.43) also function to demarcate a region as worthy of commitment and care – that is, as a sacred site. As Geco mount actions to mark out Goolengook forest as sacred country, their activities parallel the 'ecological rites' (Szerszynski, 2002) undertaken by the likes of Earth First! and the Dongas Tribe (Plows, 1995). Furthermore, the performance of obstructing logging operations has manifold sacralizing consequences. For individuals involved in direct actions – especially those engaged in 'locking-on' to heavy machinery, or perched in tree platforms or tripods for hours or even days at a time – such commitment holds a redemptive function. By 'deploying their bodies in precarious settings and ... convert[ing] themselves into flesh and blood bargaining chips' (Williams, 1998, p.9) activists may attain a kind of salvation. The tree-sit action in defence of a significant tree (and a forest coupe beyond) is a telling example of the 'life-giving action' attributed to environmental awareness and to tree planting in particular (Rival, 1998, p.18). But it is the potential it has to deliver the *ultimate* sacrifice that truly lends it its sacralizing quality.

What is the substance of this reconciliation with the sacred that the tree-sit, tripod-occupation or lock-on occasions? Conducted in relative solitude at the end of a logging-track cut deep into the forest, an anti-logging action is a deeply ambivalent event; while it may be a source of strength for the activist, it is also a ritual marker of pain and loss, for the blockade is all-too-often broken by forestry officers and police search-and-rescue teams which open up old-growth forest (the sacred) to loggers and woodchippers (sacrilege). Repeated involvement in desperate and failed attempts to defend the sacred is a distressing and traumatic experience often triggering psychological 'burn-out' and cynicism: as the 'busting' of blockades signals the encroachment of the modern 'machine' on nature's sacred remains; as the timber industry's victories are taken as a triumph of greed and shortsightedness; as the decimation of native forest (e.g. 300–400 year-old Mountain Ash) inflicts a shattering sense of personal loss; and as the habitats of native species devastated in a clear-felled, napalmed and poisoned coupe are sometimes observed as 'holocaust' zones.

Regardless, these actions, especially long term blockades, amount to transition rites, marking passage to a status akin to what Tomashow (1996) identifies as an 'ecological identity'. Activist rites assist in binding the neophyte to the sacred Other – old-growth eucalypts and the forest's threatened species become the neophyte's relations; the boundary between self and other is dissolved – engendering what eco-psychologists call the 'expansive self' (Fox, 1996). With the active performance of duty in defence of the forest, passage into a 'community of feeling' may also be achieved. Collective identification is especially evident in long-term actions like Goolengook, where occupants came to regard themselves as 'Goolengeeks'. There is a parallel here with the Dongas, who took their name from the trackways they occupied over the course of their heritage action, and who, as Plows explains (1995, p.4), 'felt part of the land, a physical extension of it, empathizing with indigenous tribes throughout the ages who had felt a spiritual connection with the land that they were torn from'. For the Dongas, this degree of empathy is easily justified because they can trace and/or imagine links to ancestors and refer to themselves as 'the nomadic indigenous peoples of Britain'. For the Goolengeeks, however, there was no such link; yet this did not prevent them from producing myths, legends, poems, plays and folksongs inspired by their extended peaceful habitation of the forest.

   While the loss of forest to which deep attachments have been formed occasions a 'crushing sense of grief and despair' among activists, the sense of desecration also binds together those who have 'borne witness' (Hoare, 1998). Contextualizing collective sacrifice, such campaign 'rites' may also effectively unite a disparate forest movement the various elements of which come to hold regions like Goolengook as movement 'icons'.[13] Furthermore, if staged media stunts are communicated by the major news networks, the threatened forest may become iconic for broader populations, whose collective response may trigger reform. This is indeed the objective of most forest campaigners: if the desecration of forest is communicated to the broader public, there is a greater likelihood that what remains will be protected, its sacred status enshrined in federal or international laws as state, national or even world heritage.[14] Using a variety of tactics, activists convey the state-sponsored sacrilege to the public. Freshly clear-felled old growth can be exploited by activists and 'ecovangelists' (Taylor, 2001, p.237) as a potent symbol of government irresponsibility and corporate greed. They may parade the stumps of 500-year-old Mountain Grey Gum on 'stump trucks' through metropolitan thoroughfares and marginal electorates. They may drop banners from bridges and buildings, hold community festivals like Goongerah's 'Celebrate and Defend' gathering, organize public education exercises like Cycle for Old Growth Forests,[15] and maintain a presence at other events such as Reclaim the Streets, Earthcore, and Psycorroboree. They may form bands (like Melbourne's Understorey), write novels (Derek Hansen's *Blockade* or Tony Quoll's self-published cyber/eco-punk novel *Escape to Goolengook*), picket suspect timber retailers, build websites, graffiti inner-city Melbourne with rousing slogans, and convey the eerie digitally-recorded spectacle of a devastated coupe to the major networks.

Feral Future

The defence of Victoria's Goolengook Forest demonstrates how independent youth formations are involved in the process of *native-becoming* in Australia. Just one example of post-settler commitment, the *terra-ist* 'fight for country' at Goolengook was motivated more by ecological imperatives than patriotic duty. The work involved in such ferality represents a departure from the known (the domestic) and a gravitation toward the uncanny. In this *terra-ist* plight, the familiar is rendered unfamiliar, and the unfamiliar familiar, a scenario of 'unsettled settledness' which, as Gelder and Jacobs (1998, pp.23–42) acknowledge, is critical to decolonization, to establishing a new relationship with the Other. As young Australians 'go feral', their intentional displacement dissolves, or at least renders uncertain, the distinction between *Other* (country, indigeneity) and *self* (settler, colonist, etc.) which informs the history of Australian nationhood.

This liminal journey may approximate the 'immanental and non-triumphalist' post-colonial spirituality that Tacey (2000, p.108) envisions will evolve in Australia. Whatever the 'feral future' looks like, it will involve the dynamic interaction of people and place. This is evident already, for example, in the work of Freya Mathews (1999a, 1999b). With the appropriate commitments from generation after generation, place – including (sub)urban place – quite literally 'infiltrates' settler identity: in time 'a place can come to accept us. We become its people. The land, or place, claims its own…[W]e become native to our world' (Mathews, 1999a, p.125). As 'going feral' is consonant with 'going native', the savage religion implicit in ferality is congruent with eco-nationalist projects like Flannery's. And the new relationship formed with place assists a post-settler identification.

Through their commitment to place and, moreover, to 'giving something back to nature', 'caring for country', preserving heritage for future generations, and 'reclaiming the future', young non-indigenous Australians are adopting custodial sensibilities and sacralizing strategies. From numerous self-identifying and indigenizing tactics evident in Australian and other settler populations, the ecological actions, performances and sacrifices described have been shown to be radical rites of enchantment. The redemptive desire to reconcile with indigenous land and people has motivated a nascent cultural, political and spiritual movement to inhabit landscape, to claim a legitimate presence, to belong to place. In reclaiming the pejorative term 'feral', used to derogate activists as invasive or pestilent, young Australians exemplify the *native-becoming*.

Notes

1 The spiritual improvement arrived at through various labours is often glossed as 're-enchantment', the anticipated 'return' to a lost or forgotten relationship with the natural world. Re-enchantment manifests variously. For instance, within New Age discourse there is a desire to remember our 'indigenous self' or 'archetype', an harmonious natural source thought to lie beneath the surface of our modern exterior (see Mulcock, 2001), and the re-awakening of which is deemed to have a significant bearing on Australian national identity (Tacey, 2000, pp.140–145). The depiction of nature as a declining bastion of harmony and purity in the world, stimulated by Romantic visions of restoring corrupted humanity to a former 'noble' condition, have more generally fed into regenerative ideologies like those rampant primitivisms wherein, for instance, Aborigines are essentialized as an idyllic 'Nature' in which Moderns are deficient, or 'blood and soil' dogmas associated with the likes of the volkish radicals of pre-war Germany who were ardent nativists concerned with over-industrialization.

2   During the nineties, Australia saw the rise of a mass movement of 'sorry
    people' engaged in the performance of a 'proliferation of apologies [made to
    indigenous Australians] on behalf of themselves and the nation' (Gooder and
    Jacobs, 2000, p.232).
3   Ricketts (2003, p.141) describes how the North East Forest Alliance (NEFA)
    blockade at Chaelundi New South Wales in 1991 became the context for the
    'subcultural' adoption of 'feral' as a term of self-identification.
4   Including antinuclear industry groups like the Jabiluka Mine blockaders
    (documented in the film *Fight for Country: The Story of the Jabiluka Blockade,*
    Written and directed by Pip Starr, produced by Bill Runting. Rockhopper
    Productions, 2001), the Keepers of Lake Eyre and the Humps not Dumps camel
    crusaders; ecologically conscious techno-tribes like Sydney's Ohms not Bombs
    and the Labrats (Strong, 2001; Brown and Peckham, 2001; St John, 2001a); and
    regenerational 'environmental sounds' parties like Melbourne's Tranceplant,
    and other conscientious reclamational events (like Reclaim the Streets, see
    Luckman, 2001).
5   An intercultural passage ritual at Captain Cook's 230-year-old landing site at
    The Foot in Sydney's Botany Bay conducted on the 23–24th of September
    2000 (see St John, 2001c).
6   Thus posing something of a competing archetype to Russell Ward's 'Australian
    Legend' (Ward, 1958): egalitarian, practical and non-authoritarian in principle,
    so often bigoted agents of environmental despoliation in practice.
7   Since in their celebration and defence of the 'earth mother', ferals embrace the
    'contaminating' and 'seductive' mother/matter typically unclean to patriarchal
    religious traditions.
8   A moratorium was placed on logging in Goolengook by the Victorian
    Government in October 2002.
9   Three legged structures constructed from saplings with a perch for a sitter.
    Often 'monopoles' (single poles) are erected above tripods to raise sitters above
    the reach of 'cherry pickers' (cranes) or above logging equipment.
10 Raised platforms built in tall trees – where activists have safety lines hooked
    onto the tree like 'umbilical cords'.
11 Attachment to roads, bulldozers and other logging equipment using chains, bike
    locks and other home made devices including 'dragons' (steel pipes cemented
    into roads into which arms are positioned – with a clip and wrist strap).
12 Activists who conceal themselves in the path of tree harvesting operations.
13 Indeed this is a view stated by long-time Geco activist John Flynn in an
    unpublished 2002 document '500 people in Goolengook in September', where
    he states: 'Goolengook is one of the most famous and recognized campaigns in
    Australian environmental history'.
14 And thus seeing the Upper Goolengook Catchment awarded 'National Park'
    status as it's added to Errinundra National Park.
15 See http://forestfreedom.org/cogf.

References

Brady, V. (1998), "'One Great World of Fire": Judith Wright's Australia: the Land of Fire', in M. Griffith and J. Tulip (eds), *Spirit of Place: Source of the Sacred*, Australian Catholic University, Sydney, pp.1–12.

Brown, I. and Peckham, M. (2001), 'Tuning Technology to Ecology: Labrats Sola Powered Sound System', in G. St John (ed.), *FreeNRG: Notes From the Edge of the Dance Floor*, Common Ground, Melbourne, pp.91–108.

Cuthbert, D. and Grossman, M. (1996), 'Trading Places: Locating the Indigenous in the New Age, *Thamyris*, vol. 3, no. 1, pp.18–36.

Dobson, A. (1995), *Green Political Thought*, Routledge, London.

Fox, W. (1996), *Toward a Transpersonal Psychology*, State University of New York Press.

Gelder, K. and Jacobs, J. (1998), *Uncanny Australia: Sacredness and Identity in a Postcolonial Nation*, Melbourne University Press, Carlton South.

Gooder, H. and Jacobs, J. (2000), 'On the Border of the Unsayable': The Apology in Postcolonizing Australia, *Interventions*, vol. 2, no. 2, pp.229–47.

Hansen, D. (1998), *Blockade*, HarperCollins.

Hastings, T. (1998), *Escape to Goolengook*. Published by AAAD aaad@iig.com.au

Hoare, B. (1998), 'A Passion for Protest: an Insider's View', in *Protest! Environmental Actions in NSW: 1968–1998*, Historic Houses Trust of New South Wales, pp.19–27.

Lohrey, A. (2002), 'Ground-swell: the rise of the Greens', *Quarterly Essay*, vol. 8, pp.1–86.

Luckman, S. (2001), 'What are they Raving on About? Temporary Autonomous Zones and "Reclaim the Streets"', *Perfect Beat*, vol. 5, no. 2, pp.49–68.

Maffesoli, M. (1996) [1988], *The Time of the Tribes: the Decline of Individualism in Mass Society*, Sage, London.

Mathews, F. (1999a), 'Letting the World Grow Old: An Ethos of Countermodernity', *Worldviews*, vol. 3, no. 2, pp.119–137.

___(1999b), 'Becoming Native: An Ethos of Countermodernity II', *Worldviews*, vol. 3, no. 3, pp.243–271.

McKay, G. (ed.) (1998), *DiY Culture: Party and Protest in Nineties Britain*, Verso, London.

Morton, J. (1996), 'Aboriginality, Mabo and the Republic: Indigenising Australia', in B. Attwood (ed.), *In the Age of Mabo: History, Aborigines and Australia*, Allen and Unwin, St Leonards, pp.117–135.

Mulcock, J. (2001), '(Re)discovering our Indigenous Selves: The Nostalgic Appeal of Native Americans and Other Generic Indigenes', *Australian Religion Studies Review*, vol. 14, no. 1, pp.45–64.

Mulligan, M. and Hill, S. (2001), *Ecological Pioneers: A Social History of Australian Ecological Thought and Action*, Cambridge University Press, Cambridge.

Plows, A. (1995), 'Eco-Philosophy and Popular Protest: the Significance and Implications of the Ideology and Actions of the Donga Tribe', *Alternative Futures and Popular Protest* Conference Proceedings, Manchester, pp.1–21.

Read, P. (2000), *Belonging: Australians, Place and Aboriginal Ownership*, Cambridge University Press, Cambridge.

Ricketts, A. (2003), '"Om Gaia Dudes": The North East Forest Alliance's Old Growth Forest Campaign', in Helen Wilson (ed.), *Belonging in the Rainbow Region: Cultural Perspectives on the NSW North Coast,*. Southern Cross University Press, Lismore, pp.121–148.

Rival, L. (1998), 'Trees, from Symbols of Life and Regeneration to Political Artefacts', in L. Rival (ed.), *The Social Life of Trees: Anthropological Perspectives on Tree Symbolism*, Berg, Oxford, pp.1–36.

Rose, D. (1996), *Nourishing Terrains: Australian Aboriginal Views of Landscape and Wilderness*, Australian Heritage Commission, Canberra.

Smith, N. (2000), 'Nature, Native and Nation in the Australian Imaginary', unpublished PhD Thesis, Latrobe University, Melbourne.

St John, G. (1999), 'Ferality: a Life of Grime', *The UTS Review – Cultural Studies and New Writing*, vol. 5, no. 2, pp.101–13.

___(2000), 'Ferals: Terra-ism and Radical Ecologism in Australia', *Journal of Australian Studies*, vol. 64, pp.208–16.

___(2001a), 'Techno Terra-ism: Feral Systems and Sound Futures, in G. St John (ed.), *FreeNRG: Notes From the Edge of the Dance Floor*, Common Ground, Melbourne, pp.109–137.

___(2001b), 'Earthdreaming for a Nuclear Free Future', *Arena Magazine*, no. 53 June/July, pp.41–44.

___(2001c), 'Australian (Alter)natives: Cultural Drama and Indigeneity', *Social Analysis: Journal of Cultural and Social Practice*, vol. 45, no. 1, pp. 122–40.

Strong, P. (2001), 'Doofstory: Sydney Park to the desert', in G. St John (ed.) *FreeNRG: Notes From the Edge of the Dance Floor*, Common Ground, Melbourne, pp.71–90.

Szerszynski, B. (1997), 'The varieties of Ecological Piety', *Worldviews: Environment, Culture, Religion*, vol. 1, pp.37–55.

___(2002), 'Ecological Rites: Ritual Action in Environmental Protest, *Theory, Culture and Society*, vol. 19, no. 3, pp.51–69.

Tacey, D. (2000), *Re-enchantment: The New Australian Spirituality,* HarperCollins, Sydney.

Taylor, B. (1994), 'Earth First's religious radicalism', in C. Chapple (ed.), *Ecological Prospects: Scientific, Religious, and Aesthetic Perspectives*, Albany: State University of New York Press, pp.185–210.

___(2001), 'Earth and Nature-Based Spirituality (Part II): From Earth First and Bioregionalism to Scientific Paganism and the New Age', *Religion*, vol. 31, pp.225–245.

Tomashow, M. (1996), *Ecological Identity: Becoming a Reflective Environmentalist*, MIT Press.

Ward, R. (1958), *The Australian Legend*, Oxford University Press, Melbourne.

Williams, D. (1998), 'Protest, Police, and the Green World View: the Search for a Brave New Paradigm', in *Protest! Environmental Actions in NSW: 1968–1998*, Historic Houses Trust of New South Wales, pp.5–18.

Index